# CommonWealth

## Self-Sufficiency and Work in American Communities, 1830 to 1993

Torry D. Dickinson

University Press of America, Inc.

Lanham • New York • London

4720 Boston Way
Lanham, Maryland 20706

3 Henrietta Street
London, WC2E 8LU England


Printed in the United States of America
British Cataloging in Publication Information Available

**Library of Congress Cataloging-in-Publication Data**

Dickinson, Torry D.
CommonWealth : self-sufficiency and work in American communities, 1830-1993 / Torry D. Dickinson.
p. cm.
Includes index.
1. Labor--United States--History. 2. Working class--United States--History. 3. Informal sector (Economics)--United States--History. 4. Neighborhood--United States--History. 5. United States--Economic conditions. 6. United States--Social conditions.
I. Title. II. Title: Common wealth.
HD8066.D53 1995
331' .0973--dc20 94-23739 CIP

ISBN 0-8191-9802-1 (cloth: alk paper)

The paper used in this publication meets the minimum requirements of American National Standard for Information Sciences—Permanence of Paper for Printed Library Materials, ANSI Z39.48–1984

*Sixteen-year-old Florence Ricci, an Italian-American living outside of Philadelphia. Ricci Family Collection, Courtesy of the Balch Institute Library.*

*To Robert, Jazz and Jeffree*
*and to improvisers everywhere*

# Contents

*The ice man making deliveries in a Philadelphia neighborhood. A. Robert Giorgio Collection, Courtesy of the Balch Institute Library.*

# *Acknowledgments*

I began this research project within the rather isolated context of graduate school, where I was taking a dissertation seminar at SUNY-Binghamton and working with the Households Research Group at the Fernand Braudel Center. But this book really did not begin there. It began when my parents said, "Enough of this racism," and "We're going to put our feet where are hearts are." They picked the family up, moved us from Columbus to Detroit, and enrolled me in an inner-city junior high at the corner of Jay and Dubois. This book started when my classmates and friends told me about sitting in the segregated upper-tier of southern movie theaters or having their homes slated to be torn down for the sake of urban renewal. I heard about capital punishment and the *debate* about it for the first time. I learned that I could play the viola in the band (transposing from oboe music) and that improvising could be fun.

But while I started to write this book in an academic context, I found that I could not finish it without going back and forth between teaching, research, and community work. The history of America's social divides, her positive cultural impulses, and the ways to a better world cannot be fully comprehended without working outside of the university's walls.

For this reason, I want to thank all those people in the university, in non-profit organizations and in community work who supported me and taught me as I engaged in this project.

First, I would like to thank the faculty and members of my dissertation committee, who helped me as I conducted my archival research and wrote up my findings. My committee included Immanuel Wallerstein, James Geschwender, Joan Smith, and Melvyn Dubofsky. The graduate students at SUNY-Binghamton were an integral part of my academic environment and I am indebted to *all* of them. For this reason, I will thank them as a group for their intellectual engagement, support and friendship.

If it had not been for the American Association of University Women (AAUW) and local members supporting the graduate fellowship program, I do not know how far my research would have progressed. I must extend a heartfelt "thank you." It was an honor receiving the first Susan B. Anthony Award and serving as an AAUW American Fellow in 1979 to 1980.

Being awarded a Revson Fellowship in Women and Public Policy by the Center for Women in Government (CWG) in 1983 was also a honor. Taking classes, working with CWG staff and the first group of Revson Fellows, and analyzing legislation influenced me enormously.

I wish to thank my students at San Jose State University in Monterey County and in San Jose. I also am indebted to the students and faculty at the Western Institute for Social Research, who are deeply involved in community work.

Staff members at many research libraries and archives helped me locate materials that enabled me to study changes in informal work. Mr. Ward Childs and the staff of the City Archives of Philadelphia, who were most helpful during the research process, granted permission for the printing of numerous photographs. The Library at the Balch Institute for Ethnic Studies granted permission for the printing of photographs. The Hagley Museum and Library granted permission for the use of a photograph. Several photographs came from the National Archives in Washington, D.C. I want to thank Mr. Frederick Miller, who was Director of Temple University's Urban Archives, for the extensive assistance that he provided. I also want to thank the staff of the Pennsylvania Historical Society for their assistance.

A great deal of my support has come from colleagues, who are working to make the world a better place. I want to thank colleagues and friends from the following organizations: Oakland's Displaced Homemaker Center, the University of Maine's Cooperative Extension Service and its public policy educators, the National Council on Aging, Wider Opportunities for Women, the Association for Women in Science, the University of California's National Center for Research on Vocational Education in Berkeley, and Centerforce (which helps at-risk families). Let me extend special thanks to Milo Smith (co-founder of the displaced homemaker movement), JoAnn Wilder, Sheila Urban Smith, Nellie Hedstrom, and Doug Dowd. I am thankful that S.O.Y. Keita believed in this project and provided constant encouragement. My family—Dick, Pat, Derry and Rink—provided a context that enabled me to write. Catherine Campaigne and Nancy Austin helped turn the manuscript into a book.

Most of all, I appreciate the day-to-day support provided by Robert Schaeffer, who has lived with this project from beginning to end. Robert's presence and help made this book more comprehensive, accessible and compelling. His advice and patience enabled me to figure out what I really wanted to say.

# *Introduction*

## History and Social Change: Connecting Past and Present

During the last century, North Americans have been losing their ability to organize and control much of their own work. In the nineteenth and early twentieth centuries, many Americans organized informal work that provided cash and in-kind income to supplement low wages from formal jobs. During this time, informal work and self-employment was a product of economic necessity. Self-employment emerged because it allowed workers to earn income outside of formal contractual employment and because it allowed them to minimize their consumption of market goods. They were able to do so partly because nearby forests and fertile land provided resources that working families could use in home-based work. By initiating, developing, and refining their own networks of petty production, marketing, and exchange, low- and moderate-income families were able to maintain an important degree of independence from employers and market-based entrepreneurs.

Today it is difficult for even elders to remember the kind of self-sufficient work and control over some market relations that once gave community life its stability and meaning. Still contemporary Americans want to become more self-sufficient and to gain greater community control over the direction of their lives, which they did in the past. Recent global economic developments have forced many working people into low-wage service jobs or out of work altogether. As a result, some people wonder if there is an alternative to the current employment system. An examination of the work relations that sustained American communities during much of the nineteenth and twentieth centuries may provide clues as to possible alternatives.

In the past, families made their living organizing much of their own work. Other families and local communities helped sustain this "economic" activity in the United States, as they still do in much of the Third World today. But as capitalist shops and factories expanded, local and state officials restricted the ability of families and communities to organize their own networks of petty production, marketing and exchange, and the type of work characteristic of more self-sufficient communities almost vanished.

By examining the diversity of and closely connected work relations in American communities of the nineteenth and twentieth centuries, it may be possible to envision new alternatives to the contemporary world of work. History and the social sciences can lead to an understanding of the past and may help Americans develop innovative solutions to the problems associated with the current system of work, particularly its relations to local communities. This historical study provides a context for understanding contemporary public policy debates and social reform initiatives related to self-employment, community revitalization, crime reduction, and relations between different community members.

Taking the long view, laboring families need not resign themselves to working for cost-cutting employers, risking unemployment, or struggling to increase the federal government's income-transfer programs. They might learn to rely on more income they generate in close-knit, community networks, networks which they organize and develop for their own benefit. By recalling income-yielding options that may be forgotten or devalued, they may identify ways to overcome persistent underemployment, joblessness and declining government-sponsored social programs.

To appreciate lost or forgotten work alternatives, this book will examine the various types of informal work carried out in different ethnic and multi-ethnic communities. By "community" I mean the people who helped sustain a network centered around informal work, informal marketing, and inter-household resource exchanges. These networks were often based in neighborhoods, though some developed over a very large geographical area. Nestled within the heart of communities was that vital building block, the family. In this study, I use "family" interchangeably with "household," the economic, cultural and emotional unit that sustained constituent members over long periods of time. Families pooled income together for one to three and even four generations. These households formed the basic building block of ethnic communities, broader ethnic groups, and economic classes. Defined in this way, families may have included both kin and non-kin members, whose work roles were shaped by families, communities, and ethnic groups.

The history of past community life prefigures contemporary and future social change, which develops along both intentional and unintentional lines. A comprehensive history of household and community work contributes to an understanding of America's past in the following ways. First, an analysis of informal work, which was once widespread, contributes to a revised understanding of how the U.S. working class was formed and how it sustained itself. Studying changes in family-controlled work means, in effect, reviewing and rewriting labor history.

Second, labor became more stratified as informal work declined and dependence on wage employment rose. The emergence of gender and age inequities have been associated with the decline of diverse types of informal work. As this study shows, the reconstruction of informal work relations can lead to a more in-depth understanding of how gender, age and ethnic stratification developed.

Third, the decline of informal work resulted in the loss of job-specific and organizational skills, which were needed to initiate and maintain informal activities. The deskilling of informal work abilities has been largely overlooked.

Last, by recognizing the diversity of work skills possessed in past communities, Americans may understand how to strengthen contemporary self-sufficiency, community development and economic development efforts. Community developers and policy makers today have seen a similarity between late-twentieth century poverty in the United States and in the Third World. As a result, some U.S. self-employment programs import and utilize Third World programs as models. The peer-lending program in Bangladesh, which helps women start up micro-businesses, is often cited as a model for poor women in America. But, with the exception of some rural and ethnic economic development efforts, there has been little attempt to build on America's own self-employment traditions, which once were a central part of community life. The search for external models has occurred, in part, because U.S. self-sufficiency traditions have not been seen as integral and vital part of American history and culture.

History and the social sciences can be used to help readers understand how historical development impacted different groups. For example, while middle-class labor did benefit from improved health, a higher standard of living, and stable incomes by the 1950s, labor lost many of its home-and job-based work skills and its ability to organize itself. A multidisciplinary approach can show how these changes took place and identify the social mechanisms that led to this change.

It is important to recognize the role that previous agents of social change played in this process. Many of the people who promoted reform in the nineteenth and twentieth centuries contributed to unexpected or undesirable changes. Business owners, state officials, social reformers, and labor union members all contributed to the decline of informal work, altering work patterns and eliminating work options for workers who had previously relied on some non-waged income to make ends meet.

Although history is often told as the story of a "dead" past, history is an ever-present force in today's world. An analysis of the early period from 1830 to 1945—when families began working less for themselves and more for others—helps to show how contemporary social divisions in the United States and around the world might be overcome.

Centuries ago, when North America became integrated into the capitalist relations being created by Western European businesses, state governments, and path-breaking entrepreneurs, the meaning of community life changed in fundamental ways. The integration of North America into the global profit-making system destroyed the pre-capitalist community and created a completely different type of community.

Although community relationships after the period of incorporation did not change as dramatically as they did during capitalism's rise, urban and industrial developments in the nineteenth and twentieth centuries profoundly transformed family and community networks. And although the process was affected by ups and downs in the economy, the shift from substantially working for oneself to largely working for others occurred in three stages: (1) the commercial and early manufacturing stage, when localities and charities assumed some responsibility for the destitute and replaced almshouses with workhouses (explored between 1830 to 1873 here); (2) the ascent of the United States as a global power stage, when early non-profit organizations and then local, state and federal governments provided pre-welfare and welfare support to low-income people (between 1873 and 1970); and (3) the decline of U.S. power stage, when the welfare state is being dismantled and support for low- and moderate-income working people is being withdrawn, a development that contributes to greater economic insecurity (explored between 1970 and 1993 here). Following 20 years of global recession and the decline of some socialist states, a new cycle of economic expansion began unfolding by 1993 or 1994. In this period, new governmental welfare strategies will be developed that will reflect economic and social choices that Americans make today and tomorrow. Although this study looks at post-1945 and current developments in relation to past transformations, it concentrates on the critical decline of informal work during the pre-welfare era, specifically from 1830 to 1945.

Nothing has shaped the structure of community life today more than the decline of informal work, which preceded the advent of the modern welfare state in the mid-1930s. In fact, it is difficult to assess contemporary work options without examining why and how communities became weakened during the stage before the United States became the leading world power in 1945.

One problem is that narrowly conceived histories of urban life after World War II, which ignore the long-term history of declining work diversity, place too much emphasis on wage employment, corporations, the state, consumerism, and the media. Studies on the division of labor typically ignore the organization and transformation of work relations outside of the factory door. The result is that this account magnifies the power of ascendant institutions.

In the United States few people in either the business or laboring classes question the emergence of bigger companies and bigger state government, largely because U.S. economic and state expansion brought material rewards for most Americans. As a result, many people assume that social options can only be explored within the context of U.S. big business and big government. The problem is that U.S. economic and political power—at least as it has been traditionally defined—has begun to slip away, while popular images of "progressive" power structures remain. This may actually prevent contemporary policy makers, business leaders, social service providers, students, or community members from seeing the full range of their social and economic options.

To understand future options, it is important to appreciate past practices, when families exercised greater control over the material world around them. Laboring people used to organize and do more work on their own. Because inadequate wages could not support all family members, working people used to design and organize "economic" support systems that helped sustain neighborhood residents. Neighborhood people undoubtedly once made local decisions about common work and marketing issues in a fairly direct, democratic fashion. But, as time went on, grassroots control of community life declined, leaving behind neighborhoods with few inter-household connections and little control over resources or income. By 1945, laboring people largely worked for others. As a result, the level of community participation and community control declined. The emergence of the modern welfare state and the rise of corporate power solidified the demise of community life, which had revolved around labor's self-sufficient work.

As family and community work relations changed, critical relationships between gender and age groups shifted. Family relations became more shaped by the *social* division of labor and the *social* definition of work roles for females and males, for young, adults, and elders. As family members acquired new social identities based on wage work outside the household, labor was splintered and families were divided. For example, as young people were thrown out of the work force and into schools, they became more socially opposed to their wage-earning and wage-spending parents. Elders, who retired or became unemployed, became devalued in relation to somewhat younger, "socially productive," and higher-paid adults. Females, denied entry into high-paid positions in wage labor, were subordinated to males, who obtained higher-paid wage employment.

As families divided along gender and age lines, these new social identity groups created new affirmative social bonds between socially similar people. "Marginalized" women, youth, elders, and culturally subordinate ethnic groups began to criticize the social inequities that resulted from these historical developments. By the 1960s, diverse social groups based on these identities waged social protests on many fronts, and demanded the country to promote greater social equality.

This historical study shows that low-income families relied heavily on income from informal work until World War II. The dissolution of family- and community-centered work is traced in relation to: changes in home-based and community-oriented work and marketing; shifts in gender and age relations; variations in the informal work patterns of ethnic communities; early state intervention in the non-waged work carried out by families; the growth in state subsidies for labor; the rise of big business and state regulation; and cyclical and secular economic developments.

Paradoxically, early state agents in localities undermined labor's self-sufficiency, reduced the ability of neighborhood people to shape their own destinies, and broke strong family bonds. In this way, local officials helped usher in corporate control and its new guardian, the modern welfare state. This historical process promoted worker dependency on the state and business, largely eliminating labor's ability to conduct its own work. As part of the creation of the modern welfare state, nineteenth and early twentieth state functionaries destroyed local initiative and relative self-sufficiency. With their conscious and unconscious actions, these early settlement workers and reformers often undermined the income-generating abilities wielded by communities and their residents. Considerable damage was wrought, as self-sufficient work with small economic rewards gradually became replaced by higher-paying wage labor positions. It was not until the end of the twentieth century that state functionaries, policy makers, business owners, and working people themselves started to recognize the economic and social value of community-oriented and regional self-sufficiency.

As a result of conscious and unintentional actions, early charity and settlement workers often undermined the income-generating abilities of community residents. They caused considerable damage when self-sufficient work was replaced by employer-based wage work. Although rewards for self-sufficient work were relatively small, work and reward was shared by many people. Income brought into the household often came in the non-monetary form of goods, which could be used by all members. Because they participated in shared work tasks, members of households and communities could more equally share the rewards of family and community efforts.

Employer-based work provided higher wages to some workers, wages that were increasingly paid in money. But really high wages were assigned to only a few people, typically adult white males. Because high incomes from shop work were not distributed widely, people who did not participate in these tasks could not make equal claims on these wages or, of increasing importance, on how wages would be spent. Economic rewards became differentiated as the unequal distribution of wage work and the unequal distribution of money wages led to unequal control over consumption. This development privileged wage workers and devalued non-waged workers, creating gross status differentials between people in these two income-generating categories. As a consequence of this development, many people found they had little ability to generate wage income or to claim wages paid to others. And because they could obtain less non-waged income and could obtain only relatively low wages on their own, they came to rely less on themselves and community networks. For their survival, socially devalued working people began relying more on high-paid household members (if there were any) and on the state.

During the stage of U.S. global dominance from 1945 to 1970, the welfare state emerged and created extensive worker dependency on the state. This was true both for middle-class and some low-income families. The heyday of the welfare state corresponded to a period of corporate expansion, high wages, and high levels of unionization in manufacturing. With the exception of domestic work and income-generating activities of low-income groups, working people organized little of their own work. Working class self-reliance and independence began to vanish in middle-income families, as families came to rely very heavily on wages from employers and state subsidies. To be sure, this generally was a period of material well-being, economic security, and even upward mobility for many groups.

But the decline of U.S. business and state power after 1970 led to the gradual breakdown of the welfare state's support for low- to moderate-income people. As business competition increased and state budgets were strained, the state began reducing some income subsidies for low-income groups. In general, entitlement payments to middle-class families largely have been sustained, though this may change in significant ways if health care and retirement programs and tax subsidies are reduced during future budget cuts. But, even with state support, some American workers started to envy the large (but shrinking) subsidies Western European countries provided to working people.

Today many people assume that the relationships between the state, business, and laboring people will remain essentially as they have been since the 1930s. But the welfare state is currently being reshaped by cyclical recession and the long-term restructuring of the world-economy. Cyclical recession and global restructuring eroded U.S. power and fiscal stability.

The fiscal crisis of the state has meant that the old welfare state, with its mild guarantees of economic security, may very well continue to crumble. The welfare state that emerged during the rise of U.S. power may be in the process of being replaced by a new type of state that minimizes the state's responsibility for labor's well-being. The decline of social transfer programs for especially low-income people is a product of the global division of labor. The transformation of social welfare policies did not occur simply because the political orientation of government officials changed. Federal and state governments began decreasing support for working people primarily because the U.S. position within the global economic system has declined. More generally, cyclical and/or secular pressures may have created the reduction of state support for working class people in many urban-industrial countries.

In the United States working people became disconnected from strong local and family networks that sustained them before the welfare state emerged. By 1970, the independent, material basis of family and community life had been drastically undermined by state actions, business maneuvers, and families' decisions to embrace consumer-oriented lifestyles.

The current stage in U.S. social history is unique. Since 1970, U.S. families have found that they had been cut off from their access to almost all informal income, with the exception of domestic work. Families have discovered that employers and state officials were no longer able to offer higher incomes or substantial income support to meet rising costs. Although business and government are cutting costs and reducing household income, most families continue to expect that most of their income will come from wages and state transfer payments.

As U.S. world power and household incomes declined, low-income people, including Third World immigrants, often tried to adjust to hard times by vending goods and sharing housing. But unless the pattern shifts, labor can anticipate a secular reduction in income support from both the state and business. Both the state and business seem to be assuming less responsibility for the working class.

The economic situation confronting low-income and some middle-income people is indeed at a critical juncture. It has been as if a large tank has been rolling back and forth over the population, crushing more people with each pass. Rather than assuming an arbitrary direction, the tank hits disproportionate numbers of low-income people, debilitating large numbers of people of color and injuring growing numbers of the hidden poor in middle-income and suburban neighborhoods. The tank's destructive capabilities are evident everywhere: homelessness, joblessness, educational inequities and high dropout rates, violent homicides and personal crimes, the widespread imprisonment of people of color, and increasing chemical dependency.

Everyone expects that the tank will continue to roll back and forth, bringing more casualties and impairing the ability of people to lead full, rewarding lives. In fact, everyone *knows* the tank will return again, but they are hoping that it will strike others and that they will be spared. But few people are trying to figure out how the tank functions, how to stop it, or how to start thinking about social change in the contemporary era.

This analogy may be an effective way of describing how some low- to moderate-income people experience the social world today, but it is limited by its emphasis on the impersonal forces of the present, which are abstracted from history. Today the dominant forces in the society often seem overwhelmingly powerful, increasingly out of control, and run from above by impersonal national and global institutions. This study shows how the personal, face-to-face aspects of community and regional control were transformed by the impersonal forces associated with economic development and state bureaucracy. As this process took place, work became more shaped by large firms and state fiscal policy, and less shaped by local people's initiative.

In the future, ordinary people, policy shapers and forward-looking organizations may have to make extraordinary interventions to bring about intentional, positive social change. Whether or not this will happen ultimately may depend on the quality of relationships between family members (including gender and age relations), the strength of community networks, the extent of connectedness between America's ethnic groups, and the ways that Americans envision community life, economic vitality, and governmental leadership.

The question here is whether the strengths associated with past work relations and communities can be created in new forms—not as products of economic necessity—but as products of what people have learned from history and where they want to go. Creating a new society may very well depend on rediscovering the lost history of community life and learning new lessons from America's past.

*Boy and man selling fruit at stand near Congress Hall, Philadelphia, 1913. Courtesy of the City Archives, Philadelphia.*

*One*

# Social Change and Community Life: Informal Work and the Creation of a Divided Working Class

## Studying the Relationship between Informal Work and Labor's Divisions

The question of how community life disintegrated in urban-industrial society has concerned historians and social scientists for the last century. Across America, people look with dismay at the lack of family and community control over the social world and wonder what happened to tightly knit communities that once exhibited greater command over their collective destiny. Is this image of closely bonded communities in the nineteenth and early twentieth centuries simply an historical mirage, a glorification of the past, which never was grounded in material life? This historical study, which reconstructs work relations in American communities, shows that working people once had greater control over the work they did and the neighborhoods in which they lived. This study argues that community life was once centered around non-waged, informal work and informal marketing networks. When informal work gradually declined between 1830 and 1945, the center of community relations disintegrated, altering social relations within families and between neighbors.

Today many scholars have conducted research both to determine how tightly knit families and communities were in the past and how community life affected female and male family members. While scholars have been carrying on this debate, the general public also has been arguing about historical relations. Some people hold up the historical image of tight communities as a positive model for today's world. Others denounce this image as a false, idealized picture of past communities and argue that work and domestic relations were oppressive and male dominated. In fact, past communities during America's industrial development actually exhibited both tendencies. They provided community-centered security for many, but they also failed to meet the needs of particular groups, including women, youth, and elders.

The world of the past carries a history of both liberating impulses and social tyranny. Past communities controlled diverse types of non-waged, income-yielding work, an aspect of work that has largely disappeared from social consciousness. At the same time, community life became increasingly oppressive, a development that originated in work relations associated with the impersonal institutions of the state and large business firms. Before the emergence of a strong state and large-scale industry, sexism and ageism were probably just as rooted in community and family life, as they were in large public and private institutions. But the roots of sexism and ageism in families and communities differed from the sources of social inequality that came from the state and industry. Over time, families and communities internalized the social division of labor, which intensified sexism, ageism and racism. As more layers of society became reorganized in concert with the hierarchical, social division of labor, sexism and ageism, racism and ethnic relations all developed within a complex, intertwined set of relationships. Just as the development of gender relations cannot be understood without looking at age and ethnic relations, racism cannot be understood without looking at gender and age relations.

This study focuses on the transformation of two central realms of community life, informal or non-waged work and the structure of gender and age relations. Because their development was interconnected and tied to the history of wage labor, informal work and gender and age divisions must be studied together, if the consequences of social change are to be grasped. In this study, informal work and gender and age relations are informed by the feminist view that all types of work and all family members need to be studied together, and studied within the context of the formation of ethnic groups. Ethnic stratification shaped the context in which work and households relationships developed. By analyzing the whole context of non-waged work situations, the archival data revealed connected relations associated with non-waged work. During the initial stage of research, the goal was simply to use archival data to identify ways that urban-based households in the nineteenth century generated non-waged income. The initial working thesis was that if income from wage labor alone was not able to sustain households, then supplementary income must have come from activities that households organized.

Initially I assumed that primarily women and girls engaged in non-waged work in urban areas and carried the burden of providing essential, supplementary income. I also assumed that basic changes associated with the decline of non-waged work took place between 1830 and 1870. But both of these assumptions proved incorrect. As it turned out, all household members did informal, non-waged work, although some distinct gender and age patterns emerged. And while informal work was on the decline by 1870, the process was slow and many people still relied on self-employment until World War II. Non-waged work was not largely abandoned until a relatively late date in U.S. history, almost one hundred years after the "Industrial Revolution" began in 1830. And after World War II, community relations associated with non-waged work continued to affect work relations.

After the first month of archival research, it was clear that the study of non-waged income provided an opportunity to document more than just household survival strategies. By examining all instances of non-waged work within households and communities, it was possible to identify changes in informal work, as well as to identify how the social division of labor affected gender, age, and ethnic relations. It quickly became clear in low-income families that children, men and elders were informal workers, just like women. The role of early state organizations and of businesses in shaping work in the home and on the street began to emerge as the research continued. Gradually, as archival data was considered alongside secondary materials, it was possible to reconstruct the periods of work-related change for families and communities, gender and age relations, industry, and the state. Although theories about the transformation of non-waged work and the rise of wage labor informed the process, the history of community life in the mid-Atlantic region was constructed from the ground up. This exploratory research should be examined in relation to future comparative studies on different spatial and temporal locations.

"Informal work," "non-waged work" and "home work" are all defined as similar concepts here. They refer to all income-generating activities initiated and carried out by working people. Some informal activities were organized and shared by groups of households, which made up "communities." Family and community life developed hand-in-hand, though there was tremendous variation in the strength of connections between family and community in different geographical areas. Non-waged activities supplemented wage income, which was distributed by employers.

Informal work, a common feature of the modern world, yields both money income and non-monetized income that does not have a capitalist market value. Domestic work and subsistence gardening are kinds of informal work. Women's Studies research often begins with the concept of "domestic work" and assumes that it was always a distinctively female activity. By contrast, this study begins with the broader category of "informal work" and traces the historical development of "women's" domestic work in this context. As it turns out, the development of "women's" domestic work, as it is thought of today, is a fairly recent creation, not a transhistorical phenomenon.

Informal work and families' internal divisions changed in different ways for different communities, which all were shaped by ethnic relationships.

Low- and moderate-income urban communities often depended on work and income generated in rural areas in the United States. Because even "urban" families received income transfers from household members in "rural" areas, the communities studied here should not be treated as completely urban or "rural," even if a core group of family members always lived in the city. In many cases, family members moved seasonally and worked in both urban and rural areas. Research findings here suggest that changes in urban labor can be best understood within a regional framework, and not within a strictly urban framework defined by city boundary lines.

Although it is difficult to accurately characterize the general income-level of community members, families that organized informal work were generally "low- and moderate-income" families. The income level of U.S. informal workers may seem low or relatively adequate, depending on the different spatial and temporal comparisons that are made. In relation to wages distributed throughout the world-economy, U.S. families that did extensive informal work in 1850 had moderate incomes. In relation to wage-dependent families in 1900, families of informal workers had low to moderate incomes. When compared to today's middle-class families, informal workers in 1930 had low incomes. As new consumer needs developed and standards of living changed, perspectives changed on what constituted low, moderate, and high incomes for laboring families. In general, it is useful to remember that at least one-half of American working families in 1850 had moderate incomes, when compared to other groups around the world. American families received high "Third World" wages and resembled Third World workers. But from the vantage point of American labor today, mid-nineteenth century U.S. communities are to be considered poor, as are most workers in the world today. In the past, members of poor American communities worked hard to share their common resources and to build a commonwealth.

The social change of community life was studied by tracing the restructuring of informal work and families' work relations primarily in four urban and rural communities in the mid-Atlantic region. The transformation of home-based work and intra-household relations was reconstructed for African-American communities from 1850 to 1945. Social change and Italian-American communities were studied in the city and in agricultural and industrial rural areas between 1870 and 1945. The shaping of informal work was analyzed for one multi-ethnic, urban neighborhood at the turn of the century. The transformation of non-waged work for German-American and other farming communities was reconstructed for the period between 1900 and 1945. All these ethnically defined communities resided part of the year in Philadelphia or in nearby rural areas in Pennsylvania, New Jersey and Delaware. Community members obtained almost all of their income from activity in the region. They received some additional support from family members who transferred income generated in other U.S. regions or abroad.

## Long-term Social Change and the Discouragement of Informal Work

Community life in low- and moderate-income areas changed as families developed closer relationships with the state and businesses. Local state agencies and early "state-like" organizations restructured working class life by discouraging labor from organizing non-waged, informal work of their own. As laboring families did less of their own work to supplement low wages, they relied more on wage work and market consumption.

This study identifies and analyzes the actions of early state-like organizations and state agencies, which contributed to the decline of most household work. It also examines the influence of industrial reorganization, rising wages, the growth of the retail market, and choices made by laboring people in this process. Informal work based in the community once enabled working people to remain relatively skilled and self-sufficient in diverse types of work. To discourage informal work, state functionaries encouraged women to take care of limited domestic responsibilities and to consume more. They simultaneously discouraged other household members from doing informal work in the home and in the streets. This process was gradual and occurred in stages, moving more families along the continuum from a heavy reliance on informal work in the mid-nineteenth century to a heavy reliance on wage labor and state transfer payments in the mid-twentieth century. For probably one-half of U.S. working people, this century-long process was if they had moved from the Third World to the First World, where most workers today rely on low-paid wage labor, informal work, and little or no assistance from the state. In the case of middle-class families who had their economic needs met by paychecks, home-based work was largely eliminated by 1945. After 1945, women's domestic work ( or housework) was one of the few surviving forms of informal work that was once extensive and diverse. In the 1950s and 1960s, women who did housework, low-income people, small producers, rural people, and recent immigrants still conducted informal work.

As large-scale industrial production and corporate control grew, the work relationships between ethnic, gender and age groups shifted. The changing social division of labor reinforced and cemented the change in home-based work that was initiated by the state. Federal and local state policies contributed to the decline of micro-businesses and small businesses, which once had sustained working people. By doing this, state officials promoted the rise of large industrialists and retailers, the new sources of employment and income. Furthermore, by dissolving informal work options and assigning household members to occupations by gender and age, early state and industrial policy solidified occupational divisions based on gender and age. Adult men secured higher paying industrial jobs while women, young people and elders became relegated to lower paying jobs.

The creation of goods, services, natural resources, and labor for sale on the capitalist market, what is called "commodification," is a central process affecting the organization of work. Extensive commodification greatly affected high-income families, but it did not make consumers out of low-income households to the same extent. Informal work was largely done by low-income households, though high-income households relied on non-monetary income from domestic work. Because low-income households in the United States still carry out non-waged work to survive, this group retains more control over the organization of its income-yielding work.

Although parastatal and state agencies have pushed working people to become "full-time" employees and consumers for one and one-half centuries, working people remained relatively independent of employer-based wages, state transfer payments, and corporate consumerism for a long time. In fact, it was not until 1910 or 1920 in the United States that it could be said that a high level of dependency on employer-based wages and the consumer market had been firmly established. And the sharp ethnic or "racial" stratification that accompanied this new dependency on non-household institutions did not really emerge until the early twentieth century. Although scholars have assumed that wage and market dependencies and working class divisions were fixed and in place by the early nineteenth century, these are actually fairly recent developments. And because the destruction of household-organized neighborhood micro-businesses and the institutionalization of the "modern" social hierarchy are relatively recent developments in the United States (and not products of early nineteenth century factory life), there may still be an opportunity to restructure work relations.

## Rewriting History: The Fundamentals of Integrating Knowledge

The shared position of subordinate ethnic, gender and age groups has often been minimized, just as the shared position of dominant groups has been. Black/Africana Studies, Ethnic Studies, Women's Studies, child and adult development, and "gerontology" have become distinct disciplines, even though they are all related. The history of wage workers is treated separately from the history of non-waged workers. Labor history rarely includes non-waged work as an integral and necessary component. The material relationship between middle-income and low-income groups has been largely ignored. In this study, changes in the historical relationships between the low-income and middle-class strata were reconsidered by reuniting related disciplines. Only by rejoining the social sciences and history is it possible to understand the common interrelated history of non-waged and wage workers, their families, and their communities.

Most studies about work never consider non-waged activities carried out by families and communities. Most scholars, with the exception of some feminists, have not noticed that something was seriously amiss when informal work was ignored. Studies by historians and social scientists that bypassed the significance of non-waged work carried out by men, women, children and elders provide only a partial picture of past social life. As a result, a double-standard of historical scholarship has emerged. Industrial production and its technical division of labor seem to be highly valued topics for scholars, while the large and changing realm of informal work has been unappreciated.

Because people are so focused on the labor force and the wage income distributed by large-scale producers, they may think it strange to read about the non-waged side of history. Reading about how local, income-yielding networks declined may bring unexpected surprises, particularly since many middle-class people, who no longer rely on these income-generating activities, do not recognize the significance of informal work for low-income groups. Not only has informal work declined in these modern times, but its significance has been deprecated by working people themselves, who often view housework as a non-productive, mindless, undervalued, female activity. Similarly, the swapping that still occurs in low-income neighborhoods is now a subject for Black/Africana Studies, but not for scholars studying class formation. Both Women's Studies and Black Studies are seen as providing material that supplements other disciplines, but they are not seen as having the capacity to redefine other disciplines. In fact, if knowledge about work done by women and African Americans is not integrated into traditional disciplines, then traditional disciplines will be incapable of developing solutions for today's problems.

Using a materialist analysis of home-based work, this project stresses the positive contributions that have been made by low- and moderate-income households and ethnic groups, whose members often have been negatively labeled "boring housewives," "the undeserving, underclass," "welfare mothers," "wild, juvenile delinquents" or "burnt-out" and "over-the-hill" elders. These "internally marginalized" groups and "invisible" workers made it possible for families and communities to sustain themselves in the face of economic adversity.

The next chapters are organized in following way. Chapter Two provides a theoretical and historical introduction to the transformation of informal and wage work, self-sufficiency, and community life. Labor, which moves from a low dependency on wages to a high dependency on wages, is described both in relation to U.S. labor history and in relation to labor in urban-industrial society. As people did less of their own work and more work for others, labor's new divisions emerged.

Chapter Three examines two early periods: 1) the period of economic contraction from 1830 to 1850, when many U.S. households relied heavily on non-waged work, and 2) the period of economic expansion from 1850 to 1873, when large-scale industrial production led to a somewhat greater dependence on wages. In general, wages from employers were so inadequate that laboring families needed to generate supplemental, non-waged income to survive. Early interventions by parastatal organizations into informal work activities are analyzed for the Philadelphia area.

Chapter Four explores the period of economic contraction from 1873 to 1897, when informal work and community networks began to break down. Secondary literature is reviewed in order to gain insight into wage and non-waged work patterns. During this period, new distinctions emerged between the informal work and the wage work carried out by females and males, by the young, adults and elders. This chapter shows how local, nascent state organizations and early state agencies discouraged informal work in the region that included Philadelphia as its urban center. Archival materials are used to reconstruct informal work patterns and to analyze informal work in African-American and Italian-American communities in the mid-Atlantic region. Gender and age divisions are considered in relation to different work contexts and production processes.

The consolidation of large-scale industry provides the historical backdrop for Chapter Five, which examines the economic expansion from 1897 to 1913. During this period of sporadic production and high levels of unemployment, urban areas began to decentralize and ethnic segregation in neighborhoods increased. This was a time when Progressives worked to minimize adverse impacts of capitalism. Social reformers in urban neighborhoods tried to fight poverty by encouraging adult males to earn more wages for market goods and by urging women and children to stay away from wage labor and street vending. Philadelphia's health officials discouraged informal work by removing farm animals from the city, which eliminated an important source of subsistence income, and by regulating some petty enterprises. Informal work patterns are examined through an analysis of records of a multi-ethnic, urban gardening project, which was managed by a parastatal organization. Using archival records, changes in informal work are analyzed for African-American, multi-ethnic, Italian-American, and rural communities throughout the mid-Atlantic region.

Chapter Six considers the period of economic contraction from 1913 to 1945, which was marked by a concentration of corporate control, high levels of unemployment and underemployment and, eventually, growing state management of working class finances. During this period in Philadelphia, municipal agencies aggressively intervened in micro-businesses by developing and enforcing regulations that raised sanitary standards, prohibiting pig and poultry raising, and restricting informal markets and second-hand shops. Changes and variations in informal work are traced through archival and secondary materials for African-American and Italian-American communities, and for women and men in multi-ethnic, industrial communities in the mid-Atlantic region.

Chapter Seven analyzes the growing reliance of families on wage income and market consumption for the period of economic expansion between 1945 and 1970 and, subsequently, for the period of economic contraction between 1970 and 1993. As families generated less non-waged income from informal work and typically relied more on the wages of adult males, clear work divisions developed between women and men, between adults and children, and between adults and elders. The fragmentation of household and community identity along these lines led to the emergence of new social identities, which created new social movements. The contemporary quest for community is associated with the decline of informal work and with the sharpening social divisions, which accompanied labor's increasing dependency on wages and market consumption. Contemporary efforts to cultivate micro-enterprises and to revitalize community life are analyzed in relation to new trends in business and underemployment.

Chapter Eight provides an overview of social change during the last 150 years. As the meaning of self-sufficiency changed in the mid-Atlantic region and in the United States, so did the meaning of community. The broad social space that once was associated with civil society and labor's activities contracted, as businesses and the state organized more work and administrative functions. As informal work declined, and wage labor became the primary way for the working class to obtain income, families and communities, gender, age and ethnic groups have all been affected in profound ways. To highlight important issues about contemporary economic development and work, selected writings of classical social scientists are reviewed in relation to the historical findings of this study. General approaches for initiating positive social change and for expanding work options are then explored within the contemporary context.

*Curbside market in a Jewish neighborhood near 4th Street and Fitzwater, Philadelphia, 1926. Courtesy of the City Archives, Philadelphia.*

# Two

# Self-Sufficiency: The Forgotten Past of Working-Class Communities in America

## Families, Work and Social Change

Many of today's political leaders, managers of social programs, and sometimes even working people themselves are struck by what they perceive to be a lack of working class self-reliance and initiative. This is ironic because about one century ago, officials of federal, state and local agencies, in conjunction with early non-profit organizations and businesses, implemented social policies that made working-class people become more dependent on non-familial, outside institutions. The establishment of labor's reliance on employers and the state, once seen as a social advancement, is now seen as problematic because homeless, underemployed, and uninsured Americans confront a shrinking pool of high-wage jobs and a reduction in state income transfers.

State agencies and parastatal organizations played a central role in persuading U.S. working-class households to rely on wage income and to decrease their reliance on their own self-sufficient, household-organized work. During the last 150 years, directors of workhouses, settlement houses, charitable organizations, and state agencies helped create a working class that became largely dependent on employers and the state. The definition of self-sufficiency itself changed, as the working class organized less of its own work and relied more on wage labor and state subsidies and services. In designing and implementing wage- and state-dependent social policies, state agencies and early "charity" organizations created many of the problems that they are trying to solve today.

But the apparent lack of self-sufficiency among low-income households in the United States is partially a myth because they continue to work somewhat on their own to survive. Although working class households or families became primarily oriented toward higher-paying wage work and market consumption, working people today still do not live by wage work alone. The modern world-economy does not provide enough wage work or sufficient wages for most households to sustain themselves—even in the best of times, even in today's advanced, industrialized countries. Enterprising household members find ways to take care of themselves, to survive in the absence of sufficient work or adequate wages. At the center of changing community structures are income-pooling households or families. These are the basic economic, multi-generational units of class that generate and share resources and the work benefits, regardless of whether they are co-residential units or units composed of familial and non-familial members.[1]

Today, one can find enterprising working people selling hot dogs or T-shirts on street corners or find children rising early to deliver the daily newspaper. One can find working people selling honey, apples or handmade weather vanes at roadside stands, hosting garage sales on the lawn, and selling goods from car and truck tailgates at weekend flea markets and swap meets. These kinds of activities provide a glimpse not only into the way that working class households "make ends meet" today, but they also provide insight into how households did so in the past.

Households used to rely to a much greater extent on income from activities they organized themselves in the home or conducted on the street, which can be described as "home work" or informal work. Instead of relying only on wage income from shop work (or from putting-out work organized by others), people made goods and sold them directly to others.[2] Enterprising household members in urban and rural U.S. settings found ways to make, swap, and sell goods and services that could generate income to supplement wage work, which alone could not provide the food, clothing, shelter and social amenities they needed. The working class sustained itself over time through income it obtained from wage labor and *non*-waged work.

In the United States between 1830 and 1945, the extension of shop work and wage labor, the growth of large-scale industry, and the rise of consumer services changed the way that working-class household members worked and lived. As time went on, most working households in the United States relied less on their own improvisational home work to provide an income and more on the shop work and money wages provided by capitalist firms. But this process was uneven. Members of some households were drawn into the orbit of shop work and money wages more than others, and some households from lower-income ethnic groups were kept at arms distance from stable employment.

Increasingly, the home-based production of goods and provision of services was assumed by capitalist firms, which led to a narrowing of the kind of work that household members did.[3] Working class families relied less on swapping and bartering with neighbors, a non-market activity, and paid for goods that were acquired through the capitalist market. In addition, as household members conducted less home work, they lost the skills associated with doing home work, a process that paralleled and accentuated the widely documented deskilling of labor in the workplace. These developments twice divided the working class. It divided households into those who relied primarily on wages from "shop work," and those who depended heavily on non-waged work, a division that typically followed ethnic lines. And it divided both types of households internally, separating household members along gender and age lines.[4]

To understand how and why the income-yielding work of laboring households changed and to appreciate the long-term consequences of this, the larger economic system must be examined. The world-economy is based on the expansion of production for profit, not only in the shop (a process already studied in great detail by many social scientists and historians), but also at home and in the streets. Changes in the organization of families' informal work, and the divisions between ethnic groups and within working households that accompanied these changes, occurred within the overall context of economic development and the social division of labor.

As the United States industrialized, working class households organized a smaller proportion of their income-yielding work and relied less on reciprocal and redistributive relationships with economically similar households. By purchasing mass-produced goods with money wages, they established tight economic links to unfamiliar producers and sellers. The goods and services they once swapped with other working class households increasingly were bought from larger producers, who set their prices in accordance with economic rules. The growing reliance on goods acquired through the capitalist system formed one part of "commodification." "Commodification" is known as the sale of more goods, services and resources, as well as the ability to labor, in accordance with the rules of the capitalist market. Commodification, in short, is the commercialization of more and more aspects of life. Labor's growing reliance on money wages and shop work to provide for its needs can be described as part of the formation of the working class, or "proletarianization." Commodification and proletarianization go hand in hand.

The history of labor's informal work in the United States in the nineteenth and twentieth centuries reveals the largely ignored, but terribly important underside of commodification and proletarianization. An in-depth examination of changes in home work and the impact of these changes on relations within and between households in the United States, particularly between 1830 and 1945, contributes to a deeper understanding of commodification and proletarianization, which generally is viewed just from the limited perspective of the shop floor, and not from the related perspective of home- and community-defined work. By looking not only at relations in the shop, but also in the home and in the community, new insights are provided on class conflict, intra-class divisions, and work initiated by labor in urban and rural areas.[5]

## Theoretical Explorations on the Interdependence of Home and Shop Work

In this study, a moving-picture camera is focused on the transformation of informal work in the nineteenth and twentieth centuries to determine how and to what extent commodification has taken place, and understand what the consequences this has had for laboring people. A moving picture of the history of family- and community-organized work is created by using archival data gathered from records of early charity, social reform, and public health organizations. This reconstruction of community life and neighborhood-based, income-yielding activities broadens traditional definitions of work, which usually just refer to employer-organized work. An analysis of archival records, rather than census data analysis, provides the best way to reconstruct shifting patterns in informal work in different ethnic communities. Unfortunately, people who gathered census data focused on wage labor and provided inconsistent, incomplete information on informal work, especially work done by women, children, and elders.[6]

By broadening the definition of work, people today can see that the work ethic has not declined, but has been reshaped to fit the bureaucratic image of the productive, industrial worker and the state-regulated, working-class family. In sharp contrast with standard perceptions about the work ethic, low-income families once exhibited a work ethic characterized by considerable independence and great self-sufficiency. By contrast, higher-income and mid-twentieth century families exhibited a work ethic of employer- and state-dependency, consistent with business- and state-organized bureaucracies.

When a moving-picture camera is used to depict stages in the history of informal work, it shows that the process of the separation of labor from the means of production and subsistence was very gradual. Family members relied on both wages and on income from household- and community-organized home work. Although the income mix gradually shifted in the direction of greater wage dependency, U.S. labor relied on households' "means of production and subsistence" to generate income. To a limited extent, this even continues to be true even today.

Although the theoretical underpinnings of this study relate to different disciplines, one central theoretical question is how does labor sustain itself in urban-industrial, capitalist society? More than other historians and social scientists, Karl Marx and his writings have influenced the way labor history and working class reproduction have been studied. For this reason, the research done here has been positioned in relation to Marx's arguments.

In *Capital,* Karl Marx made an oversimplification when he wrote that workers needed to be separated from the means of production in order to be "free" to work as wage laborers. In his theoretical formulation, Marx assumed that the wage covered the cost of subsistence, or the cost of reproduction.[7] In fact, almost all "workers of the world" were only partially separated from the means of production and subsistence. The wage only covered a part of the cost of subsistence for the vast majority of world labor, including U.S. working-class families in 1850. Because Marx based his theory on wage labor in the urban-industrial factory, he failed to see that laboring households created essential, supplementary income by organizing work of their own. They were therefore possibly "freer" from the capitalist relations than Marx imagined. Marx failed to reflect seriously on the importance of wage differentials, different production processes, and labor's supplemental income for different communities within different areas of the world-economy. If he had done so, he would have recognized the importance of informal work for labor in urban-industrialized areas, as well as in the Third World.

As Marx discovered, at the heart of capital accumulation lay the essential process of primitive accumulation, or the initial organization of production and generation of wealth in non-capitalist areas and in already incorporated areas of the world-economy. This ongoing process of primitive accumulation continuously pushes laboring people to live within expanding and deepening capitalist relations.[8] Because primitive accumulation is never ending in the modern world, more areas of work and consumption become organized within the profit-making context. During the history of the world-economy, more work became organized in the form of wage labor and working people bought more consumption goods.[9] This brought a global reduction in informal work. The growth of big business occurred partly because the state, which opened new avenues for primitive accumulation to take place, intervened on the behalf of business. This study of U.S. ethnic communities shows how the process of primitive accumulation reshaped families and communities in industrial society.

The ongoing, primitive accumulation of capital in urban-industrial areas was a strong impulse that led toward the gradual, global commodification of both work and means of everyday sustenance. It is helpful to envision a continuum of labor in the world-economy. As economic development proceeded, U.S. labor occupied a changing, fairly wide space on this continuum. At one side of the continuum, largely uncommodified labor could be found. It relied very heavily on its own work to support itself and to supplement very low wages. At the opposite end of the continuum, highly commodified labor could be found, which relied very heavily on high wages and on consumption through the capitalist market. From 1830 to 1990, U.S. labor generally moved from a mid-point on labor's continuum to the highly commodified end. This dramatic change can only be accounted for by examining how the process of primitive accumulation occurred in urban-industrial society. How businesses and the state suppressed informal work, intervened in community markets, and created new social needs in food, clothing, and shelter is part of this largely untold story.[10]

If labor in the world-economy is envisioned as part of a continuum that exhibits varying degrees of dependency on outside producers, then it can be stated that there have been essentially three groups of labor. First, on the low-wage side, one laboring group (now probably proportionately smaller than in earlier time periods) could not meet subsistence levels on a daily or generational basis. In the communities studied here, very few families formed part of this extremely impoverished group. (Starving people in contemporary Africa clearly are part of a laboring group that does not meet basic subsistence levels.)

Second, the largest group of the world-economy's laboring families has been generating sufficient low-wage and non-waged income to meet or slightly surpass subsistence levels, as these levels have been socially and historically defined. For adult male wage laborers from this group, wages typically covered the cost of sustaining the individual worker, but not the whole family. Many of the low- to moderate-income families studied in mid-Atlantic communities formed part of this very large and diverse group, though the relative size of this group within labor became smaller between 1870 and 1920. These subsistence-level families in the United States, which occupied a large middle space on labor's continuum, carried out extensive informal work.

After 1870, and especially after the turn of the century, many of the families studied here began earning higher wages, did less of their own work, and purchased more goods through the capitalist market. At this critical turning point, these families became constituted as part of the most highly commodified group on labor's continuum, where most U.S. families are today. This third group of highly commodified labor relied on high wages, extensive consumption through the capitalist market, and on a small percentage of income from non-waged work (including domestic work). Over the history of the world-economy, this privileged stratum has been labor's smallest group. Today and in the foreseeable future, some U.S. families may find that they may be forced downward from an economically advantaged position to a more intermediary stratum.

By conceiving of the stratification of labor in this way, new perspectives on "work ethic" issues emerge. On the one hand, the vast majority of laboring households in the world-economy have, in fact, worked too much, both for themselves and for others and they have received barely sufficient wages and little non-waged income for their arduous efforts. On the other hand, a current problem for U.S. labor, and for labor in other urban-industrial areas, is that households became too dependent on outside employers and shaky state transfers payments, given the historically weak commitment of business and the state to labor's well-being. Laboring people, in effect, worked too hard for others and did not control enough of their own work and marketing relations.

Business and the state helped construct the change from a more home- and community-centered work ethic to one that increasingly revolved around shop work for others. The so-called "decline of the American work ethic" was actually manufactured by and for the business class. The alleged disappearance of labor's work ethic took place because the old work ethic became transformed into a more limited, shop-centered work ethic, which characterized laboring people's extensive dependency on wage labor. In conjunction with the transformation of the work ethic, labor's "materialism" changed as it consumed less of what it directly made and bought more goods and services on the widening market.

## Historical Changes in Income Generation in the United States

Informal work probably was once a widespread phenomenon in the United States, one that thrived before World War II. Throughout the country, informal work changed in relationship to general processes of class formation, commodification, and urbanization. According to Jacqueline Jones in *The Dispossessed,* economically deprived Americans in different regions relied on foraging and subsistence activities in the nineteenth and twentieth centuries.[11] Jones' book shows that non-waged work provided a critical supplement to wages in the United States in the years since the Civil War. Evidence provided by studies on home-based work, along with documentation of non-waged work by scholars studying women and low-income ethnic groups, indicates that non-waged work has been a basic feature of work life in the United States for a long time.[12]

Documentation of various types of informal work suggests that there is nothing unique about the informal work that was carried out in the mid-Atlantic region and in the Philadelphia area.[13] The ethnically diverse communities selected for archival research here were generally representative of many communities in the United States. Non-waged work was probably more extensive in rural regions than in more urbanized areas. The general processes of change and patterns of transformation, which all were shaped by actions taken by the state, businesses and ethnic communities, probably shared a general similarity in different regions of the country, though the specific circumstances and the particular accents of social change were different. Ethnic and multi-ethnic communities and their income-sharing networks often developed across wide geographical spaces.

How did this transformation from less dependence to greater dependence on wages take place? And how did women's domestic work survive and become the primary expression of non-waged work between 1945 and the present? They did because connections between laboring families and firms deepened and widened as history unfolded. Not only did economic and social pressures move families toward the more market-oriented end of labor's continuum, but families often chose to take the road to commercialization because it promised higher wages and shorter working days. Because unions failed to see the social benefits of informal work, they played a central role in the integration of working families into an employer-centered economic system.

By participating in the system, families and communities strengthened the forces that eventually uprooted what remained of community control. Over the last two centuries, household members who participated even marginally in capitalist production processes—as farmers, artisans, and manufacturing workers—generated profits for capitalists, who then invested and reinvested the profits of their labor in the expansion of capitalist production, which helped reduce labor's own work sphere.[14] Community life became assaulted by and gradually engulfed by the penetration of the institutions of the state and the business firm.[15]

Although mid- and late-nineteenth century households linked with industrial production may have benefited from relatively high wages in certain industries, the fruits of their underpaid labor were used by capitalists to invest in enlarging their operations, thus promoting the expanded accumulation of capital. By the mid-nineteenth century, owners of large-scale firms replaced some laborers with machines.[16] When machines replaced people, branches of industry became redefined and small producers were pushed out of business, forcing households to seek new sources of wage income and revise their non-waged, income-generating strategies.[17]

Even as some direct manufacturing work became superfluous due to the application of labor-saving technology, there was an expansion of service sector jobs, jobs in distribution and transportation, and state-related employment. Typically, at least from 1870 to the mid-1980s, the most profitable firms that applied new technology in the industrial production process had large work forces. This trend toward the growth of employees in large firms was not reversed for large-scale producers until the end of the twentieth century, when highly profitable, large firms began downsizing in the 1980s.[18]

Hidden from historical view has been the critical process of the discouragement of informal work. With the exception of "adult female" domestic work, which was socially reinforced by business and state actions in the twentieth century, informal work in communities generally declined. Household dependency on wage labor increased dramatically when businesses took over activities that once had been organized by laboring households.

Skill levels required for work became defined and controlled by business managers, and not by families and local networks, thus promoting the decline of informal work skills in the working class. Families watched their options for controlling, managing, and benefiting from household work unravel and be expropriated by quick-thinking entrepreneurs. As the marketing of bread, vegetables and clothes was taken over by capitalist firms, household members were forced to find other means of supplementing wage incomes. And as more land acquired a market value, families could no longer use previously free urban spaces to build shanties or hunt game.

During the nineteenth and early twentieth centuries, wages paid by U.S. employers clearly did not cover the entire socially defined cost of reproducing wage-dependent families, including even those who relied on wages from the large, profitable firms. The significance of this fact should not be underestimated. By and large, laboring households that shared resources with economically similar households assumed responsibility for creating a sizable portion of household income. Even in this economically prosperous part of the industrial world, laboring households generated a significant proportion of their total household income throughout the multi-generational, life cycle of the household.

Identifying changes in the ways that families and community networks sustained themselves requires examining changes in the material connections between households, enterprises and the state. Traditional assumptions about how the working class survived economically need to be abandoned right from the start. The assumption that U.S. households in the nineteenth and twentieth centuries relied almost exclusively on wages to survive is false. Instead, even in the mid- to late-twentieth century, laboring households, particularly those from lower-income groups, counted on their own work efforts, community marketing relations, and inter-household income sharing to sustain themselves. Laboring households were reproduced because members pooled their income, which consisted of all that came into a household in the form of money or goods that could be consumed or used.[19] Low- to moderate-income people before World War II sustained themselves because communities organized many of their own marketing and consumption activities. The new culture of consumption defined by businesses, advertisement firms, and the thriving segment of the middle class was largely outside the realm of everyday life for labor's lower stratum before 1945.

## A Classification of Income-Generating Work and Labor's Strata

Before the historical stages of informal work can be presented in the following chapters, a review needs to be made of the different types and kinds of non-waged income-generating activities. Households pooled five general types of income.[20] First, wage income (in money or in kind) came from work in capitalist enterprises or from other employers, such as state agencies or "middle-class," professional households.

It must be emphasized here that the generation of wage income occurred within a completely different process than the generation of non-waged income through households' informal work. In the first case, wage labor was organized by and benefited the capitalist or employer, the person (or unit) who assumed the investment risks involved in setting up production. The state and its agents, of course, worked to reduce the degree of risk assumed by businessmen, reflecting the fact that capitalism was not a system of pure competition at all.[21] One of the ways that the state reduced the degree of risk for industrialists was to reshape family and community life, particularly by undermining informal work.

The breakdown of labor's sources of *non*-waged income follows. Non-waged income came from three types of informal work, as well from social relationships that yielded income transfers. As mentioned earlier, the first source of household income was wage labor. Within the category of non-waged income, the second type of income came from non-waged subsistence activities, including housework, gardening and raising animals for food (all particular kinds of subsistence activities). Subsistence work created goods that were consumed by the household. Subsistence activities utilized materials owned or bought by the household. In the past, the "means of subsistence production" probably were acquired through exchanges or sharing arrangements with neighbors, through barter, and through deals made at labor's, low-priced informal markets. Today, women's and men's domestic subsistence work usually requires making purchases through capitalist retailers. Nevertheless, First World domestic work resembles "traditional subsistence" work carried out by Third World laborers.

A third type of income came from non-waged petty commodity producing or marketing activities. This work took place within the context of informal markets, where direct producers and direct sellers met face-to-face. Petty producing and marketing also took place on the street and on a door-to-door basis, with "producers" selling directly to consumers. Low-income petty producers typically operated in informal community markets and in face-to-face relations with buyers, where prices were determined by criteria other than the standard directives of the capitalist market. In the distant past, petty producers and vendors operated within the terrain of informal, community relations, but increasingly these workers were touched by and drawn into the capitalist market's orbit.

The fourth type of income came from non-waged work associated with the renting of lodgings, land, draft animals, and equipment. For low-income people in the pre-World War II period, this work took place within informal markets and through household networks. It was also possible to generate rental income by renting in the capitalist market, but this income-generating activity was generally restricted to those with substantial resources.

Fifth, and last, income also came from transfer payments, another type of non-waged income. Transfer payments included gifts from relatives, income from charity or early state organizations, state transfer payments (including means-tested welfare income and entitlement payments such as Social Security income), and forced transfers (or theft from capital, the state, and households).[22] Historically, a major transformation occurred when the state became more involved in managing fiscal relationships between classes and in transferring non-waged income to working class families. Therefore, it is useful to make a distinction between two general categories of transfer payments: 1) transfer payments between family members and friends and 2) transfer payments made by state agencies and early state-like organizations. Small income transfers from early charity organizations, workhouses, settlement houses, and early non-profit organizations served to bridge the gap between inter-household income transfers and state transfer payments.

This study does not identify all the particular stages associated with the history of labor's informal networks. Because early social service archives and secondary literature did not provide detailed, contextual information about labor's support networks and markets, it was impossible to give specific details about the mechanisms that led to their demise. For example, there was limited information about exchanging income and goods of equal value (through bartering, sharing work, and making income transfers) and generating income by selling goods and services to other families. This lacuna will need to be addressed through future research on labor's informal organizations and networks.

The relationship between the classification of work used here and "informal work," as it is commonly defined, needs to be clarified. The concept "informal work" creates an image of people working for themselves in small-scale operations. Unfortunately, the concept typically has been divorced from the larger historical context in which informal or non-waged work developed. Studies on informal work in United States and in other industrialized countries have not focused on how self-sufficiency came to mean working for others. Here I redefine informal work to mean non-waged work.

Although scholars have used the "informal sector" to broaden our understanding of work activities, this concept has often been used to obscure more than it reveals. Scholars have typically used the informal sector to group together a hodgepodge of wage and non-waged activities, which should not be indiscriminately mixed together. Laboring for a profit-oriented company to earn wages and working for oneself are completely different. In the first case, laboring for wages occurs inside the capitalist economy, while non-waged work takes place in the personal sphere of family life, where sustaining the household is a priority. Imprecise scholars use the term "informal sector" to include "under-the-table" untaxed wage and non-waged work, wage labor organized as contract work, wage-paying homework, and household-organized marketing work. Most scholars have included some home-based and sweatshop wage labor activities in the informal sector, even though this work is organized by profit-making firms. Usually the concept of "informal work" as it is commonly used does not refer to the full range of non-waged subsistence activities that households have used to survive. What's more, the "informal sector," the "underground economy," and the "black economy" typically have been used to refer only to some income-generating activities that the state has tried to regulate, a fairly recent development.[23]

Scholars sometimes incorrectly define the informal sector as consisting only of "hidden" economic activities that government officials have identified as additional sources of tax revenue in the twentieth century.[24] According to writers who emphasize the advent of taxation, once income taxes were introduced in the early twentieth century and economic activities subsequently began to be monitored by governmental agencies, non-waged, household-organized work (with the exception of housework) suddenly fell into the "informal sector."

Women's work in the home generally has been assumed to be a non-taxable source of income for households, one that has a unique position relative to other income sources. As it has been defined in this study on U.S. communities, the informal sector has been a constant feature of the modern world, not a new addition. Here informal work refers to all non-waged work and income-generating activities (except for income from state transfer payments) that have supplemented income from wage labor.

Although taxation was not a focus here, the fear of being taxed by local, state or federal tax collectors probably did not limit low-income householders' non-waged work or force them to hide it before 1945. Instead of trying to uncover low-income people's informal activities, state officials in Pennsylvania, for example, concentrated on obtaining taxes from wealthy citizens, which included taxes on personal property, such as watches.

Although some Western and rural states imposed poll taxes on vendors and hawkers, Eastern states did not tax petty vendors.[25]

To trace household work patterns, I will roughly divide the working class into two groups. "Improvising labor" consists of households that had a relatively low degree of dependence on wages and organized much work of their own work to supplement low wages. "Monied" labor consists of households that relied heavily on income from wage labor.[26] (Monied labor includes the new middle class.) When households relied on wage labor for at least 65 to 70 percent of their total income over the course of about 10 to 20 years, they can be said to be part of "monied labor." But once some households in improvising labor became transformed into part of monied labor, economic depression often reduced their income, changed their work relations, and brought them back into improvising labor. The rough categories of improvising labor and monied labor simply summarize the grouping of households located along the continuum from less commodified to more commodified work and consumption relations.[27]

Although yesterday's American households in improvising labor tended to have low-incomes, they were not always impoverished or "poor." For example, one household might have run a successful, small producing and marketing venture. Another household might have established a set of stable non-waged activities, which were occasionally supplemented by wage labor. And though highly wage-dependent households typically had higher incomes than improvising ones, they were not necessarily economically advantaged or well-off. The classic example of this is the late nineteenth-century household that had many of its members earning very low wages by working at match, hat, clothing or food factories.

This analysis of all income-yielding work does not compare indicators that demonstrate how the relative advantages and disadvantages of class have been socially distributed (as do measures of differences based on income, educational level, and occupational classification). Here I study the changing sources of income and the changing composition of improvising and monied labor. This approach provides a means to define class formation through changes in comprehensive work relations, which are rooted in the economy and material life.

This study emphasizes the key role of the state and its sibling organizations in promoting stronger ties between households, businesses and sellers of consumer goods. Although unions sought to increase nominal wages and to increase households' ability to consume, it is doubtful that unions facilitated the immediate transformation of households from improvising to monied labor. Unions did increase the level of dependency of higher-income households on wages and on market consumption, but they probably only had a long-term, cyclical influence, which gradually created conditions that facilitated the upward mobility of many low-income households into monied labor.[28] I came across no evidence that suggested unions had a direct, immediate impact on non-waged work relations at the neighborhood or regional levels, but I did not conduct extensive research on this subject.

As households in improvising labor developed stronger links with large employers and became more integrated into market relations, they became more like households in monied labor. Between 1830 and 1945, U.S. households very gradually changed their patterns of work and consumption, which eventually resulted in a decline in the size of improvising labor.

The focus of this study is changes in informal work carried out by improvising labor. This is because improvising labor represented the largest stratum of U.S. labor in the mid-nineteenth century. Improvising labor also has been labor's largest stratum throughout the history of the modern world. In addition, it is possible that the ranks of improvising labor will greatly expand again in both cyclical and structural terms, given the decline of U.S. hegemony in the early 1970s and the depressed state of the economy in the 1980s and early 1990s. In the mid-nineteenth century, the bulk of the U.S. working class consisted of households that were only partially dependent on wage labor for their survival.

Considered as a whole, the working class—including its stratum of improvising labor—was larger than many might think. Many laborers who are treated by historians as "independent," petty-bourgeois producers, farmers and artisans were actually part of the working class because they belonged to households that had members working for capitalist enterprises. Furthermore, many household members working as apprentices in artisan shops or as day laborers on farms actually worked for small capitalists. These working people in artisanal shops and rural areas probably often relied on a high proportion of non-waged income, thereby forming part of improvising labor.

## The Rise of Divisions between Gender, Age and Ethnic Groups

As households became increasingly dependent on wage income and market consumption by 1920, there was a change in gender and age relationships within households. This, in turn, affected the social connections between members of gender and age groups outside the household and even outside of community networks. The growing dependence on wage income and market relations created more intense divisions between household members, which established new gender and age distinctions in families and society as a whole. Labor's growing integration into the industrial production process also led to more ethnic divergence. "Differences" between ethnic groups were socially and economically manufactured, as were gender and age "differences." Ethnic divergence grew out of the underlying system, which created inequities based on unequal wages, occupational segregation, unequal education, and unequal health care services. Ethnic, gender, and age differentiation expressed the racist, sexist, and ageist structure of the world-economy, which rested on work-based stratification.

By World War II adult females developed strong identities, not just as mothers and wives within the family and community, but as women within society. Similar processes occurred with adult men, female children, male children, female elders, and male elders. More generally, gender, youth, and old age assumed new social meanings, an aspect of social change that tore asunder the once-tight bonds of family and community. As a result of the ways that the market and the state penetrated family and community life, abstract social relations and personal relations have never been the same. The history of modern gender and age stratification, as well as ethnic stratification, partly had it roots in the transformation of labor's informal work.

Some scholars have already presented the case that industrialization created a divided working class and placed ethnic groups in conflict-ridden situations.[29] But this work goes further by presenting archival data indicating that gender and age relations, and not just inter-ethnic group relations, were redefined as home-based work declined. As household income sources shifted, gender and age divisions assumed new significance for households that were struggling to make ends meet. Gender and age relations shifted at the same time that new patterns of ethnic stratification emerged in wage work and in residential neighborhoods.

Although labor generally became more wage-dependent, women, young people, elders and members of lower-income ethnic groups were often kept at arms distance from steady wage work and from the material benefits of an increasingly affluent society. Women, young people, elders and economically disadvantaged ethnic groups worked for employing households and businesses, but their wages were low and employment was insecure. Although they were not marginal to the dominant system, these culturally subordinate groups found that they were marginal *within* it.

The more complete integration of women, young people, elders and low-income ethnic groups into capitalist relations and the wage work force occurred in a way that led to marginality relative to high-paid employment and the ability to acquire many consumer goods through the capitalist market. The "internal marginality" of culturally subordinate groups guaranteed large producers that they would benefit from cheap labor. At the same time, "internal marginality" also minimized the material benefits accruing to subordinate groups. Family members and different ethnic groups were increasingly defined by the complex of work force relations, consumption relations, and governmental assistance programs. Relationships between households and dominant institutions pushed gender, age and ethnic relations to become more stratified. Along many dimensions, such as sources of income and residential patterns, relations between high- and low-income ethnic groups became more unequal.

Contrary to what some scholars have argued, U.S. economic development did not result in greater economic and social equity.[30] Nor did economic development bring largely unblemished social progress.[31] The approach here differs from many perspectives on long-term social change, which often are based on assumptions derived from modernization or economistic Marxist theories. While modernization theory posits the view that economic development gradually makes the whole world better, economistic Marxist theory defines history as painful but necessary, progressive, neatly boxed stages of wage labor and industrial production, which will ultimately lead to an economic world without exploited wage laborers. This reconstruction of community life shows how people's lives today reflect the largely unknown process of the recomposition of all work and its attendant social divisions. Labor may have lost just as much as it gained. Of course, the question today is how labor can move forward, given the changes that have occurred.

According to Maurice Halbswach in *The Psychology of Social Class,* the working class is not a socially unified construction, but a hierarchical one.[32] Following a similar line of thought, this study builds on the view that social change in the modern world brought shifts in the hierarchical relationships between groups. Relationships between socially opposed groups—between women and men, for example—became institutionalized in more unequal ways as urban-industrial society unfolded.[33] This occurred partly because, as Max Weber writes, "capitalism has a free hand to alter the social distribution of the population in accordance with its needs and to determine occupational structure."[34]

Some feminist scholars have argued that gender inequality intensified as economic development proceeded, a conclusion that is supported by this archival and secondary research.[35] Ironically, the division between male and female work probably was far less rigid and "more equal" when families organized more of their own work. Goods and services produced by both female and male household members were valued because they were immediately useful to the family. But the growing distinction between creating for use and producing for exchange was accompanied by the gradual separation of home and shop work, and by the separation of housework from other non-waged work. This led to the bifurcation between subordinate, female-associated work in the home and dominant, male-associated wage labor in the shop, a recent aspect of the construction of social inequality.

The physical separation of household-organized work and wage labor contributed to gender segregation, as did the separation of housework from other non-waged work. The historical evidence suggests that when households engaged in extensive home work and/or when household-organized work and shop work both took place in the home, males and females shared more work together. When home and shop work both took place in one locale, women probably were active in both domains.[36]

For improvising labor, a stratum that decreased in relative size over time, extensive non-waged work continued to remain in the home for 75 to 90 years longer than most sociologists and historians have recognized. The process of creating a new social hierarchy with reordered work relationships took place very slowly. Most historical analysts erroneously consider the unity between the home and work to be largely broken for laboring people by the time of the so-called "Industrial Revolution." The reconstitution of work in the shop and at home, which occurred within communities defined by ethnic and class relations, reshaped ethnic groups' informal work and redefined ethnic communities. Ethnic groups in given geographical and temporal spaces developed common ways of generating income from home and shop work. These groups were composed of households at the micro-level, where they exhibited similar patterns of reproduction. Ethnic groups consumed in similar ways, established common informal markets, and participated in reciprocal relations with group members.

Ethnic groups were constantly created and recreated by economic development, intra-labor economic struggles, ethnic political struggles, the organization of business, and the organization of the state and non-profit organizations. In addition, ethnic groups themselves played a central role in defining themselves by building household-based and community networks for sharing resources. Ethnicity is a product of social processes and of decisions made by household members that respond to and attempt to reshape stratification patterns.[37] Within the context of the formation of labor's hierarchy and its ethnic groups, the following historical chapters trace the transformation of informal work, gender and age relations, and the structure of community life.

## Notes

1. See a discussion of "household" in Immanuel Wallerstein, *Historical Capitalism* (London: Verso Editions, 1983), 24. My research shows that the family or household typically is a three-generational unit that has a life cycle of about 50 to 75 years. The size of income-pooling families may change during the course

of its life cycle, as younger members begin their own households. The length of the life cycle generally depends on the economic circumstances in which household members are embedded.

2. Informal work, non-waged work and home work (used here to refer to the same set of activities) are distinct from "homework," a term that is used in other studies. "Homework" often refers to wage labor carried out at home for the benefit of an employer. Non-waged work and wage work are two entirely different work activities. Just as it is important to distinguish between wage work in the home and non-waged work, it also is important to distinguish between non-waged work that is carried out in the street and wage labor that occurs in the street.

3. Refer to R. E. Pahl's study, *Divisions of Labour* (Oxford, England: Basic Blackwell, 1984). Pahl writes, "Diversity was the norm—diversity in occupations, in opportunities for by-employment, in access to common grazing, wild game or fishing and in the particular mix of activities in specific households. Self-sufficiency reduced the need of reliance on waged labour, and most families were able to get a modest living outside the economic arena of contractual wage payments."(48)

4. Torry Dickinson, "Gender Divisions within the U.S. Working Class: Households in the Philadelphia Area, 1870–1945," eds. Joan Smith, Immanuel Wallerstein and Hans Dieter Evers, *Households and the World-Economy* (Beverly Hills: SAGE Publications, 1984), 199–211. Also Torry Dickinson and Kathie Friedman, "A Comparative Approach to the Study of Ethno-national Cultures and Households in the United States, 1870–1970." A Working Paper printed by the Fernand Braudel Center, Binghamton, New York. Presented at the Colloquium on "Households in the World-Economy" in Bielefeld, Germany, May 1982.

5. Eric H. Monkkonen, *America Becomes Urban: The Development of U.S. Cities and Towns, 1780–1980* (Berkeley: University of California Press, 1988). Monkkonen writes that many studies disassociate cities from development in the surrounding countryside.(44) Here urban and rural development were studied in relationship to each other.

6. Other than to summarize overall patterns, census records were not analyzed here. Labor's mobility during the nineteenth and early twentieth centuries made it impossible to trace the majority of households from one census period to the next.

7. Karl Marx, *Capital, Volume 1,* (New York: Vintage Editions, 1977).

8. Ibid.

9. See Joan Smith and Immanuel Wallerstein, eds. *Transforming and Creating Households* (New York: Cambridge Univ. Press, 1992). The Households Research Group of the Fernand Braudel Center for the Study of Economies, Historical Systems, and Civilizations in Binghamton, New York has studied how labor sustained itself in different areas of the world, at different points in time. As a founding member of this research group, my work began developing within this intellectual context.

10. The idea of the continuum of labor in the world-economy is introduced in Terence K. Hopkins and Immanuel Wallerstein, and Working Group Members, "Patterns of the Development of the Modern World-System," *Review,* 1, No. 2 (Fall, 1977), 111–145.

11. Jacqueline Jones, *The Dispossessed: America's Underclasses from the Civil War to the Present* (New York: Basic Books, 1992).

12. Scholars who study social policy and welfare issues often document the non-waged activities carried out by low-income households in the United States. See, for example, Michael B. Katz, *In the Shadow of the Poorhouse: A Social History of Welfare in America* (New York: Basic Books, 1986).

13. Walter Licht, *Getting Work: Philadelphia, 1840–1950* (Cambridge, MA: Harvard Univ. Press, 1992). Licht argues that a structural feature of economic life in Philadelphia in the pre-World War II period was underemployment and sporadic production. Licht makes the case that, because irregular employment was the norm in the city, families needed to develop coping strategies, which includes what I call "non-waged work." See Torry Dickinson, review of *Getting Work* by Walter Licht, *Work and Occupations: An International Sociological Journal,* 21, no. 2 (February, 1994) 127–129.

14. See Christopher Lasch, *The True and Only Heaven: Progress and its Critics* (New York: W.W. Norton, 1991). Lasch argues that the core of rebels fighting the development of capitalism included small producers, artisans, and small farmers. Many of these rebels, who had become somewhat dependent on wage labor, generated a lot of non-waged income.

15. See Immanuel Wallerstein, "The States in the Institutional Vortex of the Capitalist World-Economy," *International Social Science Journal,* UNESCO, 32, no. 4 (1980), 743–751. Economic development takes places through the global institutions of classes, the capitalist firm, the state, households and ethnic groups. The two basic classes, labor and capital, are present in relations constituting each institution.

16. See Marx, *Capital, Volume 1,* Chapters 7–17.

17. Immanual Wallerstein, William Martin, and Torry Dickinson, "Household Structures and Production Processes: Preliminary Theses and Findings," *Review* 5, no. 3 (Winter, 1982), 437–458. Also see Research Working Group on Households and Production Processes (Torry Dickinson, William Martin, Mary Ryan, and Immanual Wallerstein), "Households, Labor Force and Production Processes in the Capitalist World-Economy." The Fernand Braudel Center, Binghamton, New York, November 1, 1978.

18. An overview of the growing dominance of global corporations and the century-long development of high volume production is found in Robert B. Reich, *The Work of Nations* (New York: Vintage/Random House, 1992). Reich argues that post-1970, high-profit businesses, which now have web-like structures, have become engaged in high value production.

19. Wallerstein, Martin and Dickinson, "Household Structures and Production Processes," 438–439.

20. Ibid. Income sources are identified in this article.

21. Wage labor also occurred in other contexts (such as state employment, small business employment, or employment by a high-income household), but it grew at the rate it did because of big business.

22. Wallerstein, Martin and Dickinson, "Household Structures and Production Processes." To differentiate petty producing from production that is organized within the capitalist system, the word production is avoided when referring to non-capitalist activities, unless the word "production" is put in quotation marks. Similarly, subsistence work is not called production, unless the word is put in quotation marks. Home- and community-centered work did not constitute a "family economy," but simply developed next to an ever-expanding world economy. As Fernand Braudel writes in *Afterthoughts on Material Civilization and Capitalism* (Baltimore: The Johns Hopkins University Press, 1977), "capitalism does not overlay the entire economy and all working society; it never encompasses both of them within one perfect system all its own."(112)

23. In Alejandro Portes, Manuel Castells, and Lauren A. Benton, eds. *The Informal Economy: Studies in Advanced and Less Developed Countries* (Baltimore: Johns Hopkins Univ. Press, 1989). The authors mix subcontracting wage laborers with non-waged workers, leading to a confusion about the class relationships manifested in these "informal" work situations.

24. Alejandro Portes and Saskia Sassen-Koob, "Making it Underground: Comparative Material on the Informal Sector in Western Market Economies," *American Journal of Sociology,* 93, (1987). The authors argue that the informal sector includes "the sum total of income-earning activities with the exclusion of those that involve contractual and legally regulated employment." (31) The long history of the U.S. informal economy is bypassed in their summary: "The U.S. informal economy may be described as an outcome of the survival strategies of recent immigrants and their subsequent attempts to 'make it' in America." (48)

25. Richard T. Ely, *Taxation in American States and Cities* (New York: Thomas Y. Crowell, 1888), 166. Also refer to chart on different taxation policies. Philadelphia was the first city to impose a municipal income tax in 1939.

26. Hopkins, Wallerstein, and Working Group, "Patterns of the Development," 135. The authors describe part-life-time households (or ones that have less dependency on wages) and life-time households (or ones that have a greater dependency on wages). Both these types of households are integrated into and partially dependent on the capitalist system. Here I use "improvising labor," which essentially consists of "part-life-time households." I use "monied labor," which essentially consists of "life-time households." Improvising and monied labor were chosen because they provide an immediate image of what the primary work activities are for these strata of labor.

27. Torry D. Dickinson, "Redivided Lives: The Formation of the Working Class in Philadelphia, 1870–1945." Ph.D. Dissertation, State University of New York at Binghamton, 1983.

28. The International Workers of the World, or the Wobblies, organized mining and logging workers in rural, less industrialized western states, where non-waged work probably provided critical income supplements to low-income families.

29. See David M. Gordon, Richard Edwards, and Michael Reich, *Segmented Work, Divided Workers: The Historical Transformation of Labor in the United States* (Cambridge: Cambridge University Press, 1982); Mike Davis, "Why the U.S. Working Class is Different," *New Left Review* 123 (Sept./Oct. 1980), 3–44; Douglas Dowd, *U.S. Capitalist Development Since 1776: Of, By, and For Which People?* (New York: M.E. Sharp, 1993); W.E.B. Dubois, *Black Reconstruction in America, 1860–1880* (New York: Atheneum Press, 1971), 634–5, 706.

30. See William J. Goode, *World Revolution and Family Patterns* (New York: The Free Press, 1970), 21; Edward Shorter, *The Making of the Modern Family* (New York: Basic Books, 1975), 5, 16, 248, 278–279; Elizabeth Bott, *Family and Social Network: Roles, Norms, and External Relationships in Ordinary Urban Families* (New York: The Free Press, 1971), 60; Julie Matthaei, *An Economic History of Women in America: Women's Work, the Sexual Division of Labor and the Development of Capitalism* (New York: Schocken Books, 1982), 114, 246, 253, 277, 281.

31. For a sustained critique of the assumption that development brings progress, see Lasch, *The True and Only Heaven.*

32. Maurice Halbwachs, *The Psychology of Social Class* (Glencoe, Illinois: The Free Press, 1958), 114–116.

33. Harriet Bradley, *Men's Work, Women's Work* (Minneapolis: University of Minnesota Press, 1989). Harriet Bradley writes that "it is perhaps regrettable that [men's studies] should be developing as an endeavor separate from 'women's' or 'gender' studies."(237) This separation in disciplines has dramatic implications for theories of stratification, she argues. "[W]hile class and gender are irreducible to one another and must be seen as analytically separate, neither can be satisfactorily understood without the other."(238) She concludes by saying, "Despite the well-known methodological difficulties involved, women must be included in empirical studies of class, while in more abstract types of analysis the ways in which gender relations interact with class must be grasped."(239)

34. Max Weber, *The Protestant Ethic and the Spirit of Capitalism* (New York: Charles Scribner and Sons, 1958), 35.

35. See Gerda Lerner, "The Lady and the Mill Girl: Changes in the Status of Women in the Age of Jackson, 1800–1840," in eds. Nancy F. Cott and Elizabeth H. Pleck, *A Heritage of Her Own: Toward a New Social History of the American Woman* (New York: Simon and Schuster, 1979), 182–196; Louise A. Tilly and Joan W. Scott, *Women, Work and Family* (New York: Holt, Rinehart and Winston, 1978), 205.

36. See Claudia Goldin, *Understanding the Gender Gap: An Economic History of Women* (New York: Oxford University Press, 1990). Goldin writes, "married women were often drawn into their husbands' work when home and workplace

were physically unified, and women were more frequently employed in retail trades when the store and the house were one unit."(46) Furthermore, "the decrease over time in proprietorships and occupations of a craft nature among widows is linked to the progressive separation of home and work."(49) Goldin bases her conclusions on shared home-based work between husbands and wives in the late eighteenth century, work that includes artisanal work, huckstering and washing, and running boarding house operations. When the home and the workplace were united, Goldin argues that women made a substantial contribution to "national income."(49)

37. See Irving Louis Horowitz, "Race, Class and the New Ethnicity: The Holy Ghost of Social Stratification," in eds. Irving Louis Horowitz, John C. Leggett, and Martin Oppenheimer, *The American Working Class: Prospects for the 1980s* (New Brunswick, New Jersey: Transaction Books, 1979), 43–69. Horowitz writes that ethnicity is both "a structural and a strategic phenomenon."(610)

*Families picking strawberries in Delaware, 1870s. Courtesy of the Hagley Museum and Library. From Richard Edwards, ed.,* Industries of Delaware *(Wilmington, 1880).*

# Three

# Losing Control of Informal Work from 1830 to 1873: Low- and Moderate-Income Communities during the Rise of Industrial Production

## The Historical Context: Changes in Industrial Production and Community Life

As the size of firms began to grow in the mid-nineteenth century, charity organizations in the United States began discouraging neighborhood residents from earning income outside of the wage employment system. Initiated by non-profit boards heavily represented by business, this intervention began to nudge many workers in the community toward more wage-earning. Early predecessors to state agencies had started to intervene in informal work by the time of the economic contraction, which began in 1830 and ended in 1850. Workhouse managers tried to gain access over labor by confronting neighborhood power brokers, who provided ways for low- to moderate-income households to subsist outside of formal wage relations. Parastatal organizations tried to undermine pawnbrokers, sellers of lottery policies, sellers of second-hand goods, and renters of sleeping spaces. When the economy expanded between 1850 and 1873, increased parastatal interventions coincided with the expansion of large-scale industrial production.

In 1830, improvising labor dominated urban and rural centers, not in terms of its power or wealth, but by virtue of its relative size and weight. Improvising labor made up about 60 percent of the Philadelphia's laboring population, whereas monied labor constituted a minority. However, by 1870, improvising labor saw its limited control of the urban terrain slipping from its grasp as class relations became expressed less through family and community work relations and more through relationships with business and parastatal organizations. As commodification proceeded, divisions between labor's gender, age, and ethnic groups sharpened. Improvising labor's non-waged work in cities and in farm areas that were less dependent on the market enabled low-paid laborers to generate much of the income they needed to survive.

As this early period of development unfolded, work in the mid-Atlantic region revolved less around commercial activity on the banks of the Delaware River (as it once had) and more around factory production. This reorganization of branches of industry undermined the central role of crafts workers and artisans. The displacement of craft workers and growing intervention by local, nascent parastatal organizations into household-organized work began deflating the value that families had placed on independent work. While merchants opened and expanded shops that were frequented by high-income patrons, low-income people purchased basic staples from street vendors and peddlers. During the years of industrial growth between 1830 to 1873, many goods and services still were made and distributed through labor's own networks of marketing and exchange. Because social relations were not uniformly commodified, a wide variety of marketing and work patterns still characterized the mid-Atlantic region, which centered around the Delaware River and the City of Philadelphia.

Producers usually sold goods and services directly to consumers during the first half of the nineteenth century. Members of urban families often made customized goods for handicraft businesses, which then sold them to wealthier households. "The material belongings of most urban residents were secondhand or crudely produced by the people themselves," writes David Ward in *Cities and Immigrants.*[1] Almost all of this work was done by hand. Working class households either made most of their own goods or acquired second-hand goods through exchanges or purchases. These second-hand goods were not purchased through the capitalist market, but were acquired by households through informal community networks. Undoubtedly, these informal markets frequently were based on bartering, though archival records seldom mention the medium of exchange. In general, households making up improvising labor in this time period acquired relatively few goods and services from the capitalist market.

Marketing was not planned, nor very systematic. Urban land use was not specialized or heavily concentrated, even in urban industrial centers. When the mass market for consumer goods grew, putting-out operations hired unskilled workers and flourished in urban neighborhoods and in rural areas. Large cities in the United States had market halls, "which sold produce from the immediate hinterland, to waterfront warehouses that handled exotic staples, and to the exclusive retail trade of the affluent."[2] Before 1850, capitalist producers and merchants sold consumer goods and services to higher-income households. Small producers both worked for themselves and sometimes worked for larger producers, who paid low wages.

The economic prominence of Philadelphia, the Delaware Valley's biggest city, was due in part the fact that it had emerged as an early center of business during the colonial period, when firms exported staples (furs, lumber, stoves, iron, wheat and flour) and imported English manufactures (textiles, hardware and wine) that were purchased by wealthy households.[3]

Compared to surrounding cities and towns, Philadelphia had fairly commodified work relations for a number of reasons. The Delaware Valley's main city was located in an important agricultural belt, which made it a commercial and industrial center. Pennsylvania remained one of the six leading wheat-growing states until 1869.[4] Along with New York City and Boston, Philadelphia served as a corporate headquarters for U.S. business until 1900.[5] But while Philadelphia and its rural environs were directly tied to the world-economy, the drive toward commodification proceeded slowly. Although community life in this urban center may not have been as commercialized as working-class neighborhoods in New York City in 1850, it still exhibited evident commercialization.

Urban households were more commodified than rural ones. They spent more on perishable foods, ready-made clothing and furnishings than rural households. Between 1810 and 1840, the proportion of the population living in Eastern towns of 2,500 or more people increased from 11 to 19 percent, which expanded the base of the urban market. During this time, manufactories moved from rural to urban areas, contributing to the growing influence of manufacturers and merchants.[6]

Farmers who produced a range of goods for urban consumers used their income from petty marketing work to buy new consumer goods. For rural households, the declining price of urban goods, coupled with rising rural incomes, made market consumption seem more attractive. Businessmen in cities like Philadelphia, New York, Baltimore, and Boston distributed goods produced in the inland cities to markets outside the region and shipped goods to land-locked cities in the hinterland. Changes in the organization of enterprises brought productivity increases in manufacturing, marketing and shipping, all which lowered the prices of manufactured goods. Urban-based enterprises sold more goods and services to agricultural areas.[7]

A factory system, which relied on access to nearby coal deposits, began emerging in urban areas in the Delaware Valley by 1850. As this occurred, agriculture declined as a major industry in the valley west of Philadelphia, which had been a leading center for grain production.[8] As it became more industrial, Philadelphia's importance as a leading commercial center declined. With the rise of the large-scale, industrial production process, labor was drawn to urban settings.[9] By 1860 the Philadelphia area emerged as a leading manufacturing center. It led the United States in the production of woolen and worsted goods, carpets and hosiery. Cotton production surpassed even New England's at this time.[10]

Although they remained strong, petty producing and marketing activities in the United States began to decline as market-oriented production became more prominent. Members from laboring households found themselves going to work for others when industrialization and urbanization eroded some opportunities for cultivating vegetables, collecting firewood, fishing and trapping wild animals. Economic development shifted work and income options for some households.[11] Although this does not take into account non-monetary income from subsistence work and household transfers, the average household spent only one-third of its monetary income on manufactured goods in 1810 and still less than one-half of its monetary income in this way in 1840. On the average, urban households spent three times as much on market goods as rural households did.[12] It took a long time for rural communities to become entrenched in commercialized relations, which had started to engulf urban communities at a much earlier date.

As the economy expanded between 1850 and 1873, urban land use became more specialized. Although rural households did less petty production and gardening work than their rural counterparts, these activities remained important to urban dwellers. Capitalist production became more centralized and the consumption of market goods began to increase.

Differentiation within production and distribution, along with increasing the demand for labor, extended market areas. In order to save on transportation costs and to guarantee accessibility to markets, industries became located in central urban sites. The construction of expansive, more specialized warehouse districts led to the centralization of land use.[13]

Although retailing became somewhat more centralized in U.S. cities, vendors continued to sell their goods throughout most urban neighborhoods. Peddlers sold staples and perishable goods throughout cities, remaining outside the ambit of capitalist retailers, who controlled only some of the urban markets. Manufacturing units had not yet organized retail outlets of their own.[14]

With the growing division between industries producing means of production—which created goods primarily for capitalist producers, but still also for labor's informal workers—and those producing means of consumption for households, the demand for skilled crafts workers declined and the Jacks-of-all-trades began to lose their primary place in work.[15] But while industrial goods began replacing household manufactures by 1860, many household goods and services survived because they did not compete with business products.[16] Few of the goods and services "produced" by households were sold on the capitalist market. Instead households swapped them with other households or sold them through informal neighborhood markets.[17] These "exchanges" or swaps reflected labor's need to share scarce and necessary resources. Informal markets enabled households to acquire goods with little cash. Low- to moderate-income people determined the "value" of these informal market goods, while large producers in the profit-making business placed a price on the goods they sold.

Inter-household reciprocal swaps acted as a "countervailing force in the face of a dehumanizing market process," writes David Harvey.[18] Reciprocal relationships, which were maintained voluntarily by working-class networks, were essential to working-class households in the United States. According to David Harvey, reciprocity enabled labor to resist the commodifying aspects of the market system. After 1850, relationships of reciprocity began to weaken and community networks started to be affected by capitalist investment patterns and more socialized consumption.[19]

Although all laboring households were tied to the market economy, connections between families and employers were not as strong as historians often assume. Even adult males who labored in the 14 largest industries in mid-nineteenth century Philadelphia received an average of only $288 a year. Printers, the highest paid group of laborers, received only $370 in annual wages. Between 1850 and 1880, women wage workers labored in low-paying, "sex-typed" occupations, producing shoes and boots, hats and caps, clothing, textiles, paper, and printing and publishing. If households paid for rent, food, clothing and candles, they needed a cash income of almost $520 a year to survive. In order to keep cash expenditures low, working people ate little meat, bought goods from second-hand shops, and "scavenged the countryside for wood" for fuel. If only wages were considered, it could be said that "most workers lived at or below subsistence levels" in mid-nineteenth century Philadelphia.[20] Because families did not have enough cash from wage labor or petty producing to cover market goods, they did a lot of "invisible" non-waged work and tried to minimize buying new market goods.

The occupational breakdown of laborers associated with various production processes helps to identify the relative sizes of improvising and monied labor. In 1850, according to social historian Bruce Laurie, about 12 percent of Philadelphia's laboring population worked for artisanal shops. At this time, at least one-half of metal tradesmen, blacksmiths, butchers and bakers, along with one-fifth of shoemakers and furniture makers, worked in artisanal or craft shops. Many of these artisans suffered from unsteady wages due to sporadic production, making them seek additional employment as putting-out workers, sweatshop workers, or early assembly line workers in manufacturing establishments. About 32 percent of laborers were linked with the putting-out production process. Low-paid, male and female outworkers in putting-out shops engaged in shoemaking, tailoring and weaving. About 23 percent of laborers worked for sweatshops (small, mechanized shops that hired under 25 laborers). Only about 33 percent of laborers earned relatively "high" wages from firms that used steam or water power. After the economic downturn of 1837, one-quarter to one-third of the city's working people left Philadelphia and sought work elsewhere, though many of them returned after 1845, when employment again increased. Families were forced to rely on income from part-time wage labor and casual labor. Households reduced expenditures and often shared a rented living space with three or four other families.[21]

The archival research conducted here, in conjunction with a review of secondary research on work, indicates that improvising labor made up more than half of the laboring population in mid-nineteenth century Philadelphia. If many artisans, putting-out workers and sweatshop laborers and their families also are considered as members of improvising labor, then almost two-thirds of the laboring population may have been comprised of improvising labor in 1850. But because it is difficult to use nineteenth-century census data with accuracy, the one-half estimate may be more sound than the two-thirds estimate. For example, some highly paid artisans, who were fairly dependent on the market, actually may have been part of monied labor or were small-scale employers; they may not have been not part of improvising labor. But in less urbanized areas of the mid-Atlantic region and the United States, improvising labor may have made up an even larger proportion of the laboring population.

From 1830 to 1880 large-scale industrial production developed into the dominant production process. Although only 43 percent of wage workers were employed in firms with over 51 laborers in 1850, by 1880 this number had increased to 66 percent of wage workers. "Manufactories," large non-machine driven production units, began declining during this period. Outwork operations, utilizing home-based putting out laborers, continued until the 1870s, but then essentially disappeared. Artisans made up 12 percent of the labor force in 1850, but they comprised only 8 percent of the labor force by 1880.[22] It was not until the turn of the century that small farming units declined, when farming households found that they could no longer compete with large, commercial farmers.

## Early Parastatal Intervention into Community Life, 1830 to 1850

During the 1830s and 1840s, different classes struggled over how labor would "make ends meet." Records kept by the House of Industry, a workhouse in inner-city Philadelphia, show that workhouse managers intervened in the work activities of low- to moderate-income households and prepared household members for a long life of *wage* work. An examination of House activities reveals how improvising labor generated non-waged income and maintained low levels of cash expenditures on consumption goods. House records also show how early social reformers cooperated with business to begin reshaping improvising labor's work.

As the almshouse began disappearing as a way to manage impoverished people by the mid-nineteenth century, the workhouse emerged as the new model for dealing with low-income households. The workhouse was an early "work-for-welfare" program. It was organized around the idea that jobless people would work off the "cost" of assistance. Sometimes working people who toiled for the workhouse received a small wage, which was designed to give them a taste of the monetary benefits of wage labor. Households that received support from the House of Industry were initially drawn from the "industrious" or "deserving" poor, working people who had recently been "productive" in a way that was socially acceptable to middle-class and wealthy reformers.

Not all people who sought relief received support from the House of Industry. When relief seekers were judged by House of Industry staff to represent the "undeserving" poor, they were directed to the Blockley House for paupers, an almshouse for cast-off poor people. In mid-nineteenth century Philadelphia, about 800 people a year were denied House of Industry relief and were referred to the Blockley House, which did not direct people to reenter the work force. According to a record keeper at the House of Industry, the Blockley House supposedly included "the discharged convict, the gatherer of bones and offal, the rag picker, dog catcher and river thief."[23]

A tremendous struggle developed between the Workhouse's Board of Directors, which included prominent businessmen and highly enterprising, neighborhood employers, over access to local workers from improvising labor. The House staff worked in conjunction with the courts and police to diminish the power of local brokers and renters of tools for petty producing activities so that they could control the supply of low-paid labor.[24] Because low-paid laborers rented tools from neighborhood brokers or small-scale entrepreneurs so that they could carry out household-organized work, workhouse staff tried to eliminate access to "means of production" and directed low-income people to other kinds of income-yielding work.

Because small traders did not invest in production and took advantage of non-commodified resources, social reformers viewed small employers and traders with hostility. These resource brokers, in essence, functioned as non-capitalist adversaries of large-scale producers. The Board of Managers of the House of Industry identified local resource brokers, who partly survived off the labor of others, as enemies of progress. To gain more control over potential laborers, the House fought against the "influence of pawnbrokers, vendors of lottery policies, retailers of spirits, letters-out of places to sleep upon, and a host of others."[25]

Around 1850 workers from improvising labor and petty hirers in Philadelphia relied upon both "legal" and "illegal" income, which came from different kinds of petty marketing and petty producing work. For example, according to House of Industry records, there were 200 vendors of lottery policies, supplying 1,200 persons a day with "chances in real or counterfeit lotteries." To eliminate this source of income, the police, in cooperation with the workhouse, made a number of arrests. In 1851, the prosecution of 60 lottery vendors from just one ward was pending in the Court of Quarter Sessions.[26]

Informal workers were referred by the House of Industry's staff to labor-seeking industrialists and to monied households seeking domestic workers. By redirecting low-income people to geographically distant employers from other classes, the workhouse broke relations that households had with local petty employers and traders. Observing the economic networks in the neighborhood, House administrators noted:

> By far the largest class of them [the local urban poor] lived in a state of utter dependence upon the men who supplied their necessities. These hired men, [using] the implements of their trades, retailed out to them the bundles of straw which were to form their bed, let them the parts of a floor on which they slept; fed them on broken victuals which children made a trade of begging, and loaned them the rags they wore. Their scanty earnings, averaging about fifteen cents for each day's labor, kept them always the debtors of these men; night after night they always returned, as dogs to their masters, knowing no other home or hope.[27]

Although some laboring people depended heavily on neighborhood entrepreneurs, most low-income families had some independence from local brokers (and even from larger producers), primarily because they derived their income from so many sources.

The relationship between local resource brokers and laboring people was based partially on debt, resembling debt peonage. But while traditional debt peonage used legal and political means and economic dependency to coerce labor, resource brokers could not rely on the law, if they tried to use extra-economic measures to obtain compliance. In fact, local brokers were themselves the object of extra-economic coercion by reformers and the state. Low-income families were dependent upon small employers and traders for the resources they needed for consumption and work. Some family members may have worked directly for resource brokers, but they were not bound by the courts to work for brokers until debts were repaid. Laborers connected with resource brokers also supported themselves and their families by carrying out housework and other subsistence tasks, renting wheelbarrows or shovels to other informal workers, making goods and selling them, and engaging in casual wage labor.

The House of Industry went out of its way to recruit workers that partially depended on income from local resource brokers. Although these individuals may have been referred by staff to the almshouse at a previous time because they were seen as undeserving, the workhouse exerted considerable effort to break up community networks. If a preliminary appraisal by House staff indicated that relief seekers, who were unassociated with bondsman, lacked moral courage and a dedication to work, then staff denied them assistance.[28]

The House of Industry worked with economically deprived people from diverse backgrounds and sought out homeless youth who slept in market places or in deserted buildings. Other groups brought into the workhouse or given aid included:

> The bondsmen of certain depraved individuals upon who they live in a state of helpless dependence; who were the purveyors of everything; who rented them the offal scrip, the basket or hand barrow, with which they were to earn their daily pittance; who bought from them the rags, bones, and glass or paper they collect in the street, and paid them in the broken victuals.[29]

The work relationships described here resemble life in a company town, but in this case, the "factory town" was a non-industrial living space and work took place in the street, where "junk" was collected and resold through non-capitalist networks by resource brokers. Bondsmen rented tools to working people, who collected items in the street and then sold these items for pieces of food, an in-kind payment.

Improvising labor in the neighborhood was caught between the workhouse and local bosses in another way. Not only did House staff and local bosses struggle over who would control the supply of improvising labor, but they struggled over where improvising labor would buy and gain access to necessary resources, including water. Water was a scarce resource in low-income neighborhoods. If rented rooms had any access to water, landlords charged high rents. Petty dealers competed with landlords and with other groups over control of water. These small dealers, such as pawn shop dealers, often controlled access to water hydrants.[30]

In order to break bondsmen's control over water, the House of Industry began distributing water and selling access to showers. Since improvising households also bought wood and coal from local dealers, the House also sold coal at one-half the market price.[31] In inner-city areas at this time, water and fuel were only partially commodified.[32] Families purchased these basic necessities through informal and capitalist markets and obtained them from nascent state organizations, such as workhouses and charities.

Since the workhouse was based on the idea that self-respect only comes through labor, administrators felt a tremendous amount of satisfaction when they noted how hard the "inmates" worked for little compensation. One House administrator argued that wage labor inculcated a propensity to become market-oriented:

> The Inmates of the House of Industry were taught to feel that they were not paupers, but laborers. They were not given alms, they were paid wages. Their earnings invested under the guidance of the Managers, purchased comforts to which they had long been strangers, so that they came each day to their labor with cheerful industry. They gained habits of cleanliness. Those who rags and filth had forbidden an appeal to the charities of the street, now that they were better clad, obtained employment in decent families. Some left the city, and going into service upon the farms, were freed from evil ties, and thrived; whilst others laid aside sufficient capital to start them in petty trades.[33]

The Board of the House of Industry felt it was beneficial to encourage impoverished working people to become more self-sufficient, especially by having them work for others. Running a petty trade and working for oneself was, at this point, seen as more desirable than working for neighborhood resource brokers.

The managers of the House of Industry led the way for many subsequent social reform projects. Workhouse managers invaded, with self-righteous certainty, the economic and spatial terrain of informal work and local marketing networks in order to pull "more industrious" families into the capitalist orbit.

The Board of the House of Industry boasted that their organization developed one of the first programs to regulate and control the conditions of neighborhood life. Above the workshops, temporary living quarters were designed to further acquaint workers with the rigors and rhythms of industrial life.[34] The degree of supervision over the living quarters increased between 1850 and 1880. For people without homes or any kind of support, rooms were available to relief recipients who agreed to live according to the House's strict rules and regulations. The House wanted recipients to live within the building because it increased the Board of Directors' control over their activities. House staff served food within the House confines and temporary residents were instructed never to leave the hall. To readjust laborers' values, the new social managers provided educational instruction for children and subsequently added Christian religious instruction.[35] Bolstered by Christian doctrine of the time, the new industrial ideology encouraged laborers to abandon one work ethic, which was associated with informal work, and to adopt a new work ethic associated with wage labor in large-scale industries.

Low-income households accepting any kind of economic assistance "paid" for it by losing a certain amount of control over their everyday lives and acquiring new obligations. Whether recipients toiled in the workhouse in exchange for overnight accommodations and food, purchased coal below the retail price, received food, made use of the bath house and water, attended the medical dispensary, or used the employment service, the House exposed receiving households to unrelenting moral messages and economic sanctions. The way workhouse assistance was provided enabled the organization to meet its own goals. For example, in 1852 the managers began distributing food only to *heads* of households, a practice that identified the adult male as the primary household member who was responsible for providing income.[36]

## Nascent State Intervention in Community Life, 1850 to 1873

A variety of factors affected the movement of labor to and from relief organizations in the mid-Atlantic region, and more generally along the East Coast. First, changes in the structure of the global division of labor and the structure of capitalist production processes, including the rise of large-scale production units, altered demands for specific categories of labor (defined by ethnicity, sex and age) and for labor in specific occupations (as defined within the technical division of labor in the workshop). The growth of industrial production brought more mechanization, contributing to the decline of artisanal production and the loss of work for many crafts people, many of whom sought assistance from workhouses and charities. Second, demands for assistance changed according to cycles of expansion and contraction within the world-economy. Third, the Civil War, like other wars, displaced the population, causing some African Americans to move north in search of work. Migrating families during this period often had no alternative but to seek assistance from early state organizations. And, fourth, cycles of nature brought dramatic shifts in temperatures, from very hot to very cold. The bitter winter months forced many low-income families to seek income transfers, in money and in kind, from nascent state organizations. Although there were fewer artisans seeking assistance during the warm months when production was more regular, there were more day and industrial laborers, men without a trade, and homeless and wandering workers.[37]

From the 1830s to the turn of the century, more and more skilled laborers, whose crafts no longer provided a steady enough income, sought assistance from the House of Industry. The number of male mechanics or artisans seeking support increased, partly because they could not find employment in "skilled" or artisanal work. As production became more mechanized, growing numbers of mechanics sought assistance, who were unaccustomed to seeking housing and aid. Relief recipients in the late 1850s also included immigrants, well-educated people who became impoverished due to illness or some other misfortune, previously institutionalized from prisons, hospitals and almshouses, and migrants from other parts of the United States. Travelers seeking work pawned their clothes in exchange for food and shelter along the way, sometimes walking hundreds of miles to industrial urban centers.[38]

On the eve of the Civil War, the House of Industry distributed more aid to "foreign" than "native" male workers. At this time, only one-fourth of the total recipients had lived in the United States for some time. Most of them had recently immigrated from Ireland or England.[39] As the House of Industry temporarily oriented itself to European immigrant populations, U.S. citizens sought assistance from other local organizations.

Economic development and the reorganization of business reflected more general economic changes. Working people's economic activities and the role played by early state organizations changed accordingly. During the Civil War, business owners invested in new areas of production, increasing mechanization and centralizing financial operations on the East Coast. The growth of the railways after 1865, when railway and mining companies acquired land that previously had been cultivated, lay the groundwork for economic growth and geographical expansion. The end of the Civil War brought the political and economic unification of adjacent, but economically differentiated, areas of the North and South. Reconstruction forged closer economic ties and political unity among industrialists in the United States and weakened their economic dependence on Britain. Protective tariffs, which were erected in 1864, 1890 and 1897, stimulated the development of industrial and agricultural production during the last part of the century.[40]

Until the depression which began in 1873 and ended in 1897, Philadelphia remained the leading manufacturing center in the United States, the site of more than 260 cotton and woolen mills, the largest chemical plants in the country, publishing companies, locomotive works, and machine shops. With the increased demand for textiles, clothing, boots, and shoes during the Civil War, the demand for labor increased and wages rose in Philadelphia. Production in engineering works, machine shops, and shipyards also increased. By 1870 the lower Delaware Valley has also become the country's shipbuilding center. Although cotton, silk, woolen and worsted goods were produced in factories by 1860, weavers with putting-out hand looms produced carpets in their homes until the 1890s. The diversity of production processes allowed the Philadelphia area to remain the U.S. center for woolen and worsted goods, carpets and hosiery.[41]

Compared to other areas in the East, Philadelphia had a very large proportion of industrial workers by the time of the Civil War. The largest number of firms between 1850 and 1880 produced goods such as clothing, textiles, shoes and boots, and machine tools and hardware.[42] In this period, steel and iron-producing firms replaced textiles companies as the city's largest employers. During this time, women found wage work making hats and caps, clothing, paper, textiles, printed and published goods, and shoes and boots.[43]

By 1880 in Philadelphia, firm size grew, ownership became more concentrated and more steam power was harnessed to increase productivity. More firms employed more than 50 wage workers and one in five manufacturers relied on steam power to increase production. These big, rising industries, which produced food, fuel, chemicals and paper, required many wage laborers and substantial capital investments.[44] The production of producer goods, as opposed to consumer goods, depended on even more capital, more power-driven machinery and more wage laborers.[45] Although capital was being concentrated in this way, production processes remained diverse, with artisan shops, cottage industries, sweatshops, manufactories and industrial production units developing side by side.[46]

After the Civil War, early social management strategies and the life circumstances of low-income households began to shift perceptibly. Although the House of Industry still functioned as a workhouse and as an industrial training site, it came to resemble a social service organization. It established close ties with business and trained different groups for different types of work. As development in the North and South became linked, early social service organizations in northern cities responded to the social dislocation from the Civil War. More than two hundred freed men and women arrived at the House of Industry from different parts of the South. They were quickly referred by staff to employers in the countryside, where they found employment in domestic service, almost the only kind of wage work that European-American managers saw as appropriate for African Americans.[47]

Homeless migrants, which included artisans, former clerks, musicians and teachers, slept at charities, in almshouses, police stations, or in the street. One early social worker, who was proud of the way her organization maintained "good order among the lower class of floating population," describes lodgers arriving at the House of Industry:

> Lodgers are, in a large proportion of cases, from distant cities or country districts, and it is an interesting sight, as the evening approaches, to see them coming into the House, singly or with small groups, and to learn that they

> have come by foot from Harrisburg, Trenton, New York, Baltimore or some other distant point, with which we usually have no idea of communication other than by railroad.[48]

Walking to urban centers, rather than paying for a train or riding a horse or carriage, was part of subsistence work for enterprising working people. Homeless people displayed a cosmopolitan knowledge of the work world. When compared to members of wage-dependent households, homeless people had different sources of knowledge and exhibited a different understanding of work, which was based on the centrality of both paid and unpaid work.

Inside the workhouse walls, administrators developed new strategies for managing the poor, strategies that divided the relief population into sub-groups that were treated differently and unequally. The new social managers assigned different kinds of work to white children, to black children, to men, to white women and to black women. And they closely supervised and instructed each. The schooling or training for black and white children was divided, resulting in unequal education. The "education" for African-American children consisted of manual work, with boys taught shoe making and the girls shoe binding, which managers considered a "female" task because it resembled sewing. Black students, male and female, received dinner, clothing and a heavy dose of Christian indoctrination.[49]

While African-American children became trained in manual labor, European-American children learned how to save, consume and plan for a more privileged future. European-American children received an education centered around developing habits that would make them into prospective, industrial laborers and consumers.

> Cleanliness and good habits are enforced, tickets, indicative of merit are issued to the children, for attendance, good conduct and correct recitations; these tickets bear a value of one cent each, and are received from the children in payment for such clothing as they may need.[50]

House of Industry strategies reflected and reinforced the social division of labor that placed ethnic groups in an unequal hierarchy. When local businesses installed sewing machines in the House workroom, a move that illustrates the close collaboration between the House and garment company owners, white women were hired and trained how to operate the machines. Most of the low-paid, hand sewers that stayed in the non-mechanized sewing room were black women from the immediate neighborhood. As outside demand for white, female sewing machines operators grew, fewer white women sought assistance. White women also had more options for receiving aid because more charities assisted white applicants.[51]

The rigidity and structure of daily life at the House of Industry complemented the rigidity and fragmentation of the labor process that was characteristic of the technical division of labor in large-scale enterprises. Lodgers faced a regulated, never varying, daily routine that was designed to impose discipline and to create a new work ethic. Every move made by improvising household members was supervised closely. At 6:30 A.M. House officers woke up the "inmates" and unlocked the dormitory doors. Residents washed themselves before they attended their 7:00 breakfast of bread, meat and coffee. After breakfast, men and most of the women left the building and looked for work during the day. The remaining women assisted the Matron with her duties and matched potential domestic workers with households seeking employees. At noon, the school children were fed. At exactly 6:00, a supper of bread, meat and coffee was served. Doors were locked once again at 9:00.[52]

In the 1880s House managers tightened relief policies and intervened more directly in household work relations. For example, the House of Industry began investigating applicants to make sure that they really "deserved" income support. And, for the first time, they gave income transfers only to people having a permanent address; this facilitated investigation and social control and promoted wage dependence and consumerism. To demonstrate the importance of permanent addresses, the staff declared that 800 applicants were ineligible for relief because they gave false or incorrect addresses, were out of town at the same time they were being investigated, or were classified as simply "unworthy" of relief. Applicants thought by staff members to be "tramps" did not receive relief because they feared this would encourage pauperism.[53] Standards for relief eligibility increased, which displaced many families from relief rolls.

## Historical Summary

Archival records of Philadelphia's largest workhouse, which reveal how communities changed during a 100-year period, make it possible to reconstruct how informal and wage work was embedded in neighborhood and regional relationships. And this archival material provides insight into how and why secular, cyclical and seasonal developments reshaped noncapitalist income sources. The households studied through the House of Industry records received minimal support from wage income and purchased only basic commodities at the lowest available prices. This often meant buying or acquiring goods, not on the capitalist market, but from neighbors in the petty trades, resource brokers, or workhouse and charity staff, who catered to those with few economic resources.

Industrialists had little control over low-income households' full workday before 1870. Non-waged work done by informal workers and petty brokers impeded industrialists' access to low-income households. Informal work held consumer desires in check and limited the amount of time available for wage work. Business owners, through the House of Industry, developed strategies for penetrating local informal networks and for reallocating labor to employers outside the neighborhood. After the Civil War, social managers focused less on the role played by local petty brokers and more on dividing and resocializing the relief population so that it would be prepared for the hierarchical, segregated world of wage labor.

During the economic expansion between 1850 and 1873, labor's reliance on non-capitalist relations weakened, but the non-capitalist sphere remained an important component of urban life. Although commodification increased, which displaced some artisans, non-capitalist work relationships continued to flourish in the late nineteenth-century. Some households lost access to resources that had enabled them to do subsistence work, causing some household members to search for wage labor income. But other households continued to grow food, collect firewood, fish and trap wild animals. Low- to moderate-income household members still made their own belongings and often traveled by foot. The existence of informal markets allowed households to buy, sell and exchange second-hand clothing and other belongings. Even necessities such as water, coal and wood could be purchased or obtained outside of capitalist markets. Tools or "means of production" for petty producing work were rented from other petty producers. Many kinds of petty producing activities were found in urban settings, including the peddling of staples and perishable goods, pawnshops, gambling operations, and the renting of places to sleep. Relations of reciprocity helped households to survive with low wages (which were often paid in-kind and not in cash) and with little monetary income from informal work. But as large-scale production increased, more households relied on income transfers from parastatal organizations. By the way they redistributed limited goods to help the needy, these early state organizations helped establish ethnic, gender and age divisions, which reflected the divisions promoted within firms.

Before the United States emerged as one of the most powerful nation-states, improvising labor still retained extensive control over household work and over the allocation and valuation of non-waged work. But, when U.S. companies began to capture global profit-making after 1873, firms, parastatal organizations, and evolving state agencies pressed communities and families to surrender their control of informal work.

## Notes

1. David Ward, *Cities and Immigrants: A Geography of Change in Nineteenth Century America* (New York: Oxford University Press, 1978), 88–90.

2. Ibid.

3. Sam Bass Warner, *The Private City: Philadelphia in Three Periods of its Growth* (Philadelphia: University of Pennsylvania Press, 1978), 5; Diane Lindstrom, *Economic Development in the Philadelphia Region, 1810–1850* (New York: Columbia University Press, 1978), 15.

4. Fred A. Shannin, *America's Economic Growth: A Revision of Economic History of the People of the United States* (New York: Macmillan, 1940), 380.

5. Gabriel Kolko, *Main Currents in Modern American History* (New York: Harper and Row, 1976), 248.

6. Diane Lindstrom, *Economic Development in the Philadelphia Region, 1810–1850* (New York: Columbia University Press, 1978), 11–14.

7. Ibid. 11–14, 15, 17.

8. Ibid. 17.

9. Ward, *Cities and Immigrants,* 94.

10. Gladys Louise Palmer, *Philadelphia Workers in a Changing Economy* (Philadelphia: University of Pennsylvania Press, 1956), 8–9.

11. Stephanie Coontz, *The Social Origins of Private Life: A History of American Families, 1600–1900* (London: Verso, 1988). Coontz writes that home work for poor women differed from home work for middle-class women. "Poor women scavenged for clothing, food, and other goods (an activity that sometimes 'shaded into theft'), bartered with neighbors, peddled drink or food out of their kitchens or in the street, visited pawnshops, cooperated (or conflicted) with other women in childcare, garbage disposal, hauling water, and doing laundry, and dealt with male boarders or lodgers." (202)

12. Lindstrom, *Economic Development,* 17.

13. Ward, *Cities and Immigrants,* 94.

14. Ibid.

15. Shannin, *America's Economic Growth,* 450.

16. Rolla Milton Tryon, *Household Manufactures in the United States* (Chicago: Johnson Reprint, 1966).

17. Refer to Gary Nash's study, *Forging Freedom: The Formation of Philadelphia's Black Community, 1720–1840* (Cambridge: Harvard University Press, 1988). Nash documents extensive non-waged carried out by African Americans and the autonomous nature of this work. Non-waged work included making and selling goods, including the selling of second-hand, cast-off goods.

18. David Harvey, *Social Justice and the City* (Baltimore: Johns Hopkins University Press, 1973), 281–282, 310. Harvey argues that bonds between households loosened as geographical mobility increased. This decreased the attachment of

household members to particular locales. There is a relationship, he writes, between spatial closeness, little geographical mobility, and reciprocity.

19. Ibid. 281–282, 310.

20. Bruce Laurie, *Working People of Philadelphia: 1800–1850* (Philadelphia: Temple University Press, 1980), 10–12, 138. Also refer to Bruce Laurie and Mark Schmitz, "Manufacturing and Productivity: The Making of an Industrial Base, Philadelphia, 1850–1880", in ed. Theodore Hershberg, *Work, Space, Family and Group Experience in Philadelphia* (New York: Oxford University Press, 1981), 47.

21. Laurie, *Working People,* 16–17, 23–28, 108, 137–138.

22. Bruce Laurie and Mark Schmitz, "Manufacturing and Productivity" in Theodore Hershberg, ed. *Work, Space, Family and Group Experience,* 52, 63–64.

23. House of Industry, 1851, Report of the Managers of the Philadelphia Society for the Employment and Instruction of the Poor, 5, Urban Archives, Temple University, Philadelphia, PA.

24. Ibid. 6.

25. Ibid. 5–6.

26. Ibid. 7.

27. Ibid. 4.

28. Ibid. 1851, 6; 1850, 16.

29. Ibid.

30. Ibid. 1850, 13–14.

31. Ibid. 13–14.

32. Michael Katz, *In the Shadow of the Poorhouse: A History of Social Welfare in America* (New York: Basic Books, 1986). According to Michael Katz, it was cheaper to supply coal than food to lower-income people. When people received coal, however, they often "sold it for cash to buy other commodities."(47)

33. House of Industry Reports, 1851, 9; 1850, 15.

34. Refer to Dolores Hayden, *The Grand Domestic Revolution: A History of Feminist Designs for American Homes, Neighborhoods and Cities* (Cambridge, MA: The MIT Press, 1981). Hayden presents an overly romantic picture of settlement house activities and argues that kitchens run by parastatal organizations were similar to cooperative kitchens designed by and for labor.(151–179)

35. House of Industry Reports, 1847, 9, 12.

36. Ibid. 1847, 5.

37. Ibid. 1856, 7; 1858, 5; 1859, 6.

38. Ibid.

39. Ibid.

40. Michel Aglietta, *A Theory of Capitalist Regulation: The U.S. Experience* (London: New Left Books, 1979), 78–79; William Woodruff, *America's Impact on the World: A Study of the United States in the World-Economy, 1750–1970* (New York: John Wiley and Sons, 1975), 159.

41. Palmer, *Philadelphia Workers in a Changing Economy,* 8–9.

42. Laurie and Schmitz, "Manufacturing and Productivity: The Making of an Industrial Base, Philadelphia, 1850–1880." In ed. Theodore Hershberg, *Philadelphia: Work, Space, Family and Group Experience,* 44–45.

43. Bruce Laurie, Theodore Hershberg, and George Alter, "Immigrants and Industry: The Philadelphia Experience, 1850–1880." In ed. Theodore Hershberg, *Philadelphia: Work, Space, Family and Group Experience,* 98.

44. Laurie and Schmitz, "Manufacturing and Productivity," 46–47, 51, 57, 67.

45. Laurie, Hershberg, and Alter, "Immigrants and Industry," 99.

46. Laurie and Schmitz, "Manufacturing and Productivity," 59.

47. House of Industry Annual Reports, 1867, 5; 1868, 6–8.

48. Ibid. 1868, 6–8.

49. Ibid. 1856, 7, 10; 1852, 6.

50. Ibid.

51. Ibid. 1860, 6; 1856, 5–6; 1861, 6.

52. Ibid. 1866, 7.

53. Ibid. 1883, 8; 1884, 7.

*Storing chickens in crates for the market, Philadelphia, 1909. Courtesy of the City Archives, Philadelphia.*

*Four*

# Industrial Organization and Community Life: Changes and Continuity in Labor's Informal Work, 1873 to 1897

## The Historical Context: The Rise of Big Business and Increased State Intervention into Informal Work

As large-scale industry grew, parastatal organizations and new state agencies intervened more actively in home-based work and informal work relations based in communities. The evolving state, by helping sculpt the definition of community itself, changed the social relations that once held communities together. The meaning of community life began to shift radically during this period, and community networks and family members began to break apart. Before 1870, families in similar economic circumstances created and cultivated social relationships that sustained ethnic and multi-ethnic groups. During this early stage, strong community bonds developed in diverse urban neighborhoods and rural areas. As time passed, informal work and exchange relationships, which once had created communities, began to dissolve, leaving neighborhoods without strong inter-household connections. During the last third of the nineteenth century, local networks associated with non-waged work, began to break down in low- and moderate-income neighborhoods.

These changes may now seem almost imperceptible and even insignificant, but the cumulative impact of conscious and unintentional actions and social processes took its toll. Local governments prohibited people from giving handouts on the streets to less fortunate citizens and police arrested vagrants and prostitutes. Relief policies rewarded those with a wage-oriented work ethic and penalized others. Early social workers began making home visits to determine if applicants were truly needy and if they exhibited a work ethic that would benefit industrial culture. Parastatal organizations and state agencies defined young people, elders and women as the new dependents of adult men. Compulsory public education laws eventually removed young children from the work force. Elders began being removed from shop work and sometimes were pushed out of their adult children's homes and placed in old age homes. Early social workers promoted a new concept of womanhood, which justified the exclusion of women from the work force and defined adult women as care givers and housewives.

The economic depression from 1873 to 1897, the period when the United States became a major world power, brought increased state intervention in home-based work. New, long-term structures were created that defined the dominant features of wage-dependent "self-sufficiency" for the next 100 years. A century later, the depression of 1970 to 1993 once again restructured the inter-state hierarchy and again raised the question of what self-sufficiency should mean. Development in the late nineteenth century, therefore, set the stage for the contemporary historical period.

Development during the last decades of the nineteenth century strengthened the rule of large-scale, industrial enterprises and further separated groups of wage laborers into different branches of production. During the depression, enterprises produced goods sporadically and offered unstable wages to workers. Females and males within improvising labor generated incomes from both home and shop work, though industrialization limited employment options for adult women. Younger workers joined the labor force and often contributed wage incomes to household income pools. Children's wages provided a critical supplement to adult male and female wages and to non-waged income. Household members typically earned income from multiple occupations based in the home and the shop.

Just as employers assigned different kinds of work to different groups of laborers, parastatal organizations simultaneously separated females from males, blacks from whites when they provided economic assistance. Children, elders and women found themselves being separated from adult males because parastatal officials now viewed younger, older and female household members as less productive workers.[1] The development of these divisions occurred hand-in-hand with improvising labor's increasing dependence on wage labor, the growth in cash transactions, and the distribution of transfer payments from parastatal organizations.

After 1870, the division of the working class was directly connected to increasing mechanization. Mechanized work sites simultaneously reduced the number of necessary workers for a given operation and lowered the cost of consumer goods. As mechanization reduced the need for workers relative to machines in manufacturing, the highest-paying jobs that remained were assigned increasingly to workers who were given the privilege to work on a regular basis (white, adult male laborers), while other groups of workers were increasingly denied access to these jobs. Women, elders, children, and ethnic groups of color provided a source of cheap labor, but became "internally marginalized" within industrial culture and received few material benefits. Mechanization and the payment of cash wages encouraged improvising labor to buy goods on the capitalist market, which stimulated the expansion of industry and the further social division of labor, and to make less of their own goods.[2]

The last third of the nineteenth century in the United States marked the beginning of the transition from accumulation centered around the organization of workers to the so-called stage of "disaccumulation," where work was centered around productivity increases based more on technological advances.[3] With growing productivity in the making of industrial and agricultural goods, employers required fewer workers in production. More workers became employed in "non-productive" occupations, such as the social services, teaching, and clerical work. As these new occupations grew, employers began hiring more female wage workers.[4]

Industry expanded, capitalist relations continued to strengthen, and the depression brought economic deprivation to some laboring households.[5] In the United States, semi-finished and finished manufacturing firms grew and raw material and foodstuffs export firms declined. To stabilize business, production was reorganized to control price competition, a development that lowered prices throughout the period.[6] Technological and organizational innovations were made possible by rising profits from mechanized production. New innovations minimized the impact of growing overhead costs, which included costs for "interest on loaned capital, depreciation, insurance maintenance, leases and rents."[7] The rapid increase in capital accumulation, which began in 1870, propelled U.S. economic development, enabling the United States to become the hegemonic world power after 1945.[8]

As this structural transformation occurred, related changes affected communities in the mid-Atlantic region and in Philadelphia. Industry-based and regional shifts triggered the decline of Philadelphia as the country's manufacturing center and led to the rise of iron and steel-producing cities in the Midwest, though leather tanning, textiles and some heavy metal production remained in the lower Delaware Valley.[9]

Industries that survived in Philadelphia began operating bigger, more efficient and more specialized plants. Baldwin Locomotive Factory hired between 8,000 and 10,000 workers. William Cramp, a steel-building company, hired between 6,000 and 8,000 workers; Midvale Steel employed between 2,000 and 3,000 people; Henry Disston, a saw maker hired between 2,000 and 7,000 wage workers.[10]

By the turn of the century, agriculture on the East Coast also had changed. Increasingly, states on the East Coast (including New England, New York, New Jersey and Pennsylvania) imported foodstuffs from big cities in the Midwest. Philadelphia and other Eastern centers became secondary agricultural markets, where merchants redistributed grain to the hinterland or exported it.[11] Between 1873 and 1896, the farm population decreased from 17 percent to ten percent of the total population in the North Atlantic region.[12] Small farmers, ruined by competition with the Midwest, led the migration of laborers from farms to urban centers. By the end of the century, Jacks-of-all-trades had great difficulty competing with commercial farmers.[13]

## Supplementing Shop Wages with Income from Informal Work

An examination of wage levels in Philadelphia, which were roughly comparable to wages in New York City, provide a guide to studying the value of non-waged work. Wage incomes often came into households sporadically because work stoppages were a regular occurrence. During times when wage incomes were particularly low, home work became the focus of household activity. Conducting informal work and participating in informal markets held communities together and shaped the social identities of community members.

Previous estimates of socially necessary income levels in Philadelphia help guide the following analysis of informal work and community relations. Two detailed studies on income, which utilized 1880 data on labor force participation, provide ways to think about non-waged work. Both these studies show that wages provided insufficient support for many households. Eudice Glassberg and Michael Haines both argue that there were many low-income households, but they based their research on wage income, market prices, as well as limited census data on some additional income sources, such as boarding house operations. Despite their in-depth analyses of worker incomes, Glassberg and Haines fail to analyze the diverse and overlapping sources of income associated with the full range of informal work. At this time, non-waged work probably made up 35 to 50 percent of all income-yielding work for improvising labor. These historians assumed that laboring families purchased almost all of their goods through the market.[14] But many "consumer" goods were not purchased through the capitalist market. Some of these were acquired, for example, through swaps with neighboring households or through dealings with sellers in low-priced informal markets.

Households not only made some of their own "consumer" goods (by altering old clothes with innovative stitchery or by raising pigs for meat), but they also made some "producer" goods (by making baskets and vending apparatus.) In other words, households remained petty producing units, while also working for wages. They needed to make or acquire "means of production" to generate their income. Non-waged workers needed wheelbarrows, tools, seed, draft and food animals, and goods to make into final products before they could be sold, which required making, sharing, borrowing and buying producer goods. Working-class households sometimes needed to spend money on buying producer goods, which helps explain why "foreign-born" heads consumed more than families with "native-born heads." It seems likely that this was not consumption of "consumer" goods, but of "producer" goods. "Foreign-born" household members earned lower wage incomes and engaged in more non-waged work, which required expenditures on "means of production."[15]

Both Glassberg and Haines assume that almost all income was generated through wage labor and that almost all consumer goods were acquired through the market. These writers de-emphasize the myriad activities associated with life in low-income communities, including non-waged work, inter-household income transfers and the sharing of living spaces. These strategies for generating and stretching income would alter spending levels. Because households relied on non-waged income (in cash and in-kind forms), households did not need to reduce spending levels on consumption goods to the extent that Glassberg and Haines assumed. Instead, households replaced some consumer purchases with subsistence work, including women's housework. They also swapped with neighbors and received gifts. If families could not make, share, or borrow "producer" goods, which were necessary for their petty producing and marketing operations, they needed to rent or buy them.

Glassberg overestimates the consumer needs of low-income households, but provides occupational material that helps to substantiate her estimate of the number of households that had insufficient wage incomes. When Haines takes into account households' wages and expenditures, he has already shown that households and inter-household networks adapted to insufficient wage incomes. This helps to explain why he found so few households in severe economic stress. The households that he found in economic stress were actually those that had difficulty surviving with the combined pool of both wage and non-waged incomes, even given the supportive context of informal community relations. The conflation of behaviors associated with capitalist and non-capitalist spheres makes it impossible to understand how households' income and expenditure patterns actually developed.[16] Non-waged work both eliminated expenditures on some consumption goods and made other expenditures possible; it also incurred its own costs, which required households to spend money for some "producer" goods.

Based on House of Industry records, Eudice Glassberg developed a budget for a typical household, estimated a necessary income level, and defined the poverty line for Philadelphia in 1880. After examining the cost of consumer goods for a household of five, Glassberg developed an annual poverty budget of $643.46, of which $120 or about one-fifth went to pay for rent. As she explores income levels of Philadelphia laborers, Glassberg refers to Carroll Wright's finding that the average annual wage for men, women and children rose from $196 in 1860 to $244 in 1880, taking into account the number of days that were missed when production stopped. In determining a shortfall between wages and consumer needs, Glassberg concludes that *skilled* workers in 1880 expected shortfalls between their earnings and needs of almost $65 a year or about 10 percent. But the level of economic security from wages was considerably different for *unskilled* laborers; unskilled workers' earnings met only 58 percent of the minimal cost of living.[17] Women working in manufacturing potentially could add $5 to $6 a week to the household income pool. But employers paid less for piece work at home and women in domestic service only earned $2 to $4 a week. According to Glassberg, 50 percent of Philadelphia's people were very poor, though relief societies estimated that only 15 percent of the population sought and were granted relief allotments.[18]

When combined with her archival budget analysis, Glassberg's analysis of occupational groupings can be used to estimate the size of improvising labor. After counting males in the labor force, Glassberg estimated that high-income white collar/professional workers made up 3.2 percent of the labor force, lower-income white collar and proprietary made up 21 percent, skilled craftsmen 43.9 percent, and unskilled laborers and laborers at "other" work sites 31.9 percent.[19] In order to arrive at an estimate of the size of improvising labor, I will group together the categories that received the lowest wages and/or that organized their own work. If it is assumed that improvising labor included all unskilled laborers and laborers at other work sites (31.9 percent), one-quarter of low white collar and proprietary workers (5.25 percent) and one-tenth of skilled craftsmen (4.39 percent), then improvising labor roughly made up 41.5 percent of Philadelphia's laboring population in 1880.[20] My estimate of about 40 to 45 percent may be more accurate than Glassberg's estimate of 50 percent because, in her budget study, she overestimated the extent that households needed to purchase consumer goods on the market, but neglected to include the cost of "producer goods."

Haines tries to reconstruct hypothetical incomes of relatively well-off households, including "native white American" households, households headed by Irish-born individuals, and households headed by German-born individuals.[21] He also looked at income and expenditure information on households associated with large-scale industries, including the pig iron, bar iron, steel, bituminous, coal, coke, iron ore, cotton, woolen, and glass industries. Haines concludes that a minimum, annual budget was actually between $447 and $545 in 1880, considerably less than Glassberg's estimate.[22] Haines argues that households experiencing economic stress actually reduced their expenditures and spent 25 percent less on consumer goods than Glassberg argued was necessary. And he writes that by 1890, only a small number of households generated less than $60 to $80 per person and suffered severe economic stress. He describes households with semi-skilled and unskilled adult laborers earning at or above $60 to $80 per person as expenditure constrained.[23]

Haines' study also indicates that wage incomes of adult males greatly affected the labor force participation of other household members. When adult males had low or erratic wage incomes, parents sent their children out to earn wages. During the early and middle years of household life cycles, when children were young, the wage component of the household income packet was low. During the middle and later years of household life cycles, older laborers were paid less, but children contributed higher incomes from wage labor. When laboring children between the years of 14 and 15 are considered, 58 percent of boys and 42 percent of girls earned some wage income during a twelve-month period.[24]

Economically stressed households relied on children's wages during the economic downturn at the end of the nineteenth century. One of the main ways that households obtained wage income at this time was through child labor. Indeed, the growing reliance of low- to moderate-income households on children's wage incomes actually moved some households along the continuum from more self-reliant, improvising labor to more employer-dependent, monied labor.[25]

The decision to send children into the work force raises certain questions for scholars. Did families send children to work for wages that were necessary for survival? Or, did children's wages enable families to purchase new, "socially optional" consumption goods? And, did children's wages enable parents to buy necessary "means of production" for non-waged work? I found little material that answered these questions. The answers depend on the definition of socially necessary subsistence levels, which was defined at different levels for labor in different geographical areas and at different points in time. In the United States and the mid-Atlantic region, households were in flux and were located at different points along the "wage dependency" continuum, some exhibiting a heavy reliance on non-waged work, others a strong reliance on wage work. It is likely that children's wages were used in different ways by different types of households. Some households bought survival-level consumer goods, others purchased "producer goods" to carry out non-waged work, and while others purchased items that were still considered luxuries to many improvising households. Some probably used children's wages to cover a variety of social needs, which changed during the life cycle of households.

The extent of a household's reliance on wage income and market consumption, and consequently on non-waged work, differed along ethnic lines. Ethnic groups found that their shop and home work options were shaped by the hierarchical process of class formation, which established patterns of ethnic stratification.

A new pattern of ethnic stratification in occupations emerged for male immigrants by 1880. During this period, "older" immigrant groups found pathways leading to intra-class "upward mobility" and left their old jobs to "newer" immigrant groups. Between 1850 and 1880, Irish Americans typically held unskilled jobs while German Americans secured more skilled employment. But after this time, as white, "native"-born men and some German immigrants moved out of skilled occupations into ones requiring more formal education, the sons of Irish, English and Welsh immigrants moved into the printing, building, construction and new metal industries. Later, as Celtic and Anglo-Saxon Americans left the consumer goods industries around 1900, the new wave of immigrants from Eastern and Southern Europe entered unskilled occupations in the meat packing, needle work, and iron and steel industries.[26]

These new immigrants experienced greater residential segregation than German and Irish immigrants, who came earlier.[27] Research conducted under the auspices of the Philadelphia Social History Project indicates that segregation in Philadelphia increased between 1880 and 1920. The researchers concluded:

> [T]he low segregation scores for the "old" immigrants, the higher scores for the "new" immigrants, and the highest scores for the blacks are not evidence for the existence of an assimilation process... but are a reflection of changing structural conditions that awaited each wave of immigrants.[28]

Although residential segregation occurred in the nineteenth century, as urban historian Sam Bass Warner shows, residential neighborhoods in Philadelphia became more divided along class and ethnic lines in the twentieth century.[29] Immigrants moved into different neighborhoods, but they were segregated within these neighborhoods, as records of social service organizations indicate. Each block was divided between more desirable and less desirable housing. Although they lived in proximity to other groups, African Americans lived in back alleys and inside dark courtyards, which had no sunlight. In 1880, African Americans "were markedly segregated from native whites."[30] This segregation, which increased before and during World War I, eventually tended to restrict African Americans' petty vending and producing work to African-American neighborhoods and customers. For ethnic groups within improvising labor, both wage and informal work options developed within the context of increasing residential segregation.

It is difficult to estimate the number of women in the labor force at this time because employers subcontracted wage work to women and children, who often worked at home.[31] After analyzing census data collected by the Philadelphia Social History Project, Claudia Goldin argues that in 1880 approximately one-fifth of black women were in the labor force, while very few white women were.[32] But, if seasonal and temporary employment, part-time work, wage work based at home, and domestic wage work (including cooking, child nursing and chamber work) are all taken into account, the number of white and black women in the labor force might have been higher.[33]

Historians and social scientists typically underestimate the involvement of women, young people and older people in all types of work in the nineteenth and early twentieth centuries. Women, young people and elders probably did more wage labor than many scholars might think. These groups certainly engaged in a variety of types of informal work, though their work contributions might be described as "just housework." Working people from improvising labor did both wage labor and non-waged work; one activity did not preclude the other. Moreover, historians and social scientists overlook the contribution of men to non-waged work, including domestic work, and overestimate the importance of adult male wages within the total income packet. Work relations can only be understood by reconstructing the totality of female and male work relations.

Although the number of adult female wage workers probably was larger than some scholars may think, one structural feature of the period between 1830 and 1940 was that relatively few women earned wages from wage employment, as compared to men. Although women may have participated rather extensively in the labor force before 1830, after this time relatively few adult females (especially those drawn from the ranks of monied labor) worked for employers again until after World War I. As production units grew in size during the 1830s and 1840s, it seems that employers may have started to push adult females out of wage work. The number of wage-earning women from monied labor remained relatively low until the 1920s, when their numbers increased, particularly for married white women. Research reviewed for this study indicates that the period between 1830 and 1920 may have constituted a trough or a "U" in terms of female labor force participation, particularly for married white women.[34] In the period before 1830, both female laborers and male laborers contributed wages to households, though males contributed more wage income to households because they received higher wages. After 1830, mostly single females (including factory "girls") labored and married women did not enter the labor force in large numbers again until the 1920s.

Although households did not depend heavily on women's wages between 1873 and 1897, women and girls from improvising labor often had to take whatever wage work they could find. Although women from monied labor did little wage work at this time, women from improvising labor often found casual, wage work, when it was available.

After studying data on women, men and youth in Philadelphia who worked for more than 3,500 firms (including factories, manufactories and mercantile establishments), a factory inspector in 1893 concluded that female employment in these firms increased from 50 percent of the work force in 1880 to about 65 percent of the work force around 1890.[35] The branches of industry with the largest representation of women were textiles, carpets, hosiery, silk mills, printing and publishing, straw goods, and mercantile firms. These industries had a large number of female employees when compared to construction and machine shops, where men predominated.[36]

Employers paid lower wages to women than to men, making extensive non-waged work a necessity for households. Philadelphia women in the factory inspector's study were paid half of what men earned in similar jobs. According this study, "sales women standing beside men at the same counters, selling the same goods, and doing the same work, got much lower wages than men."[37] Some working women in the businesses studied were single parents or providers who were largely responsible for supporting dependents, either children, parents or siblings.

An analysis of the occupational structure and pay levels suggests that ageism was also being institutionalized within the labor force in Philadelphia by 1880. Employers socially defined youth and elders as groups that should receive lower wages, while males in their middle years received the highest wages. Younger adult males earned higher wages than older adult males. "Old age" for most adult male laborers meant over 40, a trend that continued in the twentieth century for many non-professional laborers who were not lifelong union members. According to Michael Haines, "a disproportionate share of younger men held the better paying occupations."[38] Men typically earned the highest wages between the ages of thirty and thirty-nine.

For improvising labor, age-integrated work relations at home and in the shop largely continued until well after 1900, even up to the 1930s. But after 1880, a declining number of elders lived with their children, the poorhouse was transformed into an old age home, and the labor movement pushed for the establishment of pensions for older workers and mothers.[39]

Although elders continued to work, the number of elders in the labor force began to drop considerably after 1900, a process that coincided with the spread of the shorter work day after 1885 and the concurrent discovery of the potential threat posed by people who, for the first time, considered themselves to be "jobless" or "occupationless."[40] William Graebner writes that "[t]he idea of a permanent and potentially dangerous residual of unemployed in some sense made age discrimination possible."[41] By 1930 only 54 percent of males over 65 and eight percent of females in this age group were in the labor force.[42]

Because labor was being displaced by large-scale production, business leaders and state officials decided to make two major social investments in labor at the end of the nineteenth century. First, they decided to develop ways of covering the retirement costs of older workers who had come to expect employment and wages by making early "Social Security" transfers from young and adult workers to older workers. Second, the business class and its allies in government decided to expand schooling, which removed younger people from the work force and placed them in schools where they could be trained for future employment. Although retirement and education appeared to benefit all workers, retirement and education policies also reinforced social inequality. Retirement was inequitable because only higher-income households that earned wage incomes were guaranteed support. And schooling was inequitable because only higher-income neighborhoods were provided with the kind of education that could train students to obtain jobs that paid high wages.

As participation by elders declined, the introduction of transfer payments in the form of pensions, which was considered a deferred wage, grew. By 1885, pensions were available for a limited group of wage laborers who had worked for business, the government and the military.[43] Transfer payments to elders replaced wages as it became more common to assume that age necessarily made people unable to work. This assumption spread even though there was no evidence to indicate that age made laborers' skills obsolete or that older workers could not learn new skills or make decisions quickly. The formation of negative stereotypes about older laborers reached new heights in the period between 1920 and 1940 and was an integral part of the process of age polarization.[44]

Because households obtained insufficient and sporadic wage income, households often found themselves with at least one unemployed household member, particularly when mechanics were deskilled and replaced by machines, a development that often impoverished households.[45] Sometimes household members refused to accept the new factory order and remained in non-waged work. Before turning to begging or the even more degrading poorhouse, Michael Katz writes that families first sought assistance and credit from landlords, grocers, and relatives or friends. "By borrowing and pawning what few valuables they had, they managed to survive a year or so" before they turned to the state and charities for help.[46] As Daniel Rodgers notes, many workers did not internalize the new industrial work ethic, but earned their keep on the streets. Police records and railroad accident rates for the end of the nineteenth century suggest that somewhere between one and six out of every one thousand people living in the United States may have been "tramps," or migrants who lived largely within the framework of non-capitalist relations.[47]

To reduce the number of migrants, state legislatures passed stricter anti-vagrancy laws. By 1900 new legislation outlawed hand-outs, encouraged the arrest of all vagrants and beggars, and established work tests as a means of separating non-industrious labor from those who allegedly deserved relief.[48] From 1893 to 1914, budget studies by public and private social workers demonstrated that most workers in New York City earned below minimal levels.[49] When public and private relief was available, it was given on completely demeaning terms.

African Americans found themselves frequently unemployed more than poor immigrants from Southern and Eastern Europe.[50] But workers in both groups moved when the location of employment changed.[51] Changing residence, then, was one household strategy to increase income. Another strategy was to conduct petty producing and rent-yielding work. Many families rented space in their homes and served food to boarders. In 1880, 20 percent of families in Philadelphia were known to take in boarders to increase household income.[52]

Households also raised non-domesticated, "farm" animals to generate income and supply food. This was often a source of conflict between the state and improvising labor. In Philadelphia there was a long history of struggle between hog owners and municipal government officials. In the partially industrialized southeastern section of Philadelphia, households raised cattle, horses, goats and pigs [and presumably chickens and ducks] in the streets and in their yards. In the 1880s, the Board of Health removed more than 1,500 pigs from the City limits, "even though this displeased the tenants, who depended on the pigs for food and garbage removal."[53]

## Racial Stratification and African-American Communities

In *The Philadelphia Negro,* W.E.B. Dubois examined how stratification affected African-American communities and structured options for both wage and non-waged work in Philadelphia's Seventh Ward.[54] African Americans had a hard time surviving economically in the 1890s, with two-thirds of the residents in the survey area earning less than $10 a week. One-tenth of the residents could not make ends meet by just doing informal work and wage work, without supplementary public assistance. Many households that relied on wage income from unskilled work and domestic service faced pauperism and needed temporary aid.[55]

According to Dubois, even though households lived most of the year in Philadelphia, household members often migrated from Philadelphia to rural areas in the surrounding countryside or to the South. Multiple migrations during the year brought household members to and from Philadelphia and their areas of origin, which often were rural parts of Maryland, Virginia and the Carolinas. Construction workers lived more cheaply during the cold winter months in the South and then returned in the summer to make bricks, ship materials, or lay asphalt. For those household members staying in the city during the winter months, rent, heat and clothing ate up a big chunk of their monetary resources. More than one-half of the residents in the survey came from the South and 30 percent were born in Philadelphia.[56]

Spatial boundaries of household life extended across hundreds of miles of territory and rhythms of work and family life fluctuated in response to economic deprivation and the hierarchical structure of wage labor. Living arrangements varied, with grandmothers in the South sometimes caring for children so that parents could work in the North. Men sometimes lived as lodgers in the city and helped support families in the rural areas. Couples without children sometimes lived together only one or two days a week because female domestic servants often lived with employer households.[57]

Between 1850 and 1880, the number of African Americans living apart from the household to which they belonged actually doubled, meaning that almost one-third of them lived away from their families. By 1880, "one out of every five adults lived and worked in a white household as a domestic servant."[58] Many African-American households were not coresidential during most of the year.

Both home and shop work defined people's occupational identities. During the 1890s, African Americans organized home work along flexible lines so that all members could simultaneously carry out different kinds of work. Many African Americans told DuBois that they had two occupations, even though they may have identified more heavily with one occupation. For example, a waiter who also worked as a petty producer identified himself as a caterer. A wage laborer who also did carpentry work said he was primarily a carpenter. Almost 30 percent of women said they were both housewives and day laborers. It is significant that non-waged work, both in terms of income security and pride about one's work, was important for these workers. Non-waged work offered an opportunity to be skilled and respected for one's work, to control and organize the work process. Wage work did not offer these benefits to men, who usually found work as servants, porters, errand runners, or unskilled laborers. Women found little satisfaction doing domestic work for others or toiling as day laborers.[59] As non-waged work gradually declined, it might be conjectured, laboring people lost their multi-occupational identities and to began to identify with their highest paying, wage-labor occupation.

Few African-American children could find wage work outside of the home and typically engaged in subsistence activities in the home. With the general decline in small shops, local trading and petty producing operations and household-organized marketing operations run by African Americans were adversely affected.[60]

During the depression, the deadly combination of low wages and high rents hit the neighborhood with a vengeance, causing households either to raise income by renting space to others or to conserve on household expenditures by renting space from other households. Almost 40 percent of households in the Seventh Ward rented rooms to unknown lodgers, and families shared living spaces with their relatives and friends.[61]

At the end of the nineteenth century, the problems of creating sufficient income and reducing expenditures were exacerbated by the decline in real wages of female, African-American domestic workers. Dubois argues that the relationship between servants and hiring households became more rigid, separating employees from employers in very clear terms. Black servants were forced to accept lower wages, including in-kind wages, as higher-paid European-American servants were seen as more desirable employees by moderate- to high-income households. By the turn of the century, thousands of African-American female servants were no longer permitted to lodge where they worked, requiring them to purchase lodging elsewhere and to accept lower real wages.[62]

## State Intervention, Gender Identity and Women's Work

The depression years forced low-income women to turn to parastatal organizations for supplemental income and "workfare." Social reformers took this opportunity to introduce these women to monied labor's conception of womanhood. Female wage workers in "sex-typed" occupations were hit harder by the depression than men in "male" wage occupations. House of Industry records show that while women were thrown out of mill work in 1873 and 1874, men from the same low-income communities did not face high levels of unemployment until five years later. House of Industry managers wrote about the poverty and distress that they saw around them. The winter of 1873 brought such economic deprivation that many women, and some men, sought outside assistance. Men became unemployed and some fathers deserted their families. Insufficient funds sometimes made it impossible for families to purchase housing and food.[63]

When many foundries and factories closed in 1893–1894, adult males applied for relief from the House of Industry during the cold winter months. Recent immigrants, particularly from England, and African Americans stopped at the workhouse, which resembled a social service organization for homeless and near-homeless people. One-half of the almost 10,000 lodgers who stayed at the House in 1896 were men between 21 and 35 years of age; one-third of the lodgers were between 35 and 50 years of age.[64]

Woman who lost their jobs at the mills also turned to the House of Industry, which distributed money and in-kind payments. Intrusive House staff inspected applicants' homes and assessed the extent of need before relief seekers were hired for House sewing room work. These women sewed garments and carpet rags for 20 cents a day. But by 1880, the House reduced the wages to its 100 female sewers to 15 cents a day. When the economy expanded at the turn of the century, wages rose from 15 cents to 25 cents a day. And for the first time in the history of the workhouse, House staff paid workers on a weekly basis, a switch intended to encourage saving for future consumption. By 1890, most women working in the sewing room were African Americans over 50 years of age, many widows and many in poor health.[65]

Along with a small money wage, the sewing room women received daytime meals at the House and were "entitled" to buy the garments they made for one-half the market price. As workers sewed garments they wanted to wear, supervisors of the sewing room encouraged them to make installment payments on the garments they were making. Sewers often made weekly payments on these garments and completed payments on them before they left the room. Working in these conditions allowed women to economize on food and fuel during the winter. Day care services also enabled Italian-American women to work in tailoring shops because they received free child care and a meal for their young ones.[66]

Early social reformers encouraged low-income families to embrace a concept of womanhood that defined women primarily as specialists in home work and child care. This definition of womanhood, in fact, reflected the definition embraced by monied labor, to which most social reformers belonged. When they held Mother's Meetings for mostly Italian-American women who sent their children to the House of Industry's school, staff members urged women to assume the primary responsibility for socializing their children. As a reward for attending Mother's Meetings, women had access to dry goods and coal at one-half the market price. At these meetings, dutiful mothers were expected to voluntarily sew garments as they discussed the challenges of raising children. Since many children went to the House school because their clothes were considered "unacceptable" for public school, mothers were blamed for neglecting their children's needs. Participants in Mother's Meetings were encouraged to purchase saving stamps for food, an activity designed to help adult women develop "modern," market-related, consumption patterns. In a similar fashion, Coal Club members, who usually were African-American, were supposed to save and consume wisely by depositing a small sum each week, so they could purchase coal at cost.[67]

While the impoverished older black women sewed their carpet rags and were served soup, bread, and tea for dinner, the adult males on the next floor were served dinners of beef stew or vegetable soup, potatoes, coffee and bread and breakfasts of good stew, coffee and bread.[68]

Early state functionaries began separating male and female relief recipients from each other, dividing households that sought assistance. By the 1890s, the House of Industry announced that social contact between the sexes and between all people on relief should be regulated and restricted, and by 1895 women and children were lodged in a separate wing. Men and women were locked securely apart and were forbidden to communicate with each other. Administrators feared women might cause moral and social disturbances if they came near men. The staff served women and men at different times to maintain the complete separation between male and female departments. Even within the sex-segregated quarters, administrators forbade residents to talk at meals or in the sleeping rooms. By 1900 this divide-and-rule policy led to the establishment of the Wayfarer's Lodge for men, when administrators passed a new rule that only male lodgers would be admitted.[69] Prototypical state agencies used gender divisions to regulate and control working people who sought economic assistance. To guarantee the maintenance of order at the House of Industry, managers arranged for City police to supervise the building in the evening.[70]

House of Industry efforts to regulate and resocialize labor by promoting womanhood, motherhood and sexual virtue were paralleled by the efforts of the Magdalen Society in Philadelphia. At the end of the 1870s, the Magdalen Society began its city-wide assault against women engaged in prostitution, which was one source of income for some improvising households.[71] Depending on support from the courts, law enforcement officials and City Hall politicians, the Magdalen Society encouraged the police to make raids on suspected prostitution operations and to distribute advertisements about the Society's Asylum to local police stations, court and municipal buildings, almshouses, and judge's parlors. Male and female missionaries stopped at brothels, hoping to convince women to change their ways.[72]

The Magdalen Society, which was concerned about the negative impact of prostitution on women and society, recognized that prostitution provided a critical source of supplementary income for some households. The Society argued that economic deprivation and low female wages forced women into prostitution. Society managers claimed that their organization attacked the root cause of prostitution by urging employers to pay higher wages to women. They blamed prostitution on business owners who took advantage of low-paid, female labor. State laws, they also argued, did not protect women from prostitution. To rid society of this "evil," they made moral appeals and offered alternative lodging to prostitutes, pregnant women, and female non-conformists.[73]

The fact that families took their young women to this institution can be seen as a sign that community bonds had begun to disintegrate. The Magdalen Society used the new power of the state to impose social control and to restrict the boundaries of acceptable sexuality. This also meant cutting off a source of income for women and their households, and cutting off income for enterprising male pimps and female madams who managed female prostitutes.[74]

In many cases, family members from English-American, Irish-American, and German-American households requested that female relatives be accepted as "inmates." Women were often institutionalized at the request of family members for the following "vices": intemperance, nervous conditions that might lead to temptation, and running with boys. Pregnant women also committed themselves, sometimes after being "ruined" under the promise of marriage. Other women became "inmates" because they were rebellious or because they had experienced sexual relations with other women. Some women rebelled against their institutionalization and successfully escaped, jumping over the wall that separated the asylum from the turbulent, ever-changing world of wage labor and informal work.[75]

## Gender and Age Identities in Italian-American Communities

Just as adult female wives and mothers and adult male wage-workers were created in opposition to each other, young people and elders were also defined as "less productive" than adults. When children were drawn into schools, they were gradually defined less as little workers and more as a fragile group that deserved an extended childhood and formal education. But this process occurred more slowly for children from improvising labor than for children from monied labor because low-income households depended on the economic contribution made by all household members. Furthermore, quality education was not widely available in low-income neighborhoods, providing less of an incentive for households to divert young workers from non-waged and wage tasks to acquiring a formal education.

The new emphasis on mothers' parental responsibilities and the related decline of child care provided by other household members became accentuated as the duration and content of childhood changed. John Modell argues that by 1920 both male and female children stayed in school significantly longer than they had before, sometimes continuing their formal education until their teenage years. Throughout the late nineteenth and early twentieth centuries, children from the higher-income areas of Philadelphia, which housed "non-immigrant" whites, stayed in school longer than children from lower-income areas.[76] In 1880 almost one-tenth of all children did not live with their parents due to "orphanhood, separation from both parents, or residence in more complex households which their parents did not head."[77] Even after compulsory schooling was established in 1895, low-income children sometimes were denied access to an education because services were distributed inequitably. Some children went to school on a part-time basis and worked during the remainder of the day. Others left school when they turned thirteen or obtained illegal work permits.

The detailed records of the Industrial School, which was run by the House of Industry, allow a contextual analysis to be made of work carried out by male and female children (including teenagers) in largely Italian-American, low-income households in Philadelphia from 1870 to 1895. The records also describe the types of work that former students secured and organized. The work relations of children attending the Industrial School changed as the social composition of the neighborhood in "South Philadelphia" changed from a predominantly early immigrant neighborhood of Irish and English Americans to a partly African-American neighborhood and later to a largely new immigrant neighborhood of Italian Americans.[78] Black and white children were segregated from each other, with black children being sent to the Western District Colored School. Students attending the Industrial School came primarily from Italian-American households, which relied on multiple sources of wage and non-waged income. Household members received wages from sweat shops and from migrant work in construction or agriculture. They generated non-waged income by making clothes and selling goods on the streets.[79]

The Industrial School gave the House a chance to educate, resocialize and discipline neighborhood children. Until its students were transferred to the public school system in 1895, the Industrial School provided an educational alternative for households that could not afford to buy clothing and shoes, a social prerequisite for attending public school. Between 1871 and 1895, there were between 20 and 100 students attending the School at any given time, 1,000 to 2,000 full- and part-time students in all.[80]

The archival records summarize the economic and demographic challenges faced by Italian-American and other low-income households. According to the teacher's records of the years 1871 to 1895, more than 100 children left school because they moved. Many of these children were members of households so poor that the children and/or their primary care givers were forced to move to asylums. During these years, the records note that 14 children and 11 parents died. Nine parents were either arrested or imprisoned, indicating the strong possibility that theft was a vital source of income for some households. In 89 instances children were sick for an extended period of time and in 11 cases a family member became injured.[81]

The Industrial School's only teacher wrote disapprovingly that Italian-American parents made their children work. Households relied upon income earned by children, particularly during the years of greatest economic duress from 1878 to 1890. Although adults may have preferred to send their children to school on a full-time basis, economic necessity often dictated that children's work skills be utilized to support the household. These records clearly show that households pooled income from wage labor earned in small shops or in large-scale production units, income-producing activities in the home (such as child care), petty commodity activities and marketing, and income distributed by state-like organizations, businesses, higher income groups, and improvising households. In some cases, theft enabled poor families to make ends meet. One-half of the children enrolled in school only attended classes one-half to three-quarters of the time, largely reflecting the extent to which they were needed to contribute to the household income pool.[82]

In order for families to supplement low wages, children needed to carry out home and street work, which included doing subsistence and petty marketing work.[83] In addition, they engaged in some wage labor. Children sold fruit from small stands in front of their houses. Parents often called on their children to help them sell goods from baskets and stands in the Italian-American neighborhoods of South Philadelphia. In some cases, parents and children were forced to beg for a living. Children "ran errands alone" and asked for alms. Parents sent their children to hotels (an early predecessor of the social-service food pantry) to buy remnants of food for ten cents a basket. Both girls and boys were known to engage in theft, a way of forcing income redistribution between households or from businesses to households. Many children searched "abroad" for wood and coal. Children cared for younger siblings while their parents worked. Boys found wage work selling newspapers and both boys and girls sold sand to help their families. Some children contributed to household income by selling oysters on the street.[84]

Parents often assigned child care responsibilities to girls. The larger girls frequently stayed home from school or left school permanently to take care of sick or younger children. This enabled mothers to look for work. By taking care of children, girls carried out a basic subsistence activity, which provided a service that was consumed directly by household members.[85]

As childhood became defined as a more protected, less productive stage of life, gender roles became clearly established in home and shop work. Girls often worked in the home while boys worked in the streets. Frequently girls left school to become wage laborers in domestic service.

Females sometimes served as domestic workers on a part-time basis and went to the school part-time.[86]

By contrast, males often left or missed school to earn non-waged income as boot blackeners, street vendors selling fruits and vegetables from carts, or sellers from the home. Boys functioned as petty entrepreneurs and performed odd jobs. Sometimes males continued going to school on a part-time basis and made a little money during the rest of the day by selling or stripping willows for basket-making.[87]

Boys found a greater variety of jobs as wage laborers than girls. They earned wages in money and in-kind from higher-income households and small business owners throughout the greater Philadelphia area. They worked as hired hands on farms in the Pennsylvania countryside, in small shops or stores, barber shops, bakeries, butcher shops, tailoring shops, shops where peas were shelled for canning, stables, and in printing firms. They sold newspapers, ran errands, carried messages, and hauled goods on the wharf.[88]

Both boys and girls found wage employment with larger-scale industrial and commercial production units. By the late 1880s, at least 40 of the School's students worked for large farms, picking vegetables and fruits. Both girls and boys were also hired to work in factories, stocking mills, and department stores. Only female students from the Industrial School worked in box, candy, and shoe factories.[89]

An analysis of the Industrial School's monthly letters indicates that some male and female children from the same households were being pulled apart spatially and socially by different types and kinds of home and shop work. In other cases, young household members remained together in a common work environment, often working with adults and elders. By tracing children's different work roles over a twenty-five year period, one can reach an understanding of how gender and age divisions were institutionalized.

Two key sets of relations help account for the ways that gender and age divisions became institutionalized, and why this process occurred in a staggered and uneven way. To frame this process within an historical context, it is necessary to explore 1) continuity and change in the dependency of households and communities on both informal work and capitalist production and 2) patterns in household relations that relate to different types of capitalist production.

Before exploring this development in greater detail, it is useful to describe the overall context of gender and age work relations. The division of child labor along the lines of gender reflected the development of the gender hierarchy in society at large, in the workshop, within households, and within community networks. Gender and age relations were defined both under the capitalist umbrella of employment and state regulation and within household networks. Both wage labor and informal work were split into stratified realms in the shop and at home, though they were being split at different rates and sometimes for different reasons. Gender and age divisions related to broad processes of social transformation, which resulted in the decline of informal work and the rise of dependency on employers.

Shop work carried out by children affected household work relations and the ways that gender and age were defined. Where wage work required children to leave the household of origin (particularly where it geographically separated sisters and brothers), it increased the degree of gender and age differentiation, leading to the polarization of family members. Wage labor relations became defined in relation to society's hierarchy. Where households organized many common work relations, the impact of the social division of labor was minimized.[90]

Informal work minimized the degree to which gender and age work roles were affected by the social and technical divisions of labor, which shaped the way that gender and age distinctions emerged in the labor force and through the state. Households that organized a large proportion of their income-yielding activities had greater control over the formation of gender and age identities than did more wage- and market-oriented households. Greater reliance on non-waged work kept household members at a distance from the new gender and age distinctions associated with commercialized life. Low-income households possessed greater control over social relations among their members than wage-dependent households did. This did not mean that households and communities necessarily elected to be egalitarian when they could. Culturally, some households were centered around male power in the community and at home, even when families had more control over the organization of informal work. But ethnic groups that depended heavily on wage labor responded more quickly to the gender and age directives of the new social division of labor.

The ways that wage labor and home work were organized shaped the degree to which household members were created as social beings. On one hand, the same or a similar work environment shaped the social identity of family members in a common direction, causing the family to exhibit social likeness. On the other hand, different work environments splintered the development of family member's social identities, causing family members to become socially unlike each other. The creation of socially similar family members occurred when members worked together. But when family members' work roles were more defined by industrial production and its gender and age distinctions, family members developed different social identities.

Industrial society imposed upon families its own definition of work roles for different family members, which separated family members along gender and age lines. These work roles were defined in relation to the new, pivotal role of the adult white male, who was defined as the most productive member of the family. Other family members were defined as less productive workers and were paid lower wages. And as more families became part of monied labor, certain family members in privileged ethnic groups—women, children, and elders—were not supposed to do wage labor, except in a minor, supplementary capacity.

Industrial society's work roles were based on gender and age distinctions, which established increasingly polarized roles for youth, adults and elders, for females and males. Although family life once centered partly around informal work and labor's informal relationships, it became more centered around industrial production and the consumer-goods market. This shift in the work orientation of improvising labor's families brought a change from family- and community-centered life to gender- and age-defined industrial life. As family members became less affected by family decisions relating to informal work, they became more defined by the capitalist social division of labor. The penetration of the social division of labor into family and community life accompanied the decline of informal work.

The so-called "breakdown" of family life, which is explored at such length today, occurred within this context. Because of their new, distinct work roles, family members thought of themselves less as a family unit and more as members of gender and age groups that were defined by industrial society. For example, boys began to see themselves as "youth" and to identify more with other youth, thus leading to the "gangs of juvenile delinquents" that emerged on urban streets at the turn of the century. Teenage girls, whose parents asked them to earn wages in industrial work sites, began see themselves as a group and identified less with their parents.

This process of acquiring industrial society's new social identities was a product of the process of individualization. Although many scholars assume that individualization allowed each person to express his or her own identity, it actually marked a shift from family and community identity to *social* group identity. Individualization meant that family members became less like each other and more like non-household members from related gender and age groups. New gender and age identities often were in conflict with household and ethnic solidarity. The process of separating household members into social groups defined by society as a whole occurred over a long period of time, and only was just beginning for improvising labor during the last third of the nineteenth century. The general acceptance of new gender and age identities had already taken place for some segments in monied labor, as the image of middle-class, "Victorian womanhood" suggests. Individualization and the development of new social group identities, which was not a simple, voluntary process at the individual level, occurred because of broad, structural changes in society.

Different family patterns were not just associated with households' informal work and general wage dependencies. Different types of capitalist production led to variations in social solidarity. Some production processes fostered household and ethnic solidarity. Other production processes created gender and age identities based on the social division of labor. A careful analysis of the life pathways followed by Industrial School students suggests that employer hiring decisions created two social patterns at opposite extremes. First, at large-scale manufacturing sites and in smaller-scale wage-employment situations, employers often hired just one member of the household. Based on gender and age considerations, these hiring decisions were made with reference to different pay levels and social understandings about what work should be done by females and males, youth, adults, and elders. As different household members began working for different employers, the social separation of household members encouraged the formation of solidarity or social identity along female or male lines. Employer hiring decisions not only separated household members, they also promoted youth, adult, and elder solidarities.

Second, when employers hired entire households to do labor-intensive agricultural work, bonds of household-based solidarity were maintained, thus minimizing the extent to which household members developed separate work identities as females and males, as youth, adults or elders. Between these two extremes fell intermediary employment situations, such as garment production in homes, where employers used many family members as wage laborers, but largely allowed adults to organize production in their own homes.

In the strawberry and blueberry fields of southern New Jersey and Delaware, migrant agricultural work reinforced household bonds and ethnic solidarity because it relied on family labor. When Italian-American households worked as a unit in the berry fields, gender and age distinctions primarily were defined by households and communities themselves, not by employers. The technical division of labor in migrant agricultural production units included all household members in the work force, though the youngest children had lighter work loads. Household solidarity among migrant workers may have been reduced to some extent when older children stayed in urban centers during the summer to earn wages from factory work.[91]

Live-in wage work, which included domestic work and working as a hired hand in small farming communities in Pennsylvania, created gender and age distinctions in much the same way that industrial employment did. When children went to work for other households, living with but not joining new households, changes began to take place within the young person's family of origin. Because sisters found domestic work and brothers found farm work, new gender distinctions within family life were planted as a result of children's wage work roles. The children's new work situations either as young, female domestics or young, male farm hands began to undermine the ties between young people and their parents, beginning to splinter family bonds. Wage labor in both urban and rural areas had the potential to accentuate divisions among household members. The critical factor for young workers may have been whether or not, and to what extent, the household of origin had become geographically separated and/or divided. Not all households with geographically separated household members had household solidarity disrupted. But the probability that this would happen after geographical dispersion occurred was greater, particularly when children lived with other households.

Older boys, who found work as live-in hired hands on farms in eastern Pennsylvania, and older girls, who found employment as live-in domestic workers, were forced to re-examine their relationships with their households of origin. Siblings from the same household were pulled in different directions, with boys and girls securing different kinds of work and moving to different places. The separation of work from the home base and the insertion of male and female children into gender-typed occupations within the labor force encouraged solidarity by gender and age group. New gender and age identities led to the break-up of solidarity within improvising labor and supplanted social ties based on household cooperation and family authority.

## Working-Class Families and the Total Income Pool

The kinds of income that households generated were influenced by the sum of household members' multiple, changing, and overlapping occupations, which were carried out in both wage and non-waged work environments. A wage-oriented picture of the allocation of household members to income-generating activities is provided by Claudia Goldin.[92] In 1880, if the adult male had a relatively high wage, it was unlikely that his children worked for wages. This changed as adult males aged; children with older fathers moved more often into wage labor. If the adult male became unemployed, then male children sought wage labor. When relatives contributed to family income, then female children carried out non-waged work in the home, such as housework.[93]

The amount of monetary income earned by household members depended on a number of work-related factors. According to Goldin, when wage-earning, female children lived at home, 86 percent of them remitted all of their wages to their families. But only one-third of wage-earning female children working away from home remitted any wages to their households of origin. By 1900, one-quarter of single female laborers between 16 and 24 years of age (not including servants and waitresses) lived in urban dwellings that were separate from their households of origin. An insight into the comparative value of generating money income at home and in the shop is provided by Goldin. Adult women who worked in the home earned 47 percent less than adult females working in factories, though this does not include subsistence income and income from all informal work.[94]

What does the relationship between low-paid wage work and non-waged activities tell us about the proportional make-up of the total household income packet? Information from diverse research projects on incomes and "shortfalls" helps to provide a very rough, composite picture of the approximate contributions made by low-income household members at this time. In 1880, at least 25 percent of household income probably came from informal work, including the housework of "stretching the wage." This 25 percent figure for informal work is supported by the "shortfall" between Eudice Glassberg's projected budget of almost $650, which was based on the market price of consumer goods, and Michael Haines' reconstituted minimal income level of between $450 and $550. Haines' interpretation is useful: the households he studied made up this shortfall largely with a 25 percent reduction in expenditures. The 25 percent shortfall roughly can be conjectured to be made up through informal work, including the housework activities of minimizing market expenditures and of making goods for direct consumption by the household.[95]

But when it is taken into consideration that many families also needed to also cover the cost of "means of production" associated with informal work (such as paying for food that families then sold on the street), it can be estimated that informal work must have provided far more than 25 percent of total income for households making up improvising labor.

Using a series of ideal-typical households drawn from archival research on household income between 1873 and 1897 provides an approach for estimating various sources of household income. Low-income households during this time may have received about 50 percent of their income from wages (earned by adult males and children), 25 percent of their income from petty production, marketing and rent, and 25 percent of their income from subsistence work. In such a household, the adult male might earn $280 a year in wages, a child might add $40 a year from wages, other children might generate $40 a year from petty marketing, the adult female and the elder female might together add $120 a year from renting out sleeping spaces and other petty producing work, and subsistence work (including housework), carried out by all family members, might contribute another 25 percent of household income in a non-monetized form.

When households earned 65 to 70 percent of their income from wages, household reproduction patterns changed and these basic units of class could be described as part of monied labor. The rough dividing line between improvising and monied labor appeared to be the reliance on wage labor for 65 to 70 percent of total household income.[96]

As incomes for adult males rose, and households became more dependent on wages and market consumption, non-waged work by other family members declined. In higher-income households in improvising labor, adult males may have contributed at least 50 percent of the total household income through wages. For example, if the adult male earned $350 a year in wages (50 percent of household income), an adult female probably contributed an additional $100 in wages (or about 10 to 15 percent of total household income), the adult female and children earned another 10 to 15 percent in petty marketing work, and the children and a relative (who were assisted by the adult female and the adult male) carried out subsistence work, which added 25 percent to the total income package.

Adult females worked as hard as, and often longer than adult males. But they were remunerated by employers at lower levels. In addition, adult females often carried out extensive non-waged work, which added vital income with a low market-value. When adult women engaged in long hours of subsistence work, such as housework, the rewards of income came through direct consumption—eating a tasty meal or wearing warm clothes—and not through more visible, monetized income. In low-income communities, families most likely valued everyone's work efforts, and not just the amount of money income that was added to the income pool. Families and community networks probably did not begin to radically change the way they valued work until children, elders and the adult female were seen as dependents of the high-paid, wage-earning, adult male.

## Historical Summary

With the rise of the large-scale, industrial production process and the rapid decline of remaining "putting-out" operations, artisanal production, non-commercial farming, and non-mechanized manufactories, laboring households became more closely linked to capitalist production units. The sporadic nature of employment, nevertheless, forced many households to find other ways to provide for their daily and generational maintenance.

For improvising labor, household members participated in diverse home work activities and often held low-paid jobs. Although children carried out subsistence work, petty producing activities, and wage work, they also sometimes attended school on a part-time basis. Children's multi-occupational pattern continued even after compulsory education laws took effect. Households became more dependent on wage labor when children contributed wage incomes to the household income pool. Mass produced consumer goods enabled households to purchase low-cost goods on the market. Rising housing costs forced many households to secure non-market housing, share living quarters, and take in boarders. Low wages and sporadic production required households to organize supplemental types and kinds of non-waged activities, including begging, "tramping," petty producing and marketing, raising draft animals for petty producing work, raising food animals for food, and prostitution.

As a response to the labor-dividing actions of enterprises and parastatal organizations, ethnic groups organized common patterns of non-waged work, which increased economic stability and, at the same time, probably created greater ethnic solidarity. Possibly these responses by ethnic groups, which led to different work patterns in different communities, may have built even higher walls between labor's ethnic groups. By the turn of the century, households of some "older immigrants" experienced upward mobility and became part of monied labor, while "newer immigrants" entered their old jobs. For the next 30 to 50 years in the United States, the ranks of improvising labor were filled by immigrants from Southern and Central Europe, and from Asia and Latin America. African Americans continued to do extensive non-waged work to supplement their very low wages. Even though African Americans had lived in the United States much longer than immigrant groups that came to the United States during the 1830s and 1840s, more recent U.S. residents from Europe largely became part of monied labor by the turn of the century. African Americans gained little economic security during the nineteenth century. The length of time working in the United States was a predictor of intra-class "upward mobility" only for European immigrants. As enterprises and parastatal organizations promoted ethnic divisions, they also continued to divide labor along gender and age lines.

The depression and the economic processes unleashed during the last third of the nineteenth century began to separate improvising labor and its communities from "traditional" and urban-based means of subsistence. The commercialization of labor's informal work occurred slowly and sporadically, transforming only some low-income households into members of monied labor. While developments during the last third of the nineteenth century set the stage for the further integration of many communities into the economic mainstream, the subsequent Progressive period inaugurated the beginning of new, social engineering. Social engineering during the next period was often carried out by well-intentioned social reformers. But as it will be shown, social reform and the spread of market values further unraveled community ties and eroded "traditional" sources of family strength.

# Notes

1. Stephanie Coontz, *The Social Origins of Private Life: A History of American Families, 1600–1900* (London: Verso, 1988). Coontz writes that "society began to be seen as a series of gender relations, divided by function, yet united by mutual need."(269)

2. Ernest Mandel, *Late Capitalism* (London: New Left Books, 1975), 186, 24, 400.

3. Martin J. Sklar, *The United States as a Developing Country: Studies in U.S. History in the Progressive Era and in the 1920s* (Cambridge, England: Cambridge University Press, 1992). Sklar argues that the disaccumulation process, a process defined by Karl Marx as the tendency for the rate of profits to fall in highly mechanized production units, required "massive shifts in capital and labor from goods production to other spheres."(35)

4. Ibid.

5. Gabriel Kolko, *Main Currents in Modern American History* (New York: Harper and Row, 1976), 35.

6. Andrew Friedman, *Industry and Labour: Class Struggle at Work and Monopoly Capitalism* (London: Macmillan, 1977), 35; Doug Dowd, *The Twisted Dream: Capitalist Development in the U.S. Since 1776* (Cambridge: Winthrop, 1974), 64.

7. Alfred Sohn-Rethel, *Intellectual and Manual Labour: A Critique of Epistemology* (London: Macmillan, 1978), 146.

8. David Brody, *Workers in Industrial America: Essays on the 20th Century Struggle* (New York: Oxford University Press, 1980), 14.

9. Gladys Louise Palmer, *Philadelphia Workers in a Changing Economy* (Philadelphia: University of Pennsylvania Press, 1956), 23.

10. Daniel Nelson, *Managers and Workers: Origins of the New Factory System in the United States, 1880–1920* (Madison: University of Wisconsin Press, 1975), 4,7,9.

11. R.W. Fogel, "A Quantitative Approach to the Study of Railroads in American Economic Growth: A Report of Some Preliminary Findings." In ed. Peter Temin, *New Economic History* (Harmondsworth, Middlesex, England: Penguin Books, 1973), 183–223.

12. Fred A. Shannin, *America's Economic Growth: A Revision of Economic History of the People of the United States* (New York: Macmillan, 1940), 352.

13. Fred A. Shannin, *The Farmer's Last Frontier Agriculture, 1860–1897,* Vol. V: Economic History of the United States (New York: Rinehart, 1945), 251.

14. Refer to Eudice Glassberg, "Work, Wages, and the Cost of Living, Ethnic Differences and the Poverty Line," *Pennsylvania History,* 46, no. 1 (January 1979) 17–58; Michael R. Haines, "Poverty, Economic Stress, and the Family in a Late Nineteenth-Century American City: Whites in Philadelphia, 1880," in ed. Theodore Hershberg, *Work, Space, Family and Group Experience in the Nineteenth Century* (New York: Oxford University Press, 1981), 240–276.

15. Glassberg, "Work, Wages, and the Cost of Living," 17–58; Michael Haines, "Poverty, Economic Stress, and the Family," 240–276, 253.

16. Ibid.

17. Glassberg, "Work, Wages, and the Cost of Living, 39, 47, 49, 57.

18. Ibid.

19. Glassberg, "Work, Wages, and the Cost of Living", 50.

20. Although at least 50 percent of laborers were associated with the improvising stratum in 1850, this number may have dropped to 40 or 45 percent by 1880. Projections by the United Nations' Regional Employment Program for Latin America (PREALC) estimate that about 50 percent of the U.S. labor force in 1900 could be considered informal workers. This estimate includes the self-employed, unremunerated family workers, and domestic servants. This report estimates that 46.5 percent of Latin American workers in 1950 could be considered informal workers. Although this type of comparison is useful because nineteenth-century U.S. improvising labor resembled labor in Latin America today, the PREALC estimate exaggerates the number of unwaged, informal workers in the United States in 1900. See Manuel Castells and Alejandro Portes, "World Underneath: The Origins, Dynamics and Effects of the Informal Economy," in eds. Alejandro Portes, Manuel Castells, and Lauren Benton, *The Informal Economy: Studies in Advanced and Less Developed Countries* (Baltimore: The Johns Hopkins Univ. Press, 1989), 16–19.

21. Haines, "Poverty, Economic Stress and the Family," 242, 250–257.

22. Ibid.

23. Ibid.

24. Ibid.

25. It seems likely that many poor families in monied labor during the steam-powered industrial revolution in mid-nineteenth century England relied heavily on wages earned by adult men and women, children, and elders. When Marx studied poor, English children and women in the factory, he may have been looking primarily at monied labor, not improvising labor. This may help to explain why he overlooked the importance of non-waged income: there was less of it in England in 1850 than there was in the United States at the same time.

26. Theodore Hershberg, Dale Light, Harold E. Cox and Richard R. Greenfield, "The Journey to Work: An Empirical Investigation of Work, Residency, and Transportation, 1850–1880." In ed. Theodore Hershberg, *Philadelphia: Work, Space, Family and Group Experience,* 166. Also see Bruce Laurie, Theodore Hershberg, and George Altar, "Immigrants and Industry: The Philadelphia Experience, 1850–1880," *Journal of Social History* 9 (Dec. 1975), 217–248.

27. Stephanie Greenberg, "Industrial Location and Ethnic Residential Patterns in an Industrializing City: Philadelphia, 1880," in ed. Theodore Hershberg, *Philadelphia: Work, Space, Family and Group Experience,* 224.

28. Theodore Hershberg, Alan N. Burstein, Eugene P. Erickson, Stephanie Greenberg, and William Yancey, "A Tale of Three Cities: Blacks, Immigrants, and

Opportunity in Philadelphia, 1850–1880, 1930, 1970." In ed. Theodore Hershberg, *Philadelphia: Work, Space, Family, and Group Experience,* 467.

29. Sam Bass Warner, *The Private City: Philadelphia in Three Periods of its Growth* (Philadelphia: University of Pennsylvania Press, 1968), 173, 182.

30. Greenberg, "Industrial Location," 216.

31. In 1890 the typical female wage laborer "was unmarried, young and a domestic servant." By 1980, the typical female wage laborer "was married, a mother and a clerical worker." See Lynn Y. Weiner, *From Working Girl to Working Mother: The Female Labor Force in the United States, 1820–1980* (Chapel Hill: The University of North Carolina Press, 1985), 5–6.

32. Claudia Goldin, "Family Strategies in Late Nineteenth-Century Philadelphia," in eds. Glenn Porter and William H. Mulligan, Jr., *Working Papers from the Regional Economic History Research Center,* 2, no. 3 (1979), 60–106.

33. Mary A. O'Reilly, *Report and Statistics of Women Wage Earners of City and County of Philadelphia* (Columbia World's Fair, Philadelphia: Avil, n.d.), probably published in 1893, 6.

34. See Ruth Sidel, *Women and Children Last: The Plight of Poor Women in America* (New York: Penguin Books, 1987), 50. Refer to Alice S. Rossi, "Sex and Gender in an Aging Society," in eds. Alan Pifer and Lydia Bronte, *Our Aging Society: Paradox and Promise* (New York: W.W. Norton, 1986), 126. Rossi bases her work partly on research conducted by Kingsley Davis, "Wives and Work: Consequences of the Sex Role Revolution," *Population and Development Review* (Sept. 1984), 397–418. See Claudia Goldin, *Understanding the Gender Gap: An Economic History of Women* (New York: Oxford University Press, 1990.) Goldin argues that in the late eighteenth and early nineteenth centuries, "women's market oriented work in cities may have been more extensive than in the 20th century." Furthermore, "women on farms and in cities were active participants when the home and workplace were unified and their participation likely declined as the marketplace widened and the specialization of tasks was enlarged."(11)

35. O'Reilly, *Report and Statistics,* 4–8.

36. Ibid.

37. Ibid. 9–10.

38. Haines, "Poverty, Economic Stress, and the Family in a Late Nineteenth-Century American City: Whites in Philadelphia, 1880," in ed. Theodore Hershberg, *Work, Space, Family and Group Experience,* 258.

39. Michael B. Katz, *In the Shadow of the Poorhouse: A Social History of Welfare in America* (New York: Basic Books, 1986), 201–204.

40. Malcolm H. Morrison, "Work and Retirement in an Older Society," in eds. Alan Pifer and Lydia Bronte, *Our Aging Society: Paradox and Promise* (New York: W.W. Norton, 1986), 346; also see Katz, *In the Shadow of the Poorhouse,* 204.

41. William Graebner, *A History of Retirement: The Meaning and Function of*

*an American Institution, 1885–1978* (New Haven: Yale University Press, 1980), 15. Eventual results of the social development of "old age" were the passing of the Social Security Act of 1935 and the selling of retirement plans to consumers by the 1960s, which had become "an identifiable commodity like any other product." (60)

42. Mimi Abramovitz, *Regulating the Lives of Women: Social Welfare Policy from Colonial Times to the Present* (Boston: South End Press, 1988), 243.

43. Katz, *Shadow of the Poorhouse,* 200–201.

44. Morrison, "Work and Retirement," 348.

45. Susan Allmendinger and David Allmendinger, Jr., eds. *The American People in the Industrial City* (West Haven, Conn.: Pendulum Press, 1973), 107.

46. Katz, *Shadow of the Poorhouse,* 47.

47. Daniel T. Rodgers, *The Work Ethic in Industrial America, 1850–1920* (Chicago: University of Chicago Press, 1978), 153, 227.

48. Ibid.

49. Melvyn Dubofsky, *Industrialism and the American Worker, 1865–1920* (Arlington Heights, Ill.: AHM, 1975), 17, 19–22.

50. Ibid.

51. Hershberg, Light, Cox, and Greenfield, "The Journey to Work: An Empirical Investigation of Work Residency, and Transportation, Philadelphia, 1850 and 1880," in ed. Theodore Hershberg, *Philadelphia: Work, Space, Family, and Group Experience,* 166.

52. Haines, "Poverty, Economic Stress, and the Family in a Late Nineteenth-Century American City," 258.

53. John F. Sutherland, "A City of Homes: Philadelphia Slums and Reformers, 1880–1918." Ph.D. Dissertation, Temple University (Ann Arbor, Michigan: University Microfilms, 1976), 39–40.

54. W.E. Burghardt Dubois, *The Philadelphia Negro: A Social Study* (New York: Benjamin Bloom, 1967), 148, 121, 223, 32–33, 37.

55. Ibid.

56. Ibid. 45, 74, 134, 165, 70. Also see Florette Henri, *Black Migration: Movement North, 1900–1920* (New York: Anchor Press, Doubleday, 1976), *passim.*

57. Dubois, *The Philadelphia Negro,* 134, 165, 70.

58. Theodore Hershberg, "Free Blacks in Antebellum Philadelphia: A Study of Ex-Slaves, Freeborn, and Socioeconomic Decline," in ed. Theodore Hershberg, *Philadelphia: Work, Space, Family and Group Experience,* 375.

59. Dubois, *Philadelphia Negro,* 99–102, 111, 45, 123.

60. Ibid.

61. Ibid.

62. Ibid. 111, 135–139.

63. House of Industry, Matron's Report, 13 February 1893; 3 March 1893; 14 September 1896. Box 4, 2, 113, United Neighbor's Association, Urban Archives, Paley Library, Temple University, Philadelphia.

64. House of Industry Annual Reports, Urban Archives, 1894, 7; 1896, 11; 1899, 8.

65. Ibid. Annual Reports, 1891, 10; 1874, 10; 1880, 8–10; 1897, 10; 1896, 12; 1890, 10; 1897, 12.

66. Ibid. 1904, 13; 1874, 10; 1901, 15.

67. Ibid. 1895, 8; 1878, 341; 1877, 8; 1901, 3; 1899, 11; 1889, 8.

68. Ibid.

69. Ibid. 1901, 9–10; 1889, 8; 1895, 7.

70. Ibid. 1889, 8.

71. Roger Lane, *Roots of Violence in Black Philadelphia, 1860–1900* (Cambridge: Harvard University Press, 1986),125–132. During the height of prostitution between 1850 to 1900, Roger Lane argues that African-American women in Philadelphia earned about $25 a week or $1000 a year. African-American women worked many years longer than white women did. White women only worked as prostitutes for an average of five or six years. Alice Kessler Harris, *Out to Work: A History of Wage-Earning Women in the United States* (New York: Oxford University Press, 1982). Alice Kessler Harris writes that William Sanger's study of 2,000 prostitutes reveals, "a quarter of New York's population of prostitutes died annually."(58)

72. Magdalen Society Records, Minutes of Annual Meetings of Board of Managers, 72–1, #35, Microfilms, 1837–1907; 1838–1850, Reel #1; 1837–1843, 1876–1889. 9 February 1900, 18; 82nd Annual Report, 1883. Refer to *Eds. Ruth Rosen and Sue Davidson, The Maimie Papers* (Old Westbury, N.Y.: The Feminist Press, 1977). *The Maimie Papers,* a collection of letters written by a Philadelphia prostitute, describes different kinds of prostitution in the late nineteenth and early twentieth centuries. Prostitution often took place in bars and brothels in open red-light districts. There were exclusive houses for the ruling class, middle-class houses, and "cribs" in tenements. In addition, streetwalkers could also be found.(xxvi) According to the editors, many prostitutes interviewed in the early twentieth century had once been unskilled workers, who had earned four to six dollars a week in wages. At the time, a living wage "for a single woman" was considered to be nine dollars a week. Domestic service provided two to three dollars a week in wages, in addition to room and board. Office work paid slightly higher wages, but required typing and stenography skills, which many women did not have. "On the average, prostitutes in American cities during the first fifteen years of the century", write the editors, earned at least fifty dollars a week and sometimes much more. (xxvii-xxviii)

73. Magdalen Society, 9 February 1900, 18.

74. Ibid. 1883, "Magdalen Society: An Institution for the Shelter and Reform of Women." Also see Christine Stansell, *City of Women: Sex and Class in New York, 1789–1860* (New York: Alfred A. Knopf, 1986). Stansell argues that, "Sexual bartering, explicit and implicit, was a common element in relations with men from the time a ["working class"] girl became sexually active. Girls and women

traded their sexual favors for food, lodging and drink."(179) Lodgers, grocers, and fathers made sexual advances at young girls.(182) A similar theme appears in Joanne J. Meyerowitz's *Women Adrift: Independent Wage Earners in Chicago, 1880–1930* (Chicago: University of Chicago Press, 1988).

75. Ibid. 20 May 1870; 25 June 1878; 9 July 1878; 27 September 1878; 14 November 1889.

76. John Modell, "An Ecology of Family Decisions: Suburbanization, Schooling, and Fertility in Philadelphia, 1880–1920," *Journal of Urban History,* 6, no. 4 (August 1980), 400, 406.

77. John Modell, Frank F. Furstenburg, Jr., Theodore Hershberg, "Social Change and Transitions to Adulthood in Historical Perspective," *Journal of Family History,* 1, no. 1 (Autumn, 1976), 15.

78. House of Industry, Annual Reports, 1915, 8. Urban Archives, Paley Library, Temple University, Philadelphia.

79. Reports of the Industrial School, Monthly Letters to the Supervisors by Elizabeth Robinson, the teacher for the entire period from 1871 to 1895. The House of Industry, 1871–1895, Urban Archives, Paley Library, Temple University. UNA, Box 4, Accnt. 2, 113.

80. House of Industry, Reports of the Industrial School, Letters written by the teacher to the Board of the House of Industry, 1871–1895.

81. Ibid.

82. Ibid. Also see Carl Werner, *An Employment History of Unskilled Male Office Workers in Philadelphia,* 1926, Thesis in Education, University of Pennsylvania, Philadelphia, 1931. Boys tended to be errand runners, deliverers and then messengers and office boys, if they were in non-industrial, wage work. If girls were hired by firms, they tended to be sellers.(57)

83. In low-income households in the Third World today, adult family members often expect children to take on major household responsibilities at a young age.

84. Reports of the Industrial School, April 1892; March 1895; Oct. 1878; May 1873; Oct. 1873; Nov. 1888; Feb. 1895; Oct. 1894.

85. Ibid.

86. Reports of the Industrial School, 1871–1895.

87. Ibid.

88. Ibid.

89. Ibid.

90. See Anthony F. C. Wallace's book, *Rockdale: The Growth of an American Village in the Early Industrial Revolution* (New York: Alfred A. Knopf, 1978). After comparing the development of divisions by sex in working class and capitalist households, Wallace argues that cooperative survival strategies in working class households probably "tended to minimize the patriarchal quality of life."(67) Wealthier households were the ones that could afford to maintain more rigid divisions between the sexes.

91. Reports of the Industrial School, May 1891.

92. See Claudia Goldin, "Family Strategies and the Family Economy: The Role of Secondary Workers," in ed. Theodore Hershberg, *Work, Space, Family and Group Experience in the Nineteenth Century,* 290–291.

93. Ibid.

94. Claudia Goldin, *Understanding the Gender Gap,* 53, 100, 186.

95. Glassberg, "Work, Wages, and the Cost of Living"; Haines, "Poverty, Economic Stress and the Family."

96. For related findings, see Kathie Friedman Kasaba, "New York City: The Underside of the World's Capital," in eds. Joan Smith and Immanuel Wallerstein, *Creating and Transforming Households: The Constraints of the World-Economy* (Cambridge: Cambridge University Press, 1992), 63–90. Also see Kathie Friedman Kasaba, *Memories of Migration: Gender, Ethnicity and Work in the Lives of Jewish and Italian Women in New York, 1870–1924* (Albany: SUNY Press, forthcoming).

*Selling produce at a sheltered urban market, Philadelphia, 1914. Courtesy of the City Archives, Philadelphia.*

# *Five*

# The Call of the Market: Come Work, Come Buy, 1897 to 1913

## The Historical Context: The Consolidation of Large-Scale Industry and State Penetration into Home Work

As large-scale industry consolidated at the turn of the century, social reform organizations and new state agencies discouraged informal work and began undermining community markets in low- to moderate-income neighborhoods. Settlement workers from middle-class backgrounds confronted working children on the street and urged mothers to keep children in school or at home. Middle-class reformers from settlement houses tried to convince mothers to keep their daughters at home and to teach them the domestic skills of cooking, cleaning, sewing, purchasing food, and balancing budgets. Social reformers attempted to reduce gambling, lottery sales, stealing, begging and prostitution, all sources of potential non-waged income in low-income neighborhoods. Municipal agencies promoted health reforms that simultaneously reduced sources of subsistence income, such as income from hog raising. Agency officials intervened in housing arrangements and fought families that shared living spaces and economized on rental payments. Hand in hand, settlement workers and doctors began developing methods to undermine neighborhood herb doctors and to introduce low-income people to more costly medical care.

By both promoting wage labor and market consumption, parastatal and state officials in the mid-Atlantic region helped reduce improvising labor to between one-third to two-fifths of the total laboring population by 1910. As the combined result of economic development, social reform, and household work and consumption decisions, support networks in labor's communities further disintegrated. As communities and their families began cracking from the combined strains of market pressures and gender and age divisions, many neighborhoods—increasingly stripped of the community content of informal work—became either residential or industrial blocks. Some local sites where informal work once thrived disappeared from the urban landscape.

Federal, state and local government efforts to expand the economy shifted households into the widening market of consumer goods and linked consumers to unknown producers. Although monied labor grew during this period, households making up improvising labor still needed to supplement wage income earned by men, women and children with various kinds of household-based work. The diversity of work activities narrowed as more income came from wage work. Generally, as more households were linked to large-scale production units, the range of household-based work conducted by household members narrowed.

In communities, the extent of wage and non-waged work diversity depended on production relations, the extent of urbanization, state policies, the strategic responses of ethnic groups, and decisions made by families themselves. Generally, intra-class divisions between laboring people sharpened during the Progressive era. Working on behalf of industrial and social reform, often well-intentioned state officials and middle-class volunteers eliminated sources of subsistence and petty producing income. In lieu of truly independent, family-run work, state officials and social reformers substituted their own work projects, which provided an economic buffer for economically stressed families. For example, parastatal organizations established "workfare" projects that allowed household members to grow their own food, an activity that previously had been controlled by families themselves.

Investors and industrialists in the United States benefited directly from economic expansion and new imperial acquisitions, which gradually created steady jobs and expanded the domestic market. During the period of economic expansion from 1897 to 1913, the United States emerged as a net exporter of finished manufactures and became dependent on raw materials from the periphery.[1] Half of these imports came from Third World countries, including from Latin America, Asia and Africa. Control over raw materials improved the strategic position of the United States and provided investment outlets at the same time.[2]

By World War I, the United States produced one-third of the world's manufactured goods and had the "greatest output of coal, iron and steel in the world."[3] By 1920, the United States refined 70 percent of the world's oil and gained greater control over raw material sources. After World War I, the United States became a massive exporter of private capital (with 50 percent going to Europe) and a major banker for the world.[4]

U.S. economic activity brought new groups of poor immigrants to the United States, many of them arriving in Philadelphia and then dispersing throughout the surrounding region. The largest increases in immigrants to Philadelphia occurred between the two decades of 1880 and 1890 and between 1900 and 1910. The arrival of new immigrants between 1880 and 1920 reduced the relative size of the Irish-American population in Philadelphia, which decreased from about 50 percent of the foreign-born population to 16 percent. The Italian-American population meanwhile increased from three-tenths of a percent of the foreign-born population in 1870 to 16 percent in 1920, with the largest increases registered between 1900 and 1920. The population from Russia and Russian-administered areas (which included many Poles) increased from one-tenth of a percent in 1870 to 24 percent of the foreign-born population in 1920, with the largest increases registered between 1900 and 1920.[5]

Between 1870 to 1920, the foreign-born population in Philadelphia increased from 183,624 to 400,744, forming about 22 percent of the population in 1920. The African-American population increased from 3.76 percent of the total population in 1870 to 7.4 percent in 1920. Along with New York, Boston, Baltimore and San Francisco, Philadelphia was a principal port of entry for turn-of-the-century immigrants. In Philadelphia, between 7,000 and 57,000 immigrants arrived each year from 1884 to 1915.[6]

After 1900, home and shop work changed in relation to the growth of large-scale industry and urbanization. Transportation and communication networks began tying together once separate urban areas. With the development of cars and trucks, the high costs associated with horse and wagon transport diminished, reducing the costs of production for industrial and commercial firms. As trucks replaced teams of horses, there was a decline in informal work associated with taking care of horses, such as making horseshoes, boarding horses, and maintaining wagons and equipment. Declining transportation costs eliminated the necessity for centralized urban areas, which eventually led to the decentralized growth pattern that has been associated with residential suburbs and suburban industry in the United States.[7]

U.S. cities became centers for financial capitalists, while industrial capitalists in construction and food processing moved to suburban areas. Central retailing, including new department stores, provided important economies of scale for distribution and sales firms. By investing in retail stores, manufacturers combined production and distribution activities in one firm, thereby eliminating the cost of middle dealers. Brand names, market franchising, declining retail prices, and the centralized location of retail businesses on transportation lines all helped markets expand.[8]

Enterprises producing consumer goods were no longer constrained by small, limited markets and began operating in wider markets, which exposed them to price competition with firms in other regions and countries. Competition between producers of consumer goods and the increase in per capita income enabled businesses to produce more mass consumer goods for the domestic market. But as David Ward notes, "[I]t was not until around 1900 that the increased purchasing power of workers meant a significant deepening of the internal market."[9] The consumption of mass-produced consumer goods did not become widespread for most laboring households until after the turn of the century.

The way in which urbanization took place divided working people. As suburbs grew and industry decentralized, as horse-drawn streetcars were replaced by electrified transit systems, spatial divisions between working class groups became solidified. After the turn of the century, monied labor's neighborhoods became increasingly separated from improvising labor, whose families lived in centrally located neighborhoods. The automobile accelerated this process by privatizing transportation to and from isolated and increasingly distant working-class neighborhoods. Eventually, the outer rim of inner-cities became the base for immigrants with long working hours and sporadic employment, while more distant suburbs housed higher-income household members with shorter working hours who had time in the working day to commute to work.[10]

Urbanization led to the division of the urban terrain along cultural lines. Increasingly rigid social barriers inhibited the relocation and movement of ethnic groups in the first half of the twentieth century. As David Harvey writes, "[T]he cultural attitudes of the inner city have always been different from those of the suburbs and it does not seem that these differences have decreased.... There have been strong forces working towards heterogeneity and territorial differentiation in the urban system."[11] The "fixing" of cultural heterogeneity meant that geographically etched relations of inequality became a basic feature of urban and suburban life in the United States.

## The Growth in Labor's Dependency on Employers and Market Consumption

Businesses paid laborers unequal wages that reflected the emerging, class-based ethnic, gender and age hierarchy. Many families in low- and moderate-income neighborhoods had a hard time making ends meet. Between 1901 and 1909 large surveys conducted by the United States Bureau of Labor and the United States Immigration Commission found that between one-fifth and one-third of the households that depended on some wage income earned less than $500 per year. This was approximately $100 less than what social workers considered to be the minimum subsistence level for urban families.[12] Official unemployment levels in the United States remained high until World War I, swinging wildly between 4.4 percent and 40 percent during the ten years prior to the war.[13] According to a 1916 report on women and child wage earners, women wage earners contributed between one-fourth to two-fifths of household wage income.[14]

Within the United States real incomes rose and standards of living changed as the country developed. After analyzing literature on changes in real wages, Melvyn Dubofsky found out that although real wages rose steadily between 1865 and 1914, working-class strata benefited differentially from rising incomes. In the first decades of the twentieth century, records and reports of public and private agencies demonstrate that many working-class households had difficulty surviving economically.[15]

Employers paid female wage workers from different ethnic groups at unequal levels.[16] Barbara Klacynska's analysis of Philadelphia's 1910 Census shows that women were occupationally segregated along gender and ethnic lines. For example, African-American women formed the largest group of domestic service workers and often worked in the homes of higher-income households. Immigrant Polish-American women found domestic work and worked in office buildings, department stores and hotels. Other European immigrant women worked as sewing machine operators, retail dealers, cigar workers and sales clerks. Irish-American women worked outside the home more than other groups of women, often working as domestic servants. Jewish women from different European countries found work in the clothing industry. Italian-American females sewed clothes in their own homes and earned wages paid by business owners. Second generation immigrants secured more skilled work as knitting and clothing machine operators. If women of European ancestry had parents who were born in the United States, then they had a better chance of finding a professional position, clerical work, work as a telephone operator, or work with a printing or publishing firm.[17]

When Klacynska analyzed the records of the Society of Organizing Charity, she found that wages earned by African-American women contributed a greater share to households' wage income than other groups of women. In addition, the records show that "native white women" tended not to participate in the labor force in the late nineteenth and early twentieth centuries. And in the late 1920s, many Polish-American women stopped producing goods at home and entered the labor force in great numbers.[18] In general, businesses benefited from women's growing participation in wage labor after 1920 and from the lengthening of workers' life spans.

## Mill Communities, the Textile Industry, and the Social Reform Movement

The history of communities in the highly industrialized, textile-producing mill area in northeast Philadelphia shows how diverse, non-waged work began to change. Although families relied on informal work, they also struggled to establish union rights. In 1903, mill workers from these communities joined the city-wide textile workers' strike, when 100,000 workers challenged company owners.[19] Social reformers and businesses counseled these families how to manage wage labor, consumption and politics. Newly married women, who were just beginning "their housekeeping careers," were urged to set up paper management systems and checking accounts so they could follow expenditures through receipts. This marked just the beginning of financial paperwork for many households, a new part of subsistence work.[20]

A local bank that earned profits through investments encouraged women to take the dollar bills they hid under their mattresses and deposit them in the bank right away. "The woman who saves," the bank advertisement read, "teaches her children also to be thrifty. . . . [O]ur great financiers have laid the foundations of their fortunes from the first nest egg in a good savings bank."[21]

Another bank promotion piece ran as follows:

> Don't be despondent: Don't lose heart, hope and faith while you have health, strength, brain, energy, ability. Take any honest work you can find and begin to save, if it's only a dollar or two each week. The dimes make the dollars and the dollars make you independent.[22]

In this fashion, local businesses and the Kensington Lighthouse, a settlement house in the mill neighborhood, worked together to demonstrate how families could place capitalist relations at the center of household decisions.[23]

Laboring communities in the Kensington mill area, where seven-eighths of the world's carpets were produced in 1900, depended on wage income from all household members who were able to secure mill work. This factory enclave resembled factory towns and enclaves in mid-nineteenth century industrial areas, where household members of different ages could be found working for low wages. In the Kensington enclave, like similar factory-town areas, households moved from improvising to monied labor because young, adult and older household members earned increasing wages and bought more market goods. Households in the mill neighborhood typically counted on teenagers' wages.[24] In addition, they depended on non-waged contributions from their mill workers and from younger household members. When the mills closed down or when work was sporadic, households sought relief payments and relief work from the Lighthouse settlement and the Union Benevolent Association. Inter-household exchanges helped provide mutual support during hard times. Neighbors maintained close ties in this relatively closed social space, where two-story homes separated by back alleys nestled up to the mill.[25]

For those workers producing carpets, upholstery, lace curtains and hosiery, labor was not well-paid, forcing all household members to earn income whenever possible. Given the nature of textile production in large factories at the turn of the century, many wage laborers found themselves temporarily out of work or waiting at their work benches for supplies to be shipped to their departments. The records of the Lighthouse mention that workers suffered from small paychecks due to inefficiencies in the production process, causing workers to wait for "want of color" or wait when "warp ran out."[26]

The settlement workers from the Lighthouse, an early human service agency, expressed concern about informal producing and vending work. Settlement workers voiced particular concern about street work that was done by children. Social reformers voiced strong objections to the presence of male child workers on the street, such as "newsies" who sold papers late in the evening, gum peddlers, and "scavengers." They did not think that gambling, stealing and begging were proper activities for young boys. When they saw young children begging for hand-outs, settlement workers argued they should be at home in their mothers' arms. Nor did settlement staff like to see young teenage girls working at the mills, partly because they might miss out on opportunities to practice cooking and sewing, which might eventually benefit their future husbands. Neighborhood people responded to reformers' criticisms by arguing that children worked because their small earnings were needed.[27]

To support their criticisms of the way households organized work, the Lighthouse staff conducted a study to find out how many boys in the neighborhood worked. Of 50 families they interviewed, 40 had boys working for an average of $1.13 a week in non-factory jobs. Older brothers often worked in the mill and sold papers in the streets. In 42 of the households surveyed, the adult male earned only an average of $10.36 a week during good times.[28]

In the Kensington mill area, budgets recorded by both male and female household members in 1920 show that women earned extra income by taking in mill workers as lodgers, who bought sleeping space, and boarders, who purchased meals along with sleeping space. Women in this neighborhood also sold lunches to men who came from other areas. Enterprising women were able to contribute additional non-waged income through subsistence housework.[29]

At this time in New York City, and probably also in Philadelphia, subsistence work organized around the transformation of food declined partly because convenience food became more available. In the words of Katharine Anthony, who studied changes in consumerism and housework in New York City, "More and more, the housewife buys these [convenience] foods: they save time and fuel—and fuel is a heavy [expensive] item."[30]

Female teen workers made substantial contributions to the household income pool from wages received for doing piece-work. Depending on how much was put into the family income package, girls received clothing and spending allowances. But spending money for teen workers was limited because the younger girls made only about two to three dollars a week in the mills.[31] Households relied heavily on teenage wage labor, which sometimes raised household dependence on wage income to at least 65 or 70 percent of total income.

The Lighthouse staff sought to capture the souls of neighborhood people to promote more "self-reliant" behavior, by which they meant greater reliance on wage labor. Staff members encouraged wise consumerism and a broader acceptance of the central role of the adult male worker. As part of their efforts, Lighthouse staff established a day nursery, organized against prostitution, supported activities for female suffrage, which they saw as an offshoot of the temperance movement, worked to shift the lunch trade from the saloons to restaurants, enrolled only healthy people as members in a beneficial or health insurance society, supported the Boy Scouts' efforts to promote discipline and good work habits, and tried to teach workers that Christianity was the true alternative to socialism.[32]

Settlement house staff developed educational programs that stressed the importance of health and cleanliness in order to counteract the habits of working people, who they regarded slothful and "dirty." For example, in a lecture on tuberculosis, one doctor emphasized that family members should never let anyone kiss a baby on the mouth. The staff stressed the importance of safety to ensure that the "breadwinner" would not be injured at work or at home. Good safety habits would reduce income losses and help guarantee financial independence from relief agencies. Social reformers directed mill families to become more careful, to prevent disease, and to make sure that they cleaned their homes and served clean food. The message from the settlement house was clear. "It is cheaper to be careful. It is modern to be careful."[33]

## State Intervention into Home and Shop Work: The Further Stratification of Labor

State and parastatal organizations simultaneously attempted to push labor into the cash nexus and minimize the potential impact of economic development on households. Without protective labor legislation and reform organizations' income subsidies, labor would have faced harder times than it did at the turn of the century.[34] By contributing to household income, state-like organizations blunted the impact of the market while state officials rolled out the welcome mat for business and ushered it into previously unexploited terrains. The Janus-faced aspect of parastatal organizations and state agencies meant that laborers began counting on some economic redistribution of wealth, which was channeled to them by social service organizations and state agencies, even while they were being deprived of the ability to generate their own kind of commonly shared wealth.

State officials promoted capitalist relations by developing a labor force that could meet the needs of business. In this capacity, state officials sought to establish a healthy, dependable, wage-oriented work force that would consume new goods and expand the domestic market, thereby helping business to profit from the manufacture of both producer and consumer goods.

During the Progressive era, state officials sought to reduce the "over-exploitation" of working people and at the same time restrict the flow of labor into capitalist industry where mechanization had reduced the demand for labor.

Most scholars who write about the Progressive period focus on the state's efforts to alleviate the negative impact of economic development on working people. As David Noble has written, the reform movement was "aimed at eliminating the horrors of industrial capitalism in order to make it work better."[35]

Social reformers, who came from the ranks of monied labor, organized the provision of social services to replace immigrant networks, supported legislation that limited working hours for women, and advocated the adoption of safety measures in the home and in industry. These advocates for reform "expanded the protective actions of government for the disadvantaged," Susan Kennedy writes.[36] Reformers from monied labor did not realize that minimizing the horrors of industrial production hurt improvising labor economically, just as much as it "protected" them. The destruction of immigrant networks removed the context in which informal work skills developed. As social reformers strived to assist improvising labor, they often unknowingly eliminated labor's self-support mechanisms that enabled households to make ends meet. Reducing wage labor hours for women and children helped industry dispense of superfluous labor more than it may have benefited laboring households, which depended on women's and children's wages. Establishing separate work standards for women further reduced their chance of obtaining adequate wages and restricted their employment options for decades to come.

Progressive reform policies in the United States were implemented by social reformers and state officials, who did not recognize the importance of informal work skills. Reformers, state officials and early social workers did not involve low- to moderate-income people in the process of making decisions about how to achieve self-sufficiency and or fight poverty. Perhaps most important of all, policy makers and program implementors only considered the option of making industry and the state bigger, without considering the option of also strengthening micro- and small businesses, while guaranteeing worker's well-being and rights through state regulations. The "bigger is better" pathway, which was used during the Progressive era and later in response to the Depression of the 1930s, laid the groundwork for future economic and state developments. This social blueprint was not questioned until the 1980s, when economic growth slowed down and the state faced a new fiscal crisis that undermined its ability to fulfill its social commitments.

According to the new social policy of the Progressive era, "self-sufficiency" no longer meant doing innovative work and running mini-enterprises to supplement wage income. Self-sufficiency came to mean depending totally on wage labor and market consumption as a means of providing for household members. This shift in the definition of "self-sufficiency" and "self-reliance," which was promulgated by a coalition of state officials, industrialists, reformers and supporters from monied labor, set the stage for corporate growth and an expanding state bureaucracy, which had few ties to labor's diverse constituencies. Working people no longer were to assume responsibility for organizing their own work, but they were to depend on employers for wages and on marketing firms for their consumption goods. "Self-reliance" became twisted to mean labor's total reliance on industrialists and merchants, a process that had already been set in motion for monied labor. Society's new edict that labor should depend on wages from firms, and not at all on its own creative abilities to work, set the stage for improvising labor's growing dependence on hand-outs from early social service organizations and, eventually, on state welfare payments.

At regional levels and in urban centers, social reformers often tried to remove households' non-waged sources of income and to undermine people's ability to work at home or in the streets. They justified the attempt to promote a greater dependence on income from employers by relying on Christian doctrine, which supplied new definitions of "self-reliance" and "self-sufficiency." Social reformers encouraged household members to reduce income-generating home work and to rely instead on wage labor and market-based consumption to take care of their needs. They told economically stressed people that they needed to become more "modern." If families wanted to make it in the new system, they would have to put all their eggs in the new basket. They assumed then that non-waged work would disappear as the economy expanded. Because it used up a portion of the working day, social reformers assumed that home work simply inhibited households' ability to survive in the market-oriented system. These reformers did not recognize the diverse work skills that informal workers possessed. They did not understand that households on the borderline between impoverishment and survival needed to have family members to work at home or in the streets. Reformers tried to raise households' income by moving working people into mass-production, mass-consumption society.

Because machines were replacing labor in large-scale production units, state officials needed to manage the over-supply of labor. In conjunction with business, organized labor, and parastatal organizations, the state sought to reduce labor surpluses by arguing that work in industry should be reserved for adult, white male wage laborers. By designating adult, white male wage laborers as the primary wage earners, other household members found that the value of their labor was depreciated.[37] Although protective legislation improved working conditions for women and children, Susan Lehrer argues that it also helped establish adult men as the primary wage earners within industry.[38] State policy, therefore, served to institutionalized the gender gap at work. Men became the primary wage earners and women were assigned the primary role of home-based reproducers of labor and subsistence workers.

By restricting the ability of women and children to work in shops or on the street, reformers consolidated the position of adult male wage laborers in industry. They also introduced sanitation and safety legislation designed to improve working conditions in factories. The factory inspection laws passed between 1885 and 1895, which barred young people under 14 from working in factories and restricted children from working more than ten hours a day or more than 60 hours a week, both improved children's health and prevented many children from earning an income.[39] After the turn of the century, when "nearly one out of five children aged from ten to fifteen years were employed," the participation of children in street and shop work declined.[40]

Pennsylvania and New Jersey passed restrictions on child and female labor more slowly than other industrial states, allowing women and children to work long hours after 1900. But between 1905 and 1915, protective legislation was introduced and some companies began welfare programs and defined work along gender lines, with companies providing more night work and longer, twelve-hour shifts to men than women.[41]

Although scholars often describe the Progressives as an anti-business movement, the state became reorganized so that it could better address business's most pressing domestic and international needs. As Doug Dowd writes, Progressivism brought far-reaching changes that "did much to take the steam out of popular discontent."[42]

Melvyn Dubofsky argues that the implementation of social reforms reduced working-class solidarity. Social reformers, law makers and business owners worked together to regularize working-class life and undo the relative isolation and separation of neighborhoods and towns. Rules for social life and work were formalized by a diverse group of social reformers, as well as by some laborers, writes Dubofsky. Although working people did not benefit from many reforms, they often pushed for state intervention to protect themselves from the economic ravages that accompanied economic expansion.[43]

Rather than promoting economic justice for laboring people, Robert Allen argues that the new social policies developed by reformers resulted in the "increasing institutionalization of racism."[44]

Not only did state officials and business leaders exercise political power in order to cultivate industrial society, they also wanted to defuse working-class interest in socialism. Union leaders who represented monied labor, state officials, and business leaders viewed improvising laborers, who lived in a different, "less desirable" way, as political adversaries.

## State Intervention into Community Life

By working to improve health conditions in the Philadelphia area, state officials reduced non-waged work options and pushed families to make larger expenditures on commercialized housing. As families felt the need to spend more on housing, they needed to earn more income—often from wage labor—to pay rent on a regular basis. Philadelphia's Bureau of Health and its sibling agencies played a major role in reducing work options for improvising labor and in changing the definition of "adequate" housing. By their actions, Bureau of Health officials also helped large businesses take over work that had generated non-waged income for improvising households. By prohibiting the raising of animals for food in residential areas, Board of Health officers helped eliminate an important source of subsistence income for improvising households. New laws restricting petty commodity production and marketing had the same effect. As food production and distribution became more regulated by city officials, the production of goods required greater capital, which made it more difficult for improvising households to participate in these activities.

In the name of good health, for example, social reformers organized a drive to remove hogs from neighborhoods, which provided an important source of subsistence income and also inexpensive food for families.[45] In 1909 the Philadelphia Housing Commission tried to convince the City to remove 20,000 hogs from urbanized sections of Philadelphia. They argued that in South Philadelphia, "Hog raisers were attracted by the prospect of free garbage, and they frequently kept their children out of school to collect it."[46] Finally, in 1912, the Housing Commission, health officials, and social service agencies convinced the City Council to pass an ordinance limiting hog raising to certain areas. Hog raisers fought back, but they lost their appeal in court.[47]

In addition to curbing certain types of non-waged work, Bureau of

Health officials also expressed concern about health conditions that were seen in relationship to low-income housing. Because Health officials viewed "crowded" housing as unhealthy, they saw much of the housing occupied by low-income households as a menace to public health.[48] And they sought to regulate households' activities, such as taking in boarders, renting out rooms, leasing or utilizing temporary shelters, and sharing a living space with others in the name of public health. Between 1897 and 1913, the Bureau worked with other city officials and arrested people for vagrancy and for taking in illegally gained income, much of it obtained by household members from renters and boarders.[49]

Bureau of Health officials also waged a campaign in low-income residential areas against "overcrowding," which reduced households' ability to reduce housing costs. Lower-income households tried to minimize housing costs by living together and pooling resources between members of different households or within large households. After a census study in 1912 concluded that most families only had two rooms in 2,964 houses, the Bureau of Health charged forward with its campaign against "unsanitary" overcrowding. Agency officials also argued that the lodging of non-family members was an "evil."[50]

Improvising households resisted public health officials, who tried to stop families from sharing living spaces. When inspectors came into the tenements, large households locked their rooms or slipped out of the building to avoid inspection. Investigators faced 852 locked rooms and 2,094 vacant rooms during their campaign against overcrowding. To avoid paying a higher rent elsewhere, tenants that did have their rooms inspected listed only some of their co-residents and hid folding beds, which were illegal in the city.[51]

Reformers expressed grave concern about various housing situations. For example, Bureau of Health records of South Philadelphia show that "Mom Hewitt" and her lodgers often defied the incursion of social reformers who intruded. Mom Hewitt was known by social service workers because she was a tough woman who supposedly lodged former prison inmates and beggars. According to inspectors, she ran her rooming house and supervised its non-waged work activities with an iron rod in her hands. As part of her petty lodging business, she ran a "function shop," where women were sent into the streets on a daily basis to beg. "They were paid five cents a basket for food which they brought in. . . . [T]his was sorted and sold over a counter to the people of the street."[52] Turn of the century beggars were given food, not money to buy food, as is typical today. Housing laws eventually provided inspectors with the means they needed to evict Mom Hewitt and her lodgers, ending their effort to sell donated, recycled food to poor people.

In another case, residents of a large 20-room tenement house fought off settlement workers and outsiders. Non-residents generally were afraid to enter tenements in low-income neighborhoods after sundown because they had no lights. According to Starr Centre settlement records, there were many stories told of people on the street who were carried into the building at night, stripped and robbed. A female janitor in the building, who also sold "policies" for a micro-gambling operation, had a reputation for fighting outside forces head-on. Settlement workers reported that she "swallowed the policy tickets when struggling with the police who were trying to gain evidence of her gambling."[53]

Until they conducted a study demonstrating that 43 percent of tenement families had lived in the United States for a long time, public health officials believed that people lived in crowded tenements because they had not been sufficiently "Americanized." Because Philadelphia was the second busiest port of entry to the United States in 1913, Bureau workers were convinced that unsanitary living conditions persisted because recent immigrants brought bad habits with them.[54] But the tenement study indicated that conditions in the United States, not cultural habits, perpetuated work and income-pooling activities that were inconsistent with the habits of monied labor.

Furthermore, the tenement dweller study proved that rigid ethnic segregation divided the tenant population. More than two thousand of the tenements housed only one ethnic group, while only two tenements housed five ethnic groups. According to the report, Italian and African Americans lived in more segregated housing than did American Jews and "native [Western European] Americans."[55]

To gain more control of the tenements, state officials and landlords issued orders forbidding overcrowding, levied fines for violations, and conducted frequent apartment inspections. The campaign against subletting questioned the appropriateness of two-family houses, furnished rooming houses, boarding houses, cheap hotels and other sublets. Officials expressed concern about conductors who installed two to six additional beds at 15 cents a night in each room during the winter months or charged men to sleep on benches, in chairs, or on the floor for five cents a night.[56] These temporary housing arrangements attest to the large number of urban, homeless working people.[57]

The claim that regulation promoted good health allowed state-like organizations to clamp down on matters previously controlled by households. For example, in 1902 a new House of Industry regulation stated that no work would be available to applicants who had not been vaccinated. A number of household members refused to be vaccinated. The House of Industry also announced a new policy in 1910 requiring that the workfare recipients of sixty-cent weekly paychecks would have to allow ongoing inspections of their homes.[58] Just as business managers sought to increase control over workers in the shop, state functionaries worked to increase their control over labor's social and economic behavior by intruding into homes and temporary living quarters. These efforts to manage the "hidden homeless" ultimately forced households to spend a larger share of their income on housing.

## Parastatal Organization of Subsistence Cultivation

Until the federal government became the principle organizer of social service programs for low-income people in the 1930s, parastatal organizations carried out this function. "Workfare" food programs, which were initially organized by parastatal organizations around the United States, helped deprive workers of their control over subsistence activities. After thousands of unemployed men marched with Coxey's Army to Washington in 1894, a gardening project—which generated subsistence food and income for low-income families—was started by an early state organization in Detroit. Parastatal-sponsored gardening projects enabled laboring households to create income from the sale or consumption of vegetables. These gardening activities were supervised and controlled by managers hired by non-profit organizations, and not directly by poor people themselves. In Philadelphia, the Vacant Lot Project, which had a combined approach of workfare, subsistence work and distributing "pre-state" transfer payments, used inner-city land that was not rented or used for pasture by its owners. The Project lasted from 1897 to 1919 and ended when land in the central part of the city was used to build homes, shops, and factories.

During the first decade of the gardening project, participating families ate a portion of the vegetables they raised and sold surplus food. For almost all the households in the Project, state-organized subsistence gardening helped cover the cost of food, but also provided income for essential clothing and rented shelter.[59]

By 1914, a small group of laborers from more commodified households also gardened on vacant lots to raise additional income that could help pay for mortgages, education for children, and supplies and clothes for school. These households formed part of the growing stratum of monied labor.[60]

Managers of the cultivation project encouraged industriousness and urged each household to accept complete responsibility for its well-being. Although gardening households had to provide their own gardening tools, the Vacant Lot Association provided one-quarter to one-half acre of rent-free land and free seed. Gardeners had to promise to chase away trespassers and to keep a record of which vegetables were sold, used or given away.[61] Project managers imposed these conditions to encourage respect for private property, reduce theft, instill obedience, and promote individual and household self-reliance.

The first gardeners in 1897 had lived in Philadelphia for an average of eighteen years, with African Americans representing 10 percent of the participating households. Households represented a wide variety of ethnic and national backgrounds.[62] Household members, who walked to garden plots from their inner-city neighborhoods, were generally urban people with little or no farming experience. The initial group of cultivators consisted primarily of unemployed, skilled laborers (including two former mill workers who walked five miles to their plots), elderly people over 50 years of age (one-third of all gardeners), disabled people, women and children.[63] Gardeners were economically disadvantaged people who had lost their wage incomes. Workfare gardeners came from groups that became socially defined by state officials and industrial managers as less productive and more marginal to the economic benefits distributed by society.

Many participating households had unsteady access to wage income and could not rely on wage income from adult males, who often lost job after job. Adult males from these units typically worked in a series of wage occupations, sometimes working in wage and non-waged jobs at the same time. Household members had numerous occupations and contributed different kinds and amounts of income to the household pool. Unsteady work as wage laborers, coupled with the creation of new social needs, put these early work-for-food recipients in an economic pressure cooker.

Even though project directors wanted to promote self-sufficiency only for individual households, low-income participants often defined gardening work as collective, income-yielding work that involved and benefited a number of households. Reciprocal, non-market work, a tradition carried out by improvising labor, continued to flourish as a survival strategy within the context of this parastatal workfare program. By promoting the new ideal of self-sufficiency for small units, project directors did not make it so because participating households remained partially grounded in another economic reality. Gardeners sometimes shared work and food, exchanging income across household boundaries. These early "food stamp" recipients often lived in multi-family dwellings. At times, they shared plots of land, worked the land together, shared the harvest collectively, and transferred income and resources among and between household members. Cultivators who had farmed plots in previous years often requested that poorer people be given access to land that would have been theirs.[64]

During the initial years of the program, the average income from growing vegetables, valued at the market rate of $62 a year, made a big difference to low-income cultivators because it supplied as much as 15 to 20 percent of total household income. With unskilled adult male laborers only making about 15 cents an hour in 1910 and averaging about $1.50 a day or $9.00 a week, adult male wages did not cover the cost of reproducing a typical laboring family of two adults and five or six children. Subsistence gardening could contribute an extra $100 worth of food each year.[65]

Vegetables were eaten right after they were harvested, canned for the winter, or sold on the street by household members. Households typically canned or preserved potatoes, tomatoes, corn, pickles, sauerkraut and catsup. In this way, households did not have to purchase these goods during the winter months, when their prices were highest.[66]

Household members often sold extra vegetables on the street. With this money, households could invest in other petty marketing ventures or purchase basic necessities. Other households simply ate the produce.

One boy used his vegetable income to invest in a vending business. Selling food—including crabs, sandwiches and coffee—at the ferry landing enabled him to generate petty marketing income. Sales increased so much that the boy expanded his operation and more than quadrupled his income from this informal work.[67]

In one case, subsistence gardening enabled one household to start a small poultry business. The adult male gardener, who became a poultry dealer, originally was a butcher. In an enterprising fashion, the household increased their savings by having the adult male till the soil while the rest of the family earned wages as live-in domestic servants. The former butcher stored his belongings with a fellow gardener, slept on the ground (thereby eliminating housing costs), and cooked his own food over an oil stove. A higher-income household that had employed the butcher's wife and children helped them acquire five acres of land in the neighborhood. Subsistence income from gardening allowed the household to purchase 100 chickens for their poultry operation, enabling the household to become petty producers.[68]

One gardener was a European-American widower who was unable to find wage work for more than six months. The whole family, which included three girls and a young boy, became weak and emaciated. The oldest girl "kept house" and did home work, while the boy labored for two to three dollars a week in wages. So that everyone could help grow food, the family moved from their one-room apartment in the heart of downtown to a small house near the garden.[69]

When these part-time gardeners marketed the relief food that they grew, they often charged higher prices than urban hucksters because their vegetables were of unusually high quality. By 1904 children developed delivery routes and visited customers regularly to take orders. Families could decide whether to consume or sell their produce. Some households directly consumed most of their crop. Others sold their vegetables for a price that enabled them to buy a larger quantity of lower-quality food from hucksters.[70]

Parastatal-run subsistence gardening provided critical economic assistance during hard times. For example, a father from a family of 11 moved West and sent home two dollars per week to his family. His twelve-year-old son gardened while his older brother earned three dollars a week as an apprentice in masonry. Another brother was paid two dollars a week for working in a mill that ran only on a half-time basis. A sister of fourteen attended school and probably engaged in subsistence work. Gardening meant there was enough food for the summer and part of the winter, and enough income to cover the monthly three-dollar rent.[71]

The idea of even one household member having a single occupation throughout his/her life is a largely an historical myth (except for some high-income U.S. families between 1945 and 1970). The traditional picture of the thrifty wife and the industrious husband does not provide an accurate description of how households maintained themselves. The following work history exemplifies the diversity of work histories, particularly for improvising labor. One truck gardener in New Jersey, who previously had been a skilled mechanic or artisan, left farming because rental costs were high and income low. After being unemployed and underemployed in Philadelphia for more than two years, the former farmer was hired as a night watchman at wages that were so low that he could not pay his rent. This former skilled mechanic, truck farmer, underemployed casual laborer, and night watchman then became a gardener in the Vacant Lot food relief program. He convinced its managers to hire him to supervise the gardens for a wage of three dollars a week. During these hard years, this multi-skilled worker said he wanted to make sure that his wife and children (who most likely had diverse work histories as well) did not have to beg in the streets.[72]

Working children contributed highly valued income to the household unit. In the case of one food relief household, two adults and five children relied on wage income from two younger children, who worked before the new child labor laws went into effect. The two girls labored in a glove factory for nine hours a day and together were paid $3.50 a week. In order to get to and from work, they walked six miles a day to eliminate transportation costs. The father commented that he would have been a tramp in the street if a credit-extending landlord had not kept the family from becoming homeless.[73]

Women also worked at home to support their households. To supplement her mechanic husband's steady, weekly income of seven to nine dollars, one mother took care of her 15 children, prepared the food, and cultivated a vegetable garden with her children's help. In addition, she washed, sewed and mended clothes.[74]

Obtaining access to means of production, such as a horse and cart, sometimes enabled relief gardeners to increase income from petty producing and marketing sources. When "reliable" male gardeners agreed to haul and plow for the Vacant Lot Association, the Association purchased horses and carts. In effect, gardeners made installment payments on the horse by working for the project managers. One adult male "did job work" for anyone who needed assistance with hauling, which enabled his household to make ends meet.[75] It is clear that improvising households often used household income to purchase "means of production," and not just to purchase food, clothing and shelter. Non-waged workers had to own or have access to "means of production," such as a horse, a cart, implements, and saleable goods to engage in petty production, marketing, and renting activities, which all yielded household income.

The Vacant Lot Project differed from most social reform projects because it experimented with gardening and farming as a means to help families become more self-sufficient. Not only did project managers allow households to sell vegetables and set up petty hauling ventures, they also hired former relief gardeners as part-time wage workers on the Association's cooperative farm in New Jersey. On this farm, managers also devised a sharecropping system, which placed more investment risk on workers' shoulders than wage labor did.[76] To socialize workers in an industrious mode, this parastatal organization adopted a labor system typically found in the South. Sharecropping gardeners worked five acres of land on shares and gave one-third of their crop to the Vacant Lot managers in return for plowed land, seed and fertilizer.[77]

An analysis of household work and budget histories for these households reveals that household income sources changed as larger-scale production units grew during the first two decades of the century.[78] Households derived less of their income from a combination of highly irregular wage labor, subsistence work, and petty commodity work and more of their income primarily from wage labor. By the end of World War I, households received more of their income from wages earned by adults and teenagers and less from subsistence and marketing work.

More commodified households relied on relief gardening to minimize economic stress during periods of unemployment or underemployment. Some fairly wage dependent, middle-class households also gardened in order to acquire funds for discretionary consumption. An older male, who had been fired from college teaching because of his political views, took up gardening because he realized he could not earn enough tutoring students "to keep the wolf from the door."[79] After 1910, rising rents, which increased faster in the city than in the suburbs, pushed households to seek alternative income sources. In 1914 more than 200 households in the garden project had been or were still receiving some wage income from heavy industry or construction work, including mill, building and railway work. Twenty-four relief households in 1914 had adult wage earners who worked in "white-collar" jobs in stores and offices. Many wage laborers faced reduced hours or long-term unemployment.[80] By 1919 the cultivation plots were also used by newly married couples and more commodified households that utilized additional income to buy consumer goods, pay for recreational activities, or save for vacations.[81]

## Informal Work and African-American Communities

The commodification of work created home- and shop-based relationships that confined subordinate ethnic groups within specialized sets of low-paying, income-yielding activities. More than other subordinate ethnic groups in the United States, African Americans found that racism severely restricted and reduced economic options in the labor force and in petty producing and marketing activities. To counter the effects of the greater economic marginalization of low-income groups in South Philadelphia, the Starr Centre (a settlement house), in conjunction with the Civic Club and the Octavia Hill Association, worked to connect more fully African-American households to capitalist institutions. Unfortunately, these organizations thought it was imperative to first break up neighborhood relations of reciprocity, which had sustained low-income households in the face of economic adversity. The Starr Centre directed it efforts at economically impoverished African Americans, who typically came from the South or had parents who came from the South. Although the main goal of the settlement house was to purchase buildings in the neighborhood, remodel them and rent out apartments to the "industrious class," settlement workers also tried to alleviate economic deprivation.[82]

To contend with their marginal employment or unemployment, African-American households often relied on income transfers from other households in the community. Noting the transfer of income between households, one settlement worker noted, "[T]here is a great deal of true charity among this class of people for each other."[83]

After her husband became ill, one older woman organized a petty lodging enterprise and rented housing space to low-income laborers. This reduced the costs of housing for everyone in the dwelling.[84]

In another household, a paralyzed mother took in washing and her daughter did the ironing. As the mother became more disabled, the daughter stopped doing wash and concentrated on providing care to her mother. Social service organizations transferred income to the household, paying for the rent, providing ice, and delivering groceries and milk. Friends of the daughter also shared their money with the economically destitute pair.[85]

To sustain themselves, poor households relied on low wages, small savings, a high level of mutual reliance among and between households, limited petty producing activities, and different kinds of subsistence work. Households in this inner-city neighborhood received little income from begging because people were so poor that they could not beg from each other.[86] Settlement workers' descriptions of this inner-city neighborhood do not indicate that working people bought goods to sell to others, purchased "means of production" or that there was a lively informal market. In fact, descriptions of households in this neighborhood indicate that they possessed few resources of any kind, which was not the case in European immigrant neighborhoods and homes.

As they grew up, African-American children often received limited and poor education, which restricted their ability to eventually secure stable, higher-paying shop work. Schools denied entrance to children if they did not have shoes, an expensive consumer good that few households in the neighborhood could afford. City officials also took schools designated for African-American children and assigned them to European-American children, removing many children from public education. In addition, the city provided few schools and little money to run them. "Blacks were the most likely to be the ones excluded and not looked after by the truant officers," one settlement worker reported.[87] In fact, the public schools became more segregated between 1880 and 1940, as mixed schools became schools for whites, as black teachers were not permitted to teach white students, and as black students were reassigned from mixed to black schools.[88]

To attend to their health, African-American households sought advice from "herb doctors" and "magic healers" in the neighborhood.[89] Women with rheumatism, ovarian troubles or cancer might consult a faith healer, a herb and root doctor or attend to their own illnesses.[90] Settlement workers viewed reliance on indigenous health practitioners as a sign of "backwardness." They argued that "herb doctors" and "magic healers" exploited local households and urged counter-education campaigns.[91] When people attended to illnesses within the context of neighborhood networks, social reformers tried to direct them to professional "experts." A clear tension developed between the cooperative efforts of households and the reformist advocates for individualized, commodified medical services.

Illness struck these households frequently. Almost 10 percent of the people visited by the Western Soup Society's "visitor" (or social worker who went to homes) in 1907 were affected by an illness and many of them were dying. The lack of subsistence-level wages created major health problems for people in the neighborhood, who had many needs and faced great suffering. Of the 203 households visited by social workers in 1913, 75 had a household member suffering from serious illness and 22 had deaths in the household. Social workers found people starving to death in cellars because they had insufficient income from work and or charities.[92]

In all the archival records examined, there was no evidence that members of other ethnic groups faced starvation.

In addition to social neglect and physical abuse, state officials conducted arbitrary police raids on African-American homes (while newspaper stories advocated violence against black people) and white individuals made vicious attacks on African-American trolley riders.[93] These actions assaulted the dignity of African Americans, living and dead. Many African-American household members feared what would happen to their bodies after they died. An older man in the neighborhood was afraid that he would be forced to spend the remainder of his life in the Soldier's Home, until his daughter convinced him to live with her. He was afraid of dying in an institution because he worried that his body would be used for scientific experiments. This man, a former soldier and a stable worker, who had watched his wife die in the Blockley asylum, could not prevent her body from being sent to medical students at the Anatomical Laboratory. To prevent such treatment, households tried to set aside money for burials and joined redistributive beneficial societies so that they could maintain their dignity at the time of death.[94]

## Multi-Ethnic Communities on the Riverfront: The Creation of Inter-Ethnic Relations

Although settlement workers sought to reduce on-going ethnic conflicts, they sometimes helped to perpetuate them by putting the lifestyle associated with monied labor on a pedestal. Social reformers often saw monied labor stripped of any ethnic content. Many social reformers felt that the ethnic content of family and community relations needed to be eradicated before ethnic conflict would disappear. Low-income ethnic groups caused ethnic conflict and the solution, reformers felt, was to mainstream and "Americanize" inner-city residents. Settlement workers at the College Settlement on Philadelphia's riverfront took a personal interest in smoothing over expressions of ethnic strife, but ethnic perspectives and distrust erupted during activities organized by the College Settlement. One settlement worker wrote, "At a moment's notice, in almost any group gathered, a sense of racial difference may spring to stronger consciousness than any bond of union as yet felt."[95] If an organizer believes that he is working with a club of boys, he "suddenly finds only individual illustrations of four or five nationalities or as many races," noted the settlement worker.[96]

Ethnic groups within improvising labor sometimes related to each other through ethnocentric assumptions, which led to derogatory exchanges. For example, at a picnic for local women and their children, which was sponsored by the College Settlement, settlement workers recorded that ethnic slurs bred more ethnic slurs. The following comments, which were recorded by settlement workers, show how the evolving social and economic hierarchy was partially accepted and perpetuated through racist ideology:

> Mrs._____ does the best she can, poor woman, but you can tell by the way her children behave what country they come from [an English-American woman speaking of an Irish-American.]
>
> I've seen a good many people in my time, and I like Mrs. _____; she's a good neighbor, but generally speaking I can't stand the Jews [an Irish-American speaking of a Jewish woman].
>
> Some Italians have the house opposite us, and we're thinking of complaining to the Board of Health. The way they live ain't decent. There's so many of them, I bet they can't pay the rent if they put five cents a piece [Jewish woman of an Italian-American household].
>
> Them Pollacks seem quiet here, but just wait till you see one of them weddings. They'll keep you awake all night all right [an Italian-American speaking of Polish-Americans].[97]

Conflicts between ethnic groups in the riverfront area also articulated divisions along the lines of religion and age.[98] The following street scene, which was recorded by a settlement worker, illustrates tensions expressed about religious differences:

> Today the air was thick with profanity. An Irish fruit vendor has offered strawberries to a Jewish woman for 6 cents a box. She tried to buy them for five. When I passed he was cursing her roundly for a [being] a Christ Killer." Less profanely, but vociferously, she was claiming to be just as good as any Christian.[99]

A settlement worker described a similar incident involving ethnic and age differences this way:

> N_____ saw some children uptown throw some things on a Jewish peddler who was passing with his basket when they came out of school. After his class [at the settlement] that night he asked me [a settlement worker] whether in Gentile sections of the city the children were taught in school to hate Jews. I said no; but he said he thought they must be, he didn't believe children naturally cruel enough for such unkindness if they were not spurred on in some way by older people.[100]

The records show that "such incidents can be multiplied indefinitely."[101]

Along with the emergence of conflicts between improvising groups, conflicts were also expressed between neighborhood people and the state. Games played by children articulated clear messages about the way that improvising labor saw the police. The game of "Cop and the Lady Bum" demonstrates that policemen were perceived as an outside force, as the following description by a settlement worker reveals:

> This game when played with the refinement of a lady, begins with the simulation of drunken disorder by a girl. Then a soap box cart—the patrol wagon—clangs around the corner, and the Lady Bum is thrust into it in the midst of hostile demonstrations by outsiders against the police. The resistance of the passenger is often followed by a collapse, her feet cease to beat the air, and dangle over the side of the box, her tongue no longer lashes, but lolls from her mouth. She remains comatose as long as possible and yields her place of honor with reluctance to the next claimant.[102]

The police may have had power of the state behind them, but the Lady Bum represented the real heroine of the neighborhood.

Neighborhood opposition developed in response to both the overt repression by police and the more covert presence of state-like organizations. Some neighborhood people may have recognized that social reform projects were designed to meet the needs of the state. The work of the College Settlement, for example, was viewed with suspicion and hostility by the community. According to a settlement worker, a small girl asked pointed questions about the settlement house and its purpose, remarking, "Well this is all right for us, but what do youse get out of it? My father says youse ain't in this business for your health."[103]

The explicit goal of the College Settlement was to persuade laboring people, who were not sufficiently dependent on wage incomes, to replace "begging, theft, alms taking" with "industry and self-sufficiency."[104] The working class was to become "self-sufficient" through a strong reliance on wages earned by working for others and by purchasing consumer goods from retail firms.

Uneven economic development and the unequal distribution of services reinforced economic inequality. Settlement workers noted, "the lower strata of the displaced population were always the last to be affected" by the distribution of resources and services.[105]

This was particularly true of public education, and led to protests from neighborhood people. A Russian-American father went to the local school and demanded an explanation as to why his child and other neighborhood children could only expect part-time schooling: "They go now morning, now afternoon, who knows when? Why can't they have as much as other children?"[106]

In communities on the banks of the Delaware River, a diverse set of economic and social activities unfolded, linking together wage and non-waged work. Fortunate male and female adults found low-paying or temporary employment in factories, while children assumed some responsibility during the daytime for home work, including child care. Little time remained, particularly for mothers, for beautifying homes and expressing the new standard of more commodified aesthetics. Instead, women spent less demanding moments washing clothes at the closest hydrant, their chief source of water. Children contributed to household income by growing vegetables in their backyards. As petty producers or wage laborers, boys earned small sums as newsboys or messengers. In order to establish greater economic stability, households created relations of reciprocity with each other, thus promoting inter-household cooperation.[107]

Although women were ultimately responsible for domestic work, the division of work along the lines of gender and age was not rigid. All household members contributed to income and rearranged their work in flexible ways to accommodate new household needs, which changed as income sources shifted. At different times during the day, female and male, young and old family members went to pick up milk for infants at the Modified Milk Station, which was run by a settlement house. Men snatched a few minutes from work to get milk for their babies and women carried babies and walked with men to the milk station. Settlement workers saw children toting heavy baskets and getting milk for younger siblings. As women began breast feeding their babies more, there was a decline in feeding babies condensed skim milk, which was diluted with water from the Schuylkill River and then sweetened or mixed with tea. Flexible work assignments within families made it possible for all members to participate in some child-rearing.[108]

Some subsistence work in the home declined by 1910, as families bought food that was easier to make. As the price of consumer goods dropped below the cost of making the same goods within the home, riverfront people changed their behavior. For example, long working days in both wage and non-waged work made it more economical to buy a piece of cheap meat rather than making soup, which required a long time to cook. Tending a slowly simmering batch of soup both reduced potential working hours elsewhere and raised fuel costs. It also became common for households to purchase inexpensive bread for one cent a loaf instead of making it themselves, which cost five cents for ingredients and fuel to make one loaf.[109] This kind of economic calculation indicated that some of improvising labor's home work was increasingly being valued both in relationship to the hourly value of similar labor in shops and the price of market goods. By the second decade of the century, the influence of the market had truly begun penetrating work organized by laboring families.

Low-income households purchased some goods on the capitalist market, but also bought goods from vendors who operated outside of the context of capitalist relations. These vendors catered to improvising labor, whose home work still took place largely outside the realm of the mass market. Riverfront people bought from second-hand stores, where cast-off, recycled goods had been sent. From these vendors, neighborhood people purchased many cast-off items, cast-off clothes, adulterated, "watered-down" or old food, such as thin blue milk, stale fish and meats, cheap bread stuffs, stale crackers, and candy for children. Local people made part of their living as street vendors and sold cast-off, recycled goods in the neighborhood. One older woman, for example, positioned herself outside the gates of public school yards, selling "toffy-on-a-stick, yellow jack and other candy," which also indicates that children had started to become consumers.[110]

## Mobile Labor and Informal Work: Italian-American Communities in the Mid-Atlantic Region

Migration between urban and rural areas, which provided a means to increase household income, shaped the formation of ethnic groups and the contexts in which home and shop work developed. Between 1900 and 1910 Italian-American males often migrated to work for labor camps. Labor camp owners organized low-wage, unskilled labor for the construction of railways, reservoirs, tunnels, quarries, and mining operations in Pennsylvania. Because the influx of Italian-American labor coincided with the drive to mine bituminous coal and speed up the transport of produced goods to buyers, 10,000 adult male Italian-American laborers from Philadelphia were organized to work in labor camps.[111] Townspeople, who lived in the areas where labor camps had been set up, resented labor camp employees because they were seen as usurpers of local jobs.[112]

Low-paid laborers at the camps received wages in money, though they sometimes received additional wages in kind (such as the provision of housing by employers). Usually employers housed laborers in cheap barracks for 20 to 60 employees, which afforded no privacy at all. As with other kinds of contemporary barrack arrangements for male laborers, cots were slept in by men working on one shift and then by men on the next shift. Some single male railroad workers slept in boxcars, indicating that the wage always did not include the provision of housing.[113]

In order to minimize expenditures so that more income could be saved for their households, male laborers from different households organized their home work collectively by setting up resource and work exchanges. Male laborers formed short-term, domestic networks that enabled them to maximize income contributions to their own households.[114] Although higher paid migrant laborers from other ethnic groups (such as Irish Americans) consumed more on goods and services, Italian-American migrants in labor camps spent their wages only when it was essential.[115] Because prices of food and clothing at the company store exceeded those in urban areas, workers had an extra incentive to reduce the level of profits accrued by the labor camp owner and to increase household income.[116]

Male Italian-American migrants in these camps were astute home workers or "housekeepers" and generated subsistence income in ways that were typically associated with women and children. Men did "housework" when it was economically advantageous to do so, particularly when women were not around.

Small groups of laborers organized some consumption relations so that they did not spend all their wages at the company store or in the dining room. By purchasing bulk items on the market and then sharing them, expenditures were minimized. According to a Works Progress Administration historical study of conditions in the labor camps, men did various kinds of subsistence work:

> Many of the men pooled their resources; cooked their own meals; washed their own clothes, etc. From the general store they bought everything they needed from clothes to food. They bought macaroni by the boxes, and this was their staple food. They bought everything in large quantities and divided the stores among themselves. For example, they bought salami, cappacola, provolone and broscuti by the whole and then cut them up for individual shares. By this method they were able to save a great deal of money on the purchase of food. Most of them preferred to do their own cooking rather than eating in the dining room operated by the general store.[117]

Subsistence work, such as cooking on barrack stoves and washing clothes, was carried out by these men in a largely private manner.

In addition to tangible, informal work skills, the collective organization of work by these men required extensive planning and organization, an ability to analyze and prioritize financial options, an ability to develop and carry out alternative work relationships, and an ability to work closely with others. When this type of informal work declined, there also was a corresponding decline in organizational skills. Just as maintaining informal markets in urban areas meant that working people developed their own vision of what might work for them and set up their organizations, informal work in labor camps required workers to have, what have been recently defined as, "professional" or "managerial" skills. The historical loss of these organizational skills was just as significant as the loss of more tangible informal work skills.

An Italian-American worker in a labor camp of this type received a small wage that only covered the cost of his reproduction. Labor camp earnings did not begin to cover the cost of sustaining his whole family. By doing domestic work and sharing resources with fellow labor camp employees, an individual was able to reduce the cost of maintaining himself. Workers saved wages in both individualistic and collective ways, enabling them to send remittances to family members in nearby cities and in Italy.

In a few instances, Italian-American men brought their family along as they moved from construction site to construction site. Although these workers were able to eliminate many cost-of-living expenses (such as paying for living spaces), part of the workers' wages probably were used for buying some food for the family. When families migrated as a unit to rural labor camps, they built huts in adjacent hillsides and eliminated housing expenses. These enterprising people brought one or two goats to provide milk and cheese. As men worked for meager wages, women, children and elders did subsistence work during the day.[118]

Agricultural labor camps for migrant, Italian-American fruit and vegetable pickers were similar to construction labor camps in terms of the kinds of subsistence work that was carried out in the barracks. But whole families of fruit pickers from Philadelphia migrated to large- and small-scale, labor-intensive agricultural units that shipped berries and vegetables to urban markets. To make it through the cold, winter months when income-generating possibilities were limited, Italian-American families migrated by train to New Jersey's and Delaware's berry fields in June, often staying until August or September.

Although pickers were recruited by contractors in the 1890s and 1900s, after 1900 farmers often recruited pickers from the previous year and drove them to the farms. When contractors or agents served as middlemen, they demanded that migrant laborers pay three fees: a job-finding fee, a fee for buying the train tickets, and a fee at the end of the summer. Contractors coerced labor and extracted payments, but they also rewarded some compliant laborers with special loans and opportunities to earn income by recruiting additional pickers.[119]

A canvas conducted by the Immigration Commission in 1909 identified 50 large and small growers in three New Jersey townships who hired more than 3,000 migrant laborers. One-half of migrants were employed by small growers who "employed from one to ten families to supplement the work of their own families."[120]

If household members picked fast enough, their wages covered expenses incurred during the winter in urban settings. In 1911 migrating households received between $500 and $700 in wages by the end of the summer. In the case of one household, the adult male, who was a junk man in Philadelphia during the winter months, and his three children doubled their monthly income when they worked in New Jersey's cranberry fields during the summer.[121]

Child labor formed an essential part of agricultural production. According to a 1911 survey, there were almost 900 children between four and 14 years of age who worked at six cranberry bogs.[122] Because families worked as units in the fields, household members tended to experience the picking season and the labor process in a similar way. Adult men, adult women, and children all started to pick cranberries at daybreak and worked until sunset. Often children, who were between three and ten years of age, followed behind their parents in the bogs and picked cranberries from the lower vines.[123] Because family members worked together and performed the same task, this production process minimized the extent to which gender and age distinctions emerged through wage labor.

Employers defined the working day as all hours when the sun was above the horizon. Thunderstorms brought periods of rest and sunshine brought laborers out to the fields again. Nature's rhythms determined the harvest cycle, moving migrants from the strawberry fields in June to the raspberry and blackberry fields or to the tomato, pepper, cucumber or sweet potato fields. Workers then relocated to the cranberry fields. By custom, all wild huckleberries belonged to the picker. Non-waged workers crated huckleberries and often sold them to farmers or to local retailers. When nature supplied plenty of berries, the pickers made $2.50 to $3.00 a day. Sometimes pickers went from house to house selling huckleberries. In addition, migrant laborers found "employment in the canning factories of Cape May, Cumberland and Salem Counties, where they peeled potatoes or skinned tomatoes for canning."[124]

During the months of laboring in agriculture, the pickers lived in employer-provided barracks that housed up to 24 households. The furniture was handmade and consisted of straw sleeping mats, tables and chairs. Like migrants in construction labor camps, farm laborers tried to limit expenditures on consumer goods. Many households brought staples with them to the farms, such as salami, sausage and cheese. Other food, including bread, was purchased from "trucks or wagons which the village storekeeper would send to various farms."[125] Migrant farm households used the summer months to save as much income as possible. Reserves from the summer helped to support the household during the winter months, which were spent in more commercialized urban settings.

## Rural Communities, the Growth of Market Relations, and the Decline of Household-Organized Work

After 1900, the commercialization of agriculture in the Pennsylvania countryside gradually affected informal work and the livelihood of German-American farming households. As the domestic market widened, farm families relied more on wage labor and purchased more goods through the market. This meant purchasing both consumer goods and "means of production," such as barbed wire and patented iron gates for fencing. About one-half of the sons and daughters of farming parents moved to towns or secured work in rural factories that were built next to railway lines.[126]

Local markets and fairs changed from ones that featured local products, which had been transported by cart, to ones featuring regional, national and even global products, which had been shipped in large quantities by train or in trucks. Curb markets often closed by 1930 because they could not compete with larger markets. At the same time that cart-pushing vendors still competed with shopkeepers, local producers had a hard time competing with larger merchants who sold goods that had been shipped from the South and the West, and from other countries. As a result, it became more difficult for local producers to make a living by selling smoked sausage, butter and eggs, fresh pork and foul at the larger markets in Philadelphia.[127]

The move away from redistributive, neighborhood markets and mixed local markets to regional and global markets indicated that large-scale market relations had begun to take hold. Once they took hold, the prices of local goods were increasingly set by global commodity chains, which linked the original informal or wage worker to every producer and merchant that helped bring the commodity to the final consumer. Commodity chains for mass consumer goods reflected competition between large production units based in different regions and countries. "Consumer-goods" commodity chains reflected global competition in much the same way that "capital-goods" commodity chains reflected competition between manufacturers of producer goods.[128]

As a result, households in the Pennsylvania countryside organized fewer subsistence activities and began buying mass-produced goods from the market. After 1900, family members sewed fewer clothes for men and women, as rural people began accepting the new standard of ready-made clothes, which had been widely accepted by men in U.S. urban areas by 1870 and by women by 1900. The baking of bread by farm households declined, as bakers began selling wares door to door. Milk trucks gradually replaced horse-drawn milk carts, which, in turn, threw independent blacksmiths, farriers (horseshoers) and hostlers (stable operators) out of business. One exception was health care. Many rural households continued to make and rely on home remedies to cure sickness as late as 1940.[129]

Inter-household relations in communities changed as families became more closely linked to business firms and the market. As households did less of their own work and became more dependent on purchased goods and wages, people from different households shared less food with each other and visited each other less. The decline in quilting bees and house-raisings meant that families engaged in less informal work together. For the first time, it was not considered "stingy" to sell food that was not consumed within the household. By 1930 relatives called first before they traveled in their new, private cars to visit kin or friends. Prior to this, a telephone call to announce or schedule a visit would have insulted hospitality providers. Holidays became commercialized, bringing a decline in Halloween trick-or-treating at rural homes (which had provided an opportunity for households to swap) and ushering in school- or government-organized parades and awards for costumes.[130]

Even after farming households discovered that there was not enough wood available in forests for fuel and fencing, nature continued to provide other resources that helped households supplement household income. Nature's gifts, however, had to be transformed into usable items through subsistence work. Wild animals in rural areas provided a source of food for immediate consumption and a source of petty producing and marketing income, if wild-animal meat was sold. Raccoons, captured with the help of hunting dogs, gave rural families a readily available source of protein. Households relied on trout fishing to provide food. Wooded areas also contained food for farm animals. By collecting acorns and chestnuts, household members were able to feed hogs and horses.[131]

An important kind of non-waged work for rural families was turtle hunting, an activity that often brought workers right to regional capitalist markets. Turtle hunters in petty producing operations placed turtles in barrels of water until they had accumulated enough to sell. When first captured, the terrapins, which were not fed in order to cleanse their intestinal tracts, were allowed to roam about the hunters' cellars freely.[132]

When turtle barrels were full, trappers notified turtle-marketing agents that it was time to collect the turtles and ship them to the market. Middlemen or agents counted the turtles and paid trappers a small amount for their petty producing work. Carrying burlap bags with 60 squirming, hungry turtles, agents boarded the train and headed toward larger markets, where turtles were bought for food.[133]

Although consumers of market-purchased turtles and "direct consumers" from turtle-trapping households both engaged in the subsistence work of transforming turtle meat into a "consumable" form, the social nature of the work preceding the final act of "consumption" was fundamentally different for these two groups. Before they could transform turtle meat through the "housework" of food preparation, market consumers bought turtles from retailers, who had bought turtles from marketing agents, who, in turn, had bought turtles from the original trappers. Thus, three work activities occurred before final turtle consumers could cook turtles for supper.

As the commodity moved from the original "producer" to the last retailer, each "producer" doubtlessly received progressively more compensation for his/her work. The non-waged work of turtle catchers was valued the least because it was informal, household-organized work, where low-income households did a lot of their own work to guarantee their survival. Turtle buyers were dependent upon the unequally valued work that was carried out by all the largely unknown previous "producers" and retailers. The system of unequal pay, therefore, was entrenched in the market system. By engaging in the market system, "modern" consumers silently participated in the unequal valuing of informal and wage work, a hallmark of the modern economic world. As the social and geographical gap between original "producers" and final consumers widened, informal work and the workers that did it became devalued in cultural and in economic terms. Urban consumers lost track of where goods came from, what skills were required for informal work, and how the informal work process was controlled by creative and independent people.

The contrast between subsistence activities carried out by turtle-buying households and turtle-catching households was striking because turtle-catching households had direct control over all aspects of their work. Even though both turtle-buying and turtle-trapping households "consumed" turtles at supper time by eating their turtle soup, turtle-trapping households directly caught, prepared and ate the turtles. They did not have to go to the market to purchase them from a retailer who was connected to a chain of merchants and workers, some located at great distance from the market. Because wages increased for some and the market widened, purchasers were able to acquire turtles through the market. Low-income turtle-catchers, who had little money and few food options, were able to eat turtles for supper only because they organized all the subsistence work involved in turtle chasing and turtle cooking.

Two kernels of modern life lie at the heart of this exposition of turtle-catching history. First, informal work was undergoing a process of deskilling and sometimes disappearance, especially for families in monied labor, who became consumers. Second, the process of remunerating working people unequally was embedded throughout the connected relations of informal work and wage labor, of informal workers and wage laborers. As work was devalued, so were the people who did it. Thus was written part of the history of America's divided working class.

Gradually, the commodification of land and the privatization of access to natural resources restricted labor's ability to benefit from nature's ecologically limited bounty in rural areas. On the one hand, this came to mean that, even for rural labor, less food was caught or grown and directly eaten by "producing" households. On the other hand, more food was purchased on the capitalist market. When market consumers prepared food for the table, they necessarily were connected to this chain of capitalist and non-waged producers. Because labor had decreasing access to land for cultivation and to wooded areas, it became more difficult to grow vegetables and catch wild animals. Food became most accessible to households that acquired income in a monetary form, which had become a prerequisite for market transactions. Each morsel of food eaten increasingly connected household members to countless, unequal, money-mediated transactions centered around businesses and markets. Whereas household-organized work once secured more of life's basic necessities, the value of informal work became supplanted by the centrality of wage labor and wages paid in money.

## Summary

Generally speaking, as "progressive" reforms made households more dependent on wage labor and market consumption, the reforms ruptured the reciprocal and redistributive relations of community life.[134] Households linked with the industrial production process grew more reliant on market consumption and turned away from remaining community markets, which offered goods for lower prices. At the same time, there was a decline in multiple wage and non-waged work relations, or work diversity based on both informal and wage work. Nonetheless, improvising labor did not disappear for a variety of reasons: industrial production remained sporadic, non-industrial production continued to be widespread in especially rural areas of the United States, the machines used in industrial production tended to make even white male labor superfluous, uneven development meant that households' incomes in improvising labor increased slowly, and industrial expansion depended on the incorporation and "internal marginalization" of low-paid laborers, which was associated with development of economic inequities between ethnic, gender and age groups.

As demonstrated by the history of mill communities, adults and younger people in improvising labor had work histories that were characterized by multiple, overlapping wage and non-waged occupations. Younger children earned wage income from textile mills, sold newspapers and gum, scavenged, begged, and stole. Teenagers labored in the mills, assisted with home work, and marketed goods in the streets. Married women carried out housework, took in boarders and lodgers, and made and sold goods to mill workers.

In general, households that had looser ties to shop work carried out a more jumbled, mixed and frequently changing set of wage and non-waged activities. Household members often generated income by doing wage labor, growing vegetables, vending food, hauling goods with a cart and horse (which required making expenditures on "means of production"), providing health care for household members, taking in sewing and wash, and doing housework. Households reduced expenditures by sharing living space, by building shacks, living in company housing in industrial or agricultural labor camps, or working as live-in domestics to avoid paying rent, by purchasing secondhand or cast-off goods from direct "producers" or vendors at curbside markets, and by continuing to do extensive housework.

By the beginning of World War I, it was clear that a growing percentage of the working class relied predominantly on wages. The size of improvising labor was still substantial, constituting probably at least one-third of the laboring population. Improvising labor was composed primarily of African Americans, "newer" Southern European and Third World immigrant groups, uprooted rural people, workers displaced from non-industrial production processes, workers displaced by machines in large-scale production units, older and younger people, women and disabled people.

But even these lower-paid groups were increasingly drawn more into the cash nexus. As families in monied labor worked for higher wages and became modern consumers, they lost sight of the chain of unequally remunerated non-waged and wage workers who created goods. Even improvising labor began to view informal work through the lens of abstract market transactions. The expanding market place made informal work and the work relations of improvising labor more and more invisible. As inequities of the system were buried by the market's abstract mystique, the cultural memory of community bonds and diverse work skills began to fade.

## Notes

1. Gabriel Kolko, *Main Currents in Modern American History* (New York: Harper and Row, 1976), 197; Doug Dowd, *The Twisted Dream: Capitalist Development in the U.S. Since 1776,* (Cambridge: MA.: Winthrop, 1974), 206.
2. Kolko, *Main Currents,* 202.
3. William Woodruff, *America's Impact on the World, A Study of the United States in the World-Economy, 1750–1970* (New York: John Wiley and Sons, 1975), 159.
4. Gabriel Kolko, *Main Currents,* 198, 202, 211.
5. Caroline Golab, *Immigrant Destinations* (Philadelphia: Temple University Press, 1977), 168–172, 208–209.
6. Ibid.
7. David Ward, *Cities and Immigrants: A Geography of Change in Nineteenth Century America* (New York: Oxford University Press, 1978), 86–87, 94, 99–100.
8. Ibid.
9. Ibid. 85–103.
10. Ibid. 125.

11. David Harvey, *Social Justice and the City* (Baltimore: Johns Hopkins University Press, 1973), 190.

12. Daniel T. Rodgers, *The Work Ethic in Industrial America, 1850–1920* (Chicago: University of Chicago Press, 1978), 15.

13. Melvyn Dubofsky, *Industrialism and the American Worker, 1865–1920* (Arlington Heights, Ill.: AHM, 1975), 17, 19–22.

14. Ruth Rosen and Sue Davidson, eds. *The Maimie Papers* (Old Westbury, N.Y.: The Feminist Press, 1977), xxvii.

15. Dubofsky, *Industrialism and the American Worker,* 13–14, 17.

16. For studies of women and occupational segregation, refer to Louise Lamphere, *From Working Daughters to Working Mothers: Immigrant Women in a New England Industrial Community* (Ithaca: Cornell University Press, 1987), especially Chapter 3, "Working Daughters, Ethnic Neighborhoods, and Family Strategies," 92–170. Also see Leslie Woodcock Tentler, *Industrial Work and Family Life in the United States, 1900–1930* (New York: Oxford University Press, 1979).

17. Barbara Mary Klaczynska, "Working Women in Philadelphia, 1910–1930." Temple University Ph.D. Dissertation, 1979. (Ann Arbor, Michigan: University Microfilms, 1970) 15–16, 23, 31, 40–41. In addition, see Barbara Klaczynska, "Why Women Work: A Comparison of Various Groups—Philadelphia, 1910–1930," *Labor History* 17 (Winter 1976), 73–87. Also see Carol Ann Golab, "The Polish Communities of Philadelphia, 1870–1920: Immigrant Distribution and Adaptation in Urban America." Ph.D. Dissertation, University of Pennsylvania, 1971. (Ann Arbor, Michigan: University Microfilms, 1971), 334.

18. Barbara Klacynska, "Working Women," 15–16, 23, 31, 40–41.

19. Records of the Kensington Lighthouse, Pennsylvania Historical Society, Philadelphia, PA. *Kensington Lighthouse Annual Report,* 1903, 19.

20. Kensington Lighthouse, Pennsylvania Historical Society, Philadelphia, PA. Advertisement in the *Lighthouse Lantern,* a settlement house newsletter, Jan. 1913.

21. Ibid. Nov. 1914.

22. Ibid. Nov. 1915.

23. *Kensington Lighthouse Annual Report,* 1903, 19.

24. Contemporary households in Sao Paulo, Brazil that rely on some income from factories employ a similar strategy: they increase the number of wage laborers in the unit, and rely on piecework and petty vending in the informal sector. See Helen Safa, "Women, Production and Reproduction in Industrial Capitalism: A Comparison of Brazilian and U.S. Factory Workers," in eds. June Nash and Maria Patricia Fernandez Kelly, *Women, Men and the International Division of Labor* (Albany, New York: SUNY Press, 1983), 102–103.

25. Kensington Lighthouse, 21st Annual Report, 1915; May 1903 Annual Report, 9; Feb. 1905 Annual Report, 10th Report, 11–12.

26. Ibid. May 1903 Annual Report, 12–13; Feb. 1905 Annual Report, 12; Dec. 1910 Annual Report, 17.

27. Ibid. *Lighthouse Lantern,* Aug. 1912, 7.

28. Ibid.

29. Ibid.

30. Katherine Anthony, *Mothers Who Must Earn: West Side Studies* (New York: Survey Associates, Russell Sage Foundation, 1914), 146.

31. Kensington Lighthouse, May 1903 Annual Report, 17.

32. Ibid. 10th Annual Report, Feb. 1905, 13; May 1903 Annual Report, 13; Sept. 15, Flyer; Flyer, 1913–1914, 13; Dec. 31, 1912 Annual Report, 8; Nov. 21–26, 1912 *Lighthouse Lantern,* 10, 12; Dec. 1912 *Lighthouse Lantern,* 8; May 1914 *Lighthouse Lantern.* Settlement houses tried to get neighborhood people to resist consuming alcoholic beverages. The physical layout of saloons in the Kensington mill neighborhood, like other saloons, most likely was designed with the mills' work day in mind. Open spaces, rather than spaces crowded with seats, made it easier to accommodate mill workers at noon and after work. See Richard B. Stott, *Workers in the Metropolis: Class, Ethnicity and Youth in Antebellum New York City* (Ithaca: Cornell University Press, 1990), 220.

33. Ibid. May 12 *Lighthouse Lantern,* 6; Oct. 1914 *Lighthouse Lantern.*

34. Maurice Halbwachs, *The Psychology of Social Class* (Glencoe, Ill.: The Free Press, 1958), xii.

35. David F. Noble, *America by Design: Science, Technology and the Rise of Corporate Capitalism* (New York: Alfred A. Knopf, 1977), 60.

36. Susan Estabrook Kennedy, *If All We Did Was to Weep at Home: A History of White Working-Class Women in America* (Bloomington, Indiana: Indiana University Press, 1979), 134, 141, 149, 155–156.

37. See Michael B. Katz, *In the Shadow of the Poorhouse: A History of Social Welfare in America* (New York: Basic Books, 1986), 181–184. Katz identifies eugenics and state-sponsored sterilization programs, immigration restriction, the abolition of child labor, and retirement as means to eliminate laborers. In addition to these mechanisms, women became more excluded from the labor force through protective legislation.

38. Susan Lehrer, "Origins of Protective Labor Legislation for Women, 1900-1925." Ph.D. Dissertation, SUNY-Binghamton (Ann Arbor: University Microfilms, 1980).

39. Daniel Nelson, *Managers and Workers: Origins of the New Factory System in the United States, 1880–1920* (Madison: University of Wisconsin Press, 1975), 125–127, 132, 141.

40. Lynn Y. Weiner, *From Working Girl to Working Mother: The Female Labor Force in the United States, 1820–1980* (Chapel Hill: University of North Carolina Press, 1985), 85.

41. Daniel Nelson, *Managers and Workers,* 125–127, 132, 141.

42. Doug Dowd, *The Twisted Dream,* 261.

43. Melvyn Dubofsky, *Industrialism and the American Worker,* 75–76, 82.

44. Robert L. Allen with Pamela P. Allen, *Reluctant Reformers: Racism and Social Reform Movements in the United States* (Washington, D.C.: Howard Uni-

versity Press, 1974), 265, 268–269.

45. Like many Third World countries, non-domesticated animals in U.S. cities and rural areas were storehouses of value to low-income people; animals functioned as household-run "savings accounts." Hogs, cattle or chickens could easily be converted into food for direct use or " 'rolled' over in value through the sale of mature [animals]" and the raising of young ones. Households utilized the strategy of keeping animals so they could be sustained in hard times, as well as during more economically stable periods. In this way, "savings [were] kept in the ... unit. They were not thrown into circulation." In Stephen Gudeman, *The Demise of a Rural Economy: From Subsistence to Capitalism in a Latin American Village* (Boston: Routledge and Kegan Paul, 1978), 57.

46. John F. Sutherland, "A City of Homes: Philadelphia Slums and Reformers, 1880–1918." Ph.D. Dissertation, Temple University (Ann Arbor: University Microfilms, 1976), 163.

47. Ibid.

48. John Sutherland, "Housing the Poor in the City of Homes: Philadelphia at the Turn of the Century," in eds. Allen F. Davis and Mark H. Haler, *The Peoples of Philadelphia: A History of Ethnic Groups and Lower-Class Life, 1790–1940* (Philadelphia: Temple University Press, 1974). Sutherland writes that "tumbledown wooden shacks and lean-tos" were found in the back of rear alley courts. "Damp cellar dwellings existed, and the cellars or first floors of some houses might contain bakeries, butcher shops, goats, pigs, chickens, and geese. Push cart operators often stored their produce in their dark rooms." Crowded living quarters also doubled as work spaces.(184)

49. Bureau of Public Health, City Archives, Philadelphia. 1915 Annual Report, 358–361.

50. Ibid. 1912 Annual Report, 476.

51. Ibid. 1912 Annual Report, 477.

52. The Starr Centre Records (a settlement house), The Pennsylvania Historical Society, Philadelphia, PA. Starr Centre Reports, "History of a Street," 1901, 7, 11, 13, 15, 17, 19, 31–32, 35–36; 1907 Report, 10.

53. Ibid. "History of a Street," 1901, 37; 1909 Report, 6.

54. Bureau of Public Health, 1913 Annual Report, 319–321; 1914 Annual Report, 323–324, 329, 331, 352.

55. Ibid.

56. Ibid. 1912 Annual Report, 498.

57. Michael B. Katz argues that today "homelessness, and indeed urban poverty, have become a different sort of problem than in the past because these [mutual support] networks either have attenuated or have disappeared." He writes that urban redevelopment destroyed the basis of many neighborhood networks. National chains replaced local retailing merchants (which once extended credit because of personal relationships). Few local labor markets exist, reducing the prospect of neighborhood-based employers hiring friends or local people. He also speculates

that family members move a lot, eliminating a source of free housing for people who become homeless. See *The Undeserving Poor: From the War on Poverty to the War on Welfare* (New York: Pantheon Books, 1989), 190–191.

58. House of Industry Annual Reports, 1904, 13; 1910, 10.

59. Vacant Lot Association, Pennsylvania Historical Society, Philadelphia. 4th Annual Report, 1901, 3; 1st Annual Report, 1897, 1; 3rd Annual Report, 1900, 3; 14th Annual Report, 1910, 8–9; 13th Annual Report, 1909, 6; 16th Annual Report, 1912, 8; 19th Annual Report, 1915, 7.

60. Vacant Lot Association. 4th Annual Report, 1901, 3; lst Annual Report, 1897, 1; 3rd Annual Report, 1900, 3.

61. Ibid. 1st Annual Report, 1897, 3–7.

62. Ibid. 13th Annual Report, 1909, 5, 9; 12th Annual Report, 1908, 6, 7, 9; 17th Annual Report, 1913, 9; 2nd Annual Report, 1898, 4, 9; 3rd Annual Report, 1899, 7.

63. Ibid. 1st Annual Report, 4, 7.

64. Ibid. 13th Annual Report, 1909, 5, 9; 12th Annual Report, 1908, 6, 7, 9; 17th Annual Report, 1913, 9; 2nd Annual Report, 1898, 4, 9; 3rd Annual Report, 1899, 7.

65. Ibid. 14th Annual Report, 1910, 8–9; 13th Annual Report, 6; 16th Annual Report, 1912, 8; 19th Annual Report, 1915, 7.

66. Ibid. 1st Annual Report, 1897, 7.

67. Ibid.

68. Ibid. 11.

69. Ibid.

70. Ibid. 2nd Annual Report, 1898, 2; 3rd Annual Report, 1899, 8.

71. Ibid. 1st Annual Report, 1897, 8–9.

72. Ibid. 11–12.

73. Ibid. 12.

74. Ibid. 2nd Annual Report, 1898, 10.

75. Ibid. 6th Annual Report, 1904, 8.

76. Refer to Ronald Takaki, *Strangers from a Different Shore: A History of Asian Americans.* (New York: Penguin Books, 1989) 188–189. At the turn of the century, sharecropping often was used in the South and in new agricultural areas in the West, such as California. With the sharecropping system, direct producers assumed greater risks than with the contract system, where laborers received a wage for planting and picking a crop for a pre-arranged amount. With sharecropping, landowners displaced more of the risk in production to direct producers. Although sharecroppers carried the burden of assuming more risk, they also might get a larger economic payment in the end, if the crop was abundant and the price for the crop high. Sharecropping enabled low-income people to engage in production, even if they did not have means of production, which were provided by the landowner.

77. Vacant Lot Association. 3rd Annual Report, 1899, 7; 11th Annual Report,

1907, 12–14, 10; 5th Annual Report, 1901, 6; 1903 Annual Report, 5–6; 9th Annual Report, 1905, 7.

78. Sam Bass Warner, Jr., *The Private City: Philadelphia in Three Periods of its Growth,* (Philadelphia: University of Pennsylvania Press, 1968), According to Warner, by 1920 to 1930 three-quarters of all manufacturing workers were hired in large-scale production units.(162)

79. Vacant Lot Association. 11th Annual Report, 1907, 13.

80. Ibid. 18th Annual Report, 1914, 5.

81. Ibid. 18th Annual Report, 1914, 5; 23rd Annual Report, 1919, 6.

82. The Starr Centre Records, Pennsylvania Historical Society, Philadelphia. "History of a Street," 1901, 7, 11, 13, 15, 17, 19, 31–32, 35; 1907 Report, 10.

83. Ibid. "Some of the Individual Cases Helped," Occasional Paper #4, 23 May 1913, 6.

84. Ibid.

85. Ibid.

86. 1907 Report, p. 5; 1906 Report, p. 14.

87. Ibid. 1907 Report, 10; "History of a Street," 1901, 84.

88. Vincent P. Franklin, *The Education of Black Philadelphia: The Social and Educational History of a Minority Community, 1900–1950* (Philadelphia: University of Pennsylvania Press, 1979), 39–40, 59. In 1950 85 percent of black elementary students in the public school system attended schools that had black majorities. Of this group, 63 percent attended schools that were between 90 to 100 percent African-American.(168)

89. Eugene D. Genovese *Roll Jordan, Roll: The World the Slaves Made* (New York: Pantheon Books, 1974). Genovese argues that the deeper meaning of folk medicine was not its contribution to science, though this was partly the case. Folk medicine enabled black people to use religion as a defense against slavery and racial oppression. In doing so, folk medicine reinforced culture and helped it flourish.(228–231)

90. Starr Centre Records, 1910 Report, 23.

91. Ibid. 1911, 13.

92. Records of the Western Soup Society, Urban Archives, Paley Library, Temple University, Philadelphia. "Report of the Visitor," covering April 1, 1907 to November 1907, Box 1, Account 130, #5.

93. Starr Centre Reports, Oct. 1907, 4; Article by R. Wright, Jr., in Starr Centre files on racism, 1907, 9; January 1900, 4.

94. Starr Centre Reports, "Some of the Individual Cases Helped," Occasional Paper #4, 23 May 1913, 9, 14; January 1900, 6. In *Roll Jordan, Roll,* Genovese addresses the problem of asserting life when people die within an oppressive economic and social context. "Respect for the dead signifies respect for the living—respect for the continuity of the human community and recognition of each man's [person's] place within it."(202)

95. The College Settlements Association Records, The Pennsylvania Histori-

cal Society, Philadelphia, Annual Reports, 1905–1914. 18th Annual Report, 1907, 53.

96. Ibid. 53.

97. Ibid. 58–59.

98. Caroline Golab, *Immigrant Destinations* (Philadelphia: Temple University Press, 1977), 55. In the 1880s and 1890s, almost 40 percent of Philadelphia's Jewish immigrants—who came from various Eastern European countries—worked in the garment industry. Around 1915, almost all garment workers who worked on a full-time basis within industrial settings were Jewish, with many of them women. Also see Maxwell Whiteman, "Philadelphia's Jewish Neighborhoods" in eds. Allen F. Davis and Mark H. Haller, *The Peoples of Philadelphia: A History of Ethnic Groups and Lower Class Life, 1790–1940* (Philadelphia: Temple University Press, 1974). Jewish immigrants also relied upon non-waged income from subsistence work (like raising goats in more rural areas), peddling, ragpicking, or selling handicrafts and used clothes. (233–234, 247)

99. The College Settlements Association Records, The Pennsylvania Historical Society, Philadelphia, Annual Reports, 1905–1914, 17th Annual Report, 1906, 59–60.

100. Ibid. 17th Annual Report, 59–60.

101. Ibid. 17th Annual Report, 1906, 59–60.

102. Ibid. 25th Annual Report, 1914, 17.

103. Ibid. 18.

104. Ibid. 9.

105. Ibid. 20th Annual Report, 1910, 18; 16th Annual Report, 1905, 30.

106. Ibid. 18th Annual Report, 1907, 62; 20th Annual Report, 1910, 67.

107. The Starr Centre Records, The Pennsylvania Historical Society. Annual Report, November 1903, 5; 1912, 15; 1909, 15; 1907, 1–4; 1906, 5; 1902, 12.

108. The Starr Centre Records, Report of 1900, 10; 1916, 12; "Summer Appeal," leaflet, no date; 1907, 25; 1906, 11; 1904, 1.

109. Ibid.

110. Ibid. 1907, 1–4; 1906, 5; 1902, 12.

111. Ethnic Survey, Balch Institute for Ethnic Studies, Philadelphia. Survey was conducted by the Works Progress Administration, 1938–1941. Microfilm. Di Maria, 3 December 1940, 1–2; "Interviews on Italian Workers;" Shradley, 21 March 1940, 4.

112. Ibid. Palazzi, "Italians in Labor," interview with Pelleicciotti.

113. Balch Institute for Ethnic Studies, Photograph Collection, Crystal Water Company, photographs of Italian families and their residences.

114. Ethnic Survey, Job #26, from interview with Barardino, 26. In the literature, there are examples of these short-term domestic networks in other contexts. For example, see the study by Joanne J. Meyerowitz, *Women Adrift: Independent Wage Earners in Chicago, 1880–1930* (Chicago: University of Chicago Press, 1988). Young, single working women often pooled income and shared resources

together. Young women formed domestic networks when they were in the process of moving from their household of origin to transitional living arrangements. They then started new households, typically at the time of their marriage. Households often pushed grown female children out of family residences and made these grown children cover the cost of their own reproduction. Sometimes these young women also helped to cover the cost of reproducing their household of origin. Another study of short-term domestic networks was written by Carol Stack, *All Our Kin: Strategies for Survival in a Black Community* (New York: Harper and Row/Harper Colophon, 1975).

115. Balch Institute, Photograph Collection, Crystal Water Company.

116. Ethnic Survey, From Italians in Labor Camps, 7; from Bulletin of Department of Labor, Vol. II, No. 9, 113–126.

117. Ethnic Survey, Palazzi, 2–3; Interview with Giuseppe Stante by Pennsylvania Writers' Project, 2; Di Maria, 1–3.

118. Crystal Water Company Photographs, Balch Institute for Ethnic Studies, Philadelphia, PA. These photographs depict labor camp life and living conditions.

119. Ethnic Survey. Fanelli, 19 June 1940, 1; Interview with Teti, 9, from Bulletin of Department of Labor, Vol. II, 113, 128; "The Survey of The Charity Organization Society, 9–11; Interview with Tote, 10.

120. Ibid. Bonze, 2 April 1940, l; from *Immigrants in Industry,* Part 24, "Recent Immigrants in Agriculture," Vol. 2, 3, Hammonton, New Jersey and Vicinity, South Jersey Berry Picking.

121. Ibid. Italian Migrant Farm Workers, Fanelli, 1; Milberry, Chapter 4 of "Italians in Philadelphia," 11–4-38; 5–6; original source from "The Survey," The Charity Organization Society, New York, 7 January 1911. Vol. 25, 508, 605–610. Also see Fanelli, 1; "The Survey" of The Charity Organization Society, 9–11; including interview with Tote, 10.

122. Ibid. Italian Migrant Farm Workers, quote from Fanelli, 1; Milberry, Chapter 4 of "Italians in Philadelphia," 14 November 1938; original source from "The Survey," The Charity Organization Society, New York, 7 January 1911. Vol. 25, 508, 605–610.

123. Ibid. from "The Survey" of the Charity Organization Society, written by Emily Fogg Meade, 10; Fanelli, 2.

124. Ibid. Bonze, 2 April 1940, from "Recent Immigrants in Agriculture," Vol. 2, Hammonton, New Jersey and Vicinity, 5.

125. Ibid. "The Survey" of the Charity Organization Society, written by Emily Fogg Meade, 10–11; interview with Tote; Fanelli, 2.

126. Balch Institute for Ethnic Studies, Ethnic Survey, Pennsylvania Dutch and German American Farmers, West and North of Philadelphia, Records of a Farmer, 2–3, 9; "Clothing, 1875–1893."

127. Ibid. 6, 11, 15.

128. Immanuel Wallerstein, *Historical Capitalism* (London: Verso Editions, 1983). "It was not inevitable—it was not even common— that every subprocess

in this commodity chain was commodified.... Profit is often greater when not all links in the chain are in fact commodified."(16)

129. Ethnic Survey, Records of a Farmer, 3, 6, 9, 11, 15; "Clothing, 1875–1893." Also refer to Rosara Lucy Passero, "Ethnicity in the Men's Ready-Made Clothing Industry, 1880–1980: The Italian Experience in Philadelphia." Ph.D. Dissertation, University of Pennsylvania. (Ann Arbor: University Microfilms, 1978), 7–8, 19.

130. Ethnic Survey, Records of a Farmer, 2, 10, 12.

131. Ibid. "Raccoon Hunt;" "Trout Fishing;" Gerber, interview.

132. Ibid. 1904 Interviews, "Turtle Hunting."

133. Ibid. 1904 Interviews, "Turtle Hunting."

134. A similar approach is used today in the area of welfare reform. Improvising households are "stabilized" so that they can became dependent on employers, and not on state transfer payments.

*Buying and selling at a large indoor market in southeastern Pennsylvania's farm country, ca. 1930. Courtesy of the National Archives, Washington, D.C.*

# *Six*

# The Decline of Informal Work and Changes in Community Life: The Creation of New Ethnic, Gender and Age Inequities, 1913–1945

## The Historical Context: The Concentration of Corporate Control and Growing State Management of Working-Class Life

As corporate control became more concentrated, the state increased its intervention into home work in substantive ways. By providing different subsidies to labor's strata, the state began managing the finances related to the daily and generational reproduction of the working-class. When informal work options eroded and improvising labor demanded state subsidies, state officials realized that they would need to provide state transfer payments to low-income households. During the 1930s, working people demanded that the state protect them from economic changes. Partly because working families knew that businesses did not just operate with local conditions in mind, they pushed the Roosevelt administration to recognize the right of workers to organize trans-regional labor unions of their choice. New federal policies guided companies' more daring impulses, widened the domestic market, and eventually curbed social protest. As the state established means-tested income transfers for increasingly state-dependent improvising households, it simultaneously established non-stigmatized entitlement payments for monied households. This governmental entitlement policy divided monied from improvising labor and stigmatized the latter, which now partly depended on governmental welfare.

Before this major change in state organization and working class support took place, the state and social reform organizations continued to assault the heart of community life, its marketplaces and informal work relations. State officials intensified efforts to eliminate "traditional" kinds of subsistence work and implemented new vending and packaging relations that reduced petty producing and marketing work. Directing pregnant women to hospitals, health officials discouraged neighborhood midwives from attending home births and helped reduce midwifery, a kind of informal work that had been well-rooted in community life. Health officials fought "overcrowding" and tried to get working-class families to spend more income for their own private dwellings and apartments. At the same time, landlords and police evicted tenants who were unable to make rental payments. State agencies and charities moved away from serving home-cooked food to relief recipients and began ladling out mass-produced canned soup, evidence that market consumption was well-established.

Between World War I and World War II, household-organized work declined even further than it had in the previous period. This lead to more wage and state dependency, which brought the development of new gender, ethnic, and age inequities. By this time, both improvising and monied labor had become significantly more dependent on wage labor and market consumption. The transformation of households from improvising to monied labor accelerated, even though the depression years temporarily pushed some monied households back into improvising labor. By 1920, the intervention of state officials and the effects of competition from large-scale firms eliminated many options for subsistence, petty producing and petty marketing work, diminishing opportunities for non-waged income. Instead of obtaining income from its own household-organized work, improvising labor relied more on supplementary income from increasingly bureaucratic state agencies and non-profit organizations.

Although improvising labor continued to rely on inter-household income sharing and informal work and curbside markets, which brought non-waged "producers" together, these activities registered a significant decline by 1930. The declining availability of subsistence work, petty producing work, and petty marketing activities also led to the decline of sources of low-cost, "petty producer" goods for poor consumers. And laboring households paid a steep price for their dependence on wage labor. Because they had become so dependent on wage labor and market consumption by 1930, both improvising and monied labor suffered greatly during the depression. During the depression, many employer-dependent family members were thrown out of wage work, returned to non-waged work, reduced expenditures on consumer goods, and sought state transfer payments.

Labor's relationship to employers and state officials changed in critical ways between 1913 and 1945. As the state became stronger, state officials began transferring, or redistributing, small amounts of income between business and labor and between groups within the working class. Income redistribution provided some stability for a society based on class inequality. Economic depression consolidated the position of large-scale industry and placed state officials in the position of managing relations between capital and labor, and relations among members of the working class.

Labor turned to the federal government for assistance and relied less on support from parastatal agencies, local and state governments, benevolent employers and firms, and labor's own household-organized efforts. Skilled laborers saw labor unions as an effective means of redressing grievances with employers and with the federal government. By 1920, labor no longer attempted to establish a shorter working day, which both would redistribute wages to a wider group of laborers and get businesses to plan for upswings and down-swings in the economy.[1] Because business did not completely provide the means for labor to survive, labor turned to the state to make up the difference.

Income transfers from the state, which helped support households, also served to further divide recipients of entitlement-based unemployment and Social Security benefits from means-tested welfare benefits. Corresponding lines between monied and improvising labor, as well as between men and women, adults and elders, blacks and whites were drawn in new ways. Divisions between working people were being institutionalized through new, income-related state policies and state programs. Improvising labor, which suffered from higher levels of unemployment and underemployment, gradually began relying on the state for supplemental, means-tested income and subsequently conducted even less informal work.

## Firms, the State and Household-Organized Work

As mass production expanded and as the state helped expand the domestic market by managing the finances associated with capitalist growth, laboring households increasingly geared their activities toward the purchase of mass-produced consumer goods and less toward household-organized work. After World War I, settlement workers tried to teach neighborhood people that, if they saved more income and paid more taxes, they would become more interested in electoral politics and in exercising their citizenship rights. Settlement workers urged households to save money: "A man with $1,000 saved is a better citizen than one without a cent."[2] By increasing their reliance on wages and consumer goods, households making up improvising labor supported the dominant economic trends and further erased their own informal networks from the social map.

The highly technological division of labor within large-scale production units made high wages possible for adult male wage laborers, the kind of worker employed by capital-intensive firms. Industrial production in the United States was exceptionally capital intensive, Gabriel Kolko argues, requiring a disciplined labor force that could endure "exhausting, alienating labor."[3] During the nineteenth and first half of the twentieth centuries, labor in industry had been deskilled. Deskilling pushed machinists down the ladder of labor's hierarchy, as industrialists replaced them with machines and with workers who possessed little mastery of work in the shop.[4] As part of the structural change in work, the deskilling of work in the shop corresponded with the deskilling of work at home. This twofold process of deskilling had tremendous ramifications for laboring people, which went far beyond income. The deskilling of home and shop work undermined labor's creative ability to organize and control work, and its ability to define work relations at home and in neighborhoods.

During the nineteenth and early twentieth centuries, the number of craft workers declined drastically. By World War I, only one-fifth of workers engaged in creating goods were considered to be crafts people, and some of these may have been primarily wage laborers and not independent producers or artisans.[5] In 1919 there were twice as many unskilled factory jobs in the United States as there were in 1899. By 1947, unskilled factory jobs increased by 40 percent over the 1919 level.[6]

After 1880, industry depended more on using low-paid laborers in production, particularly new, low-paid immigrants. In 1910 foreign-born workers made up 45 percent of the country's unskilled work force in the United States. Foreign-born people and those with foreign-born parents made up 58 percent of the population of the largest cities in the United States. As the depression that began in 1913 took hold and economic growth slowed, the U.S. government began shutting the door to new immigrants, ending open immigration in 1924.[7]

It was access to lower-paid labor, which depended on its own efforts to supply much of its material needs, that enabled rapid industrialization to take place in the late nineteenth and twentieth centuries.[8] The expansion of large-scale production and growing profits from mechanization meant that stratification within the working class became more rigid, according to Suzanne de Brunhoff.[9] During the first decades of the twentieth century, business managers began recruiting labor drawn from areas within the United States, as well as from regions in Latin America, including the Caribbean. Of the four million Southerners recruited from 1910 to 1940, one-half were white laborers and one-half were African-American laborers. In order to increase wage income, households moved within and between regions in the United States. European-American and African-American laborers often moved from the South to eastern cities because southern employers paid very low wages.[10] David Brody argues that from 1870 to 1929, employers recruited new laborers "from America's own countryside."[11] During these two economic cycles of boom and bust, which altered the character of industry and home work, "probably half of all rural-born children moved cityward."[12]

Labor migrated from Europe, Asia and Latin America and U.S. rural areas to U.S. cities, and sometimes laborers migrated from urban and rural areas back to their original starting points. One-third of immigrants returned to their country of origin, though many returned to the United States again. European-American households from mountainous or farming areas often moved back to rural areas, though many households returned again to cities. Although farm income fell by one-half, nearly 500,000 new farms were started in the Corn Belt and in Appalachia during the 1930s, illustrating the cross-over between urban and rural ways of working.[13] Scholars typically underestimate the rural and non-waged work skills possessed by U.S. working people, and the extent to which urban workers created non-waged work anew.

The growth in state power resulted in less control by working people over home and shop work. The New Deal signaled the point when the state began handling more of the cost of sustaining laboring families. The state started to define new ways of supporting and financing the relationship between capital and labor. The redefinition of relations between the state, business and labor after 1930 contributed to the creation of ethnic clusters, which were newly defined along the lines of means-tested income and state entitlement income. Differentiated state subsidies, including means-tested and entitlement income transfers, simultaneously alleviated poverty and exacerbated patterns of stratification between households and among household members.

Although labor tried to gain control over the conditions of shop work and receive higher wages, state officials and business managers also tried to gain greater control over labor and the conditions of wage labor between 1870 and 1930. Before the state and business could exercise greater control over labor and its wage payment, argues Suzanne de Brunhoff, it was necessary for the following conditions to be met. Most laborers had to rely on wages, enabling workers to see the nominal wage, not non-waged income, as their primary source of income. State fiscal programs needed to link public and private finances. In addition, labor needed to organize itself so that it could influence state policy. Both early state organizations and subsequent state agencies, according to de Brunhoff, were "essentially permanent sites of class confrontation" and "arose from the material conditions embodied by the existence of the [heavily capital-dependent and state-directed] labor market."[14]

The New Deal enabled the state to transfer shares of income unequally, both within labor and between labor and business. The state's redistribution of income eventually consolidated divisions between improvising and monied labor and between groups defined by gender and age. In addition to supplementing the income of selected low-income groups, transfer payments drew clear distinctions between recipients of means-tested income (largely from improvising labor) and recipients of other entitlement payments (predominantly from monied labor). Contrary to popular myth, both lower- and higher-income households depended on state support. It was just that the forms of support were different, and this made all the difference in the world to culturally dominant groups, such as monied labor and white males. According to Mimi Abramowitz, Old Age Insurance and the 1939 amendments to the Social Security Act, "penalized working women, rewarded full-time homemakers, punished husbandless women, and neglected women once their reproductive and care taking responsibilities declined."[15] As Michael Katz writes, "[social insurance] reinforces inequality," partly because the New Deal was based on the old distinctions between the worthy and the unworthy poor.[16] Walls were created, Katz writes, "between social insurance and public assistance that preserved class distinctions and reinforced the stigma attached to relief or welfare."[17] These distinctions became the basis on which welfare reforms were built in the 1960s, when nearly 16 percent of the population lived in poverty.

During the 1930s, New Deal programs affected diverse groups. In 1933, low-income households started receiving income from the Civilian Conservation Corps, a public works program. The Federal Emergency Relief Act provided temporary assistance to needy people and their dependents. Farmers received aid through the Agricultural Adjustment Act, which provided price supports and widely available cheap credit. The National Industrial Recovery Act helped business by limiting production and fixing prices. Labor unions grew as hours and wages became regulated and as the Wagner Act established new collective bargaining procedures. The Works Progress Administration moved unemployed people from direct relief to work projects. And, in 1935, the Social Security Act provided unemployment insurance for laid-off workers, Old Age Insurance for retired workers, and federal aid to states for assisting unemployed elders, blind people and orphans.[18]

To end stagnating production, underconsumption and unemployment, a new global economic policy (known as Keynesianism) was instituted by many European and North American states.[19] In order to stimulate the economy and support the creation of government relief jobs, the federal government began borrowing money and going into debt. Growing state intervention in the 1930s took place within the context of the new global policy that was designed to extend credit both to industries and consumers, and thereby contribute to economic expansion.[20] Increasing investments and expenditures in the world and subsequent increases in world prices occurred as the dollar became established as the international reserve currency and the money of account. This development contributed to the rise of the United States as the major world power.[21] The establishment of the Bretton Woods system in 1944 (which created a gold standard and valued currencies in relation to the dollar) and the International Monetary Fund marked the beginning of U.S. hegemony, or its emergence as the world's most powerful nation-state.

The extension of credit cushioned the economic crisis by "loosening the bond between money and commodities," writes de Brunhoff.[22] State transfer payments and benefits created a greater temporal separation between wage work and payment of the wage. According to Ernest Mandel, inflation displaced the risk of business investments outside of production and relocated it globally "within the whole terrain of commodity circulation," making everyone using money assume part of the risk of production.[23] Labor partly experienced this change through rising prices, rising wages and greater debts. The credit card, which encouraged household debt, became a symbol of working-class households' monetary investment in production and in the economic system.

The New Deal established relatively systematic state management of the relationship between money and labor. After 1930, the state began managing the nominal wage. In addition, it managed the mutual dependence of improvising and monied labor and the dependence of both on consumer goods.[24] By economically and politically bifurcating ethnic clusters into differential and unequal dependencies on state transfer payments and the wage, the New Deal solidified a new pattern of ethnic stratification that became clearly established between 1910 and 1920.

Expanding consumerism resulted from the decline of home work, the erosion of community markets, and changes in industrial production. Using heavy advertising and product promotion, corporations attempted to create social bonds based on consumer markets. Increased consumption by households was seen as a means to maintain social control and to help big business realize profits through increased consumer sales. Consumerism arose in the 1920s because of aggressive corporate efforts, and not as an automatic result of the evolution of earlier patterns of consumption, writes Stuart Ewen. Monied labor, in particular, purchased mass consumer goods and developed wardrobes that would help household members retain their jobs in the labor force.[25]

In an intensive study of Middletown during the mid-twenties, researchers found that the Midwestern town was becoming rapidly commodified. Robert S. Lynd and Helen Merrill Lynd write, "[T]he money medium of exchange and the cluster of activities associated with its acquisitions drastically condition[ed] the other activities of people."[26] Furthermore, the researchers concluded, "Living in all its aspects leans more upon money than ever before."[27]

Consumer expenditures for durable goods rose. By 1930 both urban and rural households had become accustomed to purchasing many household goods through the capitalist market, including clothes and a variety of other consumer products. But during hard times, improvising households became somewhat disengaged from the market and once again took up subsistence activities like gardening.[28]

After 1930, changes in household income-generating activities became related to the premise—which was made by business leaders, state officials and monied households alike—that the wage relation was an integral part of production and a central feature of state fiscal management. Workers would largely live by wages alone, with the major exception that the state would supply some transfer payments. As home work and natural resources continued to be commodified, the nominal wage emerged as the centerpiece of negotiations between labor, the state and business.

Business managers had long counted on the "invisible," informal work that yielded supplemental income for low-income families, but business had never acknowledged that home work provided the basis that made it possible for them to exploit laboring households. When non-waged income sources changed and reduced potential income levels for groups that were relatively marginal to large-scale production, business and the state paid little attention. The generation of non-waged income in the 1930s foreshadowed informal work controversies of the 1980s and 1990s, which focused public attention on the earning of non-waged income from drug transactions, window washing and street vending operations, and uninsured, under-the-table child-care work ("nanny" work), and begging by homeless and near homeless people.

After 1945, state management of the relationship between big business and labor developed hand-in-hand with changes in industrial production. Production became more specialized as greater automation was applied to the production of producer and consumer goods. Ownership became more concentrated and multi-national corporations controlled a greater share of total production. Automation was facilitated by data processing machines and computer systems. Multi-national corporations within highly industrialized countries exported more machines, equipment and vehicles to the Third World. Corporate managers became preoccupied with selling a growing array of consumer goods to working-class households.[29]

## Hungry Families, Work Relations, and Informal Support Networks

During the 1920s, three-quarters of all Philadelphia's workers engaged in manufacturing earned wages from firms that had industrial production processes. In textile mills and metal working shops, production still took place sporadically, imposing economic uncertainty and periods of temporary unemployment on its laborers.[30] Women wage laborers, who produced clothing and tobacco, as well as doing laundry work, continued to receive wages that were one-half those of male wages in 1920.[31]

During the trough of the depression, more than 60 percent of workers in Philadelphia were not employed full-time, forcing households to respond to the adverse impact of unemployment and underemployment. The unemployment rate for African Americans was more than twice as high as it was for whites in 1936. During these depression years, white households had much higher incomes on average than black households. And adult white males fared better than other laborers. According to Gladys Louise Palmer, in 1936, "workers in single worker families were predominantly males in the most employable age groups, while workers in multi-worker families were predominantly secondary workers with a much wider range of employment characteristics."[32] Economically privileged families tended to rely on one main wage earner, while low- and moderate-income families relied upon the contribution of many household members, producing complex household income pools.

Compared to the newer iron and steel plants in the Midwest, Philadelphia's factories were small and locally owned.[33] When the full impact of the depression hit firms and their employees in Philadelphia, owners and managers implemented more efficient methods of operation and cost-saving techniques. The records from one company's waste-elimination campaign show that workers were encouraged to function as industrial engineers as they carried out their work, anticipating the industrial reorganization campaigns in the 1980s. To cut production costs, workers were asked to shut down unused machines, rely on sunlight instead of coal, and avoid loafing ("the worst form of waste"). In addition, managers urged laborers to anticipate when new stock would be needed because late orders delayed shipments, led to overtime costs and express bills, and extended the amount of time before profits could be realized. But managers warned workers that over-stocking could also increase costs because it led to depreciation, a loss of storage room and extra inventory work, and tied up capital.[34] Laborers were expected to save their jobs by increasing earnings for their employers.

After 1913, improvising households tried to buffer themselves from the cold economic winds by delving into tried-and-true and experimental kinds of home work. In the case of Slavic households in Johnston, Pennsylvania, a social worker noted that households derived income from a combination of wage labor, taking in lodgers, engaging in subsistence work like chopping and carrying in wood, raising farm animals, and organizing the child birth process.[35] Self-reliance" continued to characterize improvising households in more rural areas until almost 1940. Geographical isolation in rural areas meant little state intervention and economic assistance, few employment options, more options for informal work, and tighter connections between families.

After reviewing literature on employment conditions during this period, Caroline Golab concludes that working people found it difficult to survive on wages alone. This finding is supported by a 1914 study of immigration and unemployment conducted by the Pennsylvania Department of Labor and Industry. Between June 1913 and June 1914, the study concludes, one-fourth of the men who normally would have been employed were forced to change occupations or to become unemployed. Adult males, again, fared better than younger people, who had particularly high unemployment rates.[36] Married women were particularly disadvantaged because they faced bans forbidding the employment of married women, in addition to facing historically low wages.[37]

Another study conducted by the Metropolitan Life Insurance Company in 1915 found that more than ten percent of wage earners in policy-holding families were unemployed and 20 percent of the wage earners were only working part-time. In the textile, clothing, building and metal industries, one-fifth of laborers had been out of work more than six months. Laborers born outside of the United States tended to be located in industries with high rates of unemployment. The insurance company's report, which was prepared for the municipal government of Philadelphia, concluded that unemployment was permanent and increasing.[38]

Unsteady work for "employed" laborers compounded the unemployment problem. Pennsylvania workers in 1916, on the average, did not work more than 287 days a year out of the normal 312 days per year (or six days a week). Even when adult male laborers received wages for 312 days of work each year, an unlikely event, their wages did not support the adult wage worker and other household members. With the average daily wage in Pennsylvania at $2.76 in 1916, the adult laborer who worked 300 days a year received only $825. This was below the State Department of Labor and Industry's poverty guideline of $900 per year for a family of five.[39]

The depression in the United States forced some low-income households to rely on a larger proportion of non-waged income, as it simultaneously pushed some higher-income households to adopt new work relations and to share with relatives and friends. Even for those industrial households that allocated some household income for life insurance, the Metropolitan Life Insurance Company discovered that 24 percent of these households in 1913 had at least one adult wage earner who was completely unemployed.[40] Real wages fell, as laborers faced reductions in hours and in pay. Between 1929 and 1932, wage incomes in the United States declined by one-third.[41] According to Irving Bernstein, lower-income households felt the impact of declining real wages more than higher-income households did because "the wages of the unorganized workers fell more rapidly than did those of the organized during the depression."[42]

To stretch their income pooling efforts, families often migrated between parts of the United States. During the depression's hardest years, some families migrated back to farms only to find that farm incomes had also fallen by the 1930s.[43] Sometimes families temporarily split apart, with members going in different directions. According to Bernstein:

> Men, young and old, have taken to the road. They sleep each night in a new flop house. Day after day the country over, they stand in bread lines for food which carried with it the suggestion 'move on,' 'we don't want you.' In spite of the unpalatable stew and the comfortless flop houses, the army of the homeless grows alarmingly. Existing accommodations fail to shelter the homeless; jails must be opened to lodge honest job-hunters. Destitution reaches the women and children. New itinerant types develop: women vagrants' and 'juvenile transients.' There are no satisfactory methods of dealing with these thousands adrift.[44]

"Many older sons in families on relief left home so that the younger children would have more to eat," writes Irving Bernstein.[45]

The Women's Bureau noted that between 1932 and 1933, the number of women migrants (usually women under 30 years of age) increased by 60 percent. Older workers, African Americans, women, those born outside of the United States, and recent labor-force recruits faced the highest levels of unemployment.[46]

Local relief organizations and small businesses developed and distributed alternative sources of income during the trough of the depression. Philadelphia's mayor established a committee that organized fruit peddling operations, a way to help labor earn income. Restaurants were encouraged to save leftover food for unemployed people. Plots of land were set aside so that jobless people could grow vegetables.[47]

The distribution of relief itself became more commodified. Many relief workers no longer bent over large kettles of simmering soup, which had been made from scratch for hungry people seeking nourishment. Instead relief organizations bought cheap, mass-produced canned soup and then heated it for relief recipients. Social service organizations often distributed canned soup and factory-produced bread, instead of homemade food. Hungry people then took the food home and served it from their own kitchen tables.[48]

Household members from improvising labor and from once-secure monied labor protested they were not being sufficiently supported by either business or the state. Protesters in Philadelphia demanded cash, not food orders, clothing or medical care. They wanted "more consideration at the hands of interviewers and caseworkers, and, above all, something nearly approaching adequacy."[49]

Unemployed people in Philadelphia faced police repression when they staged demonstrations directed at City Hall. Groups began looting and demanding that storekeepers and drivers of delivery trucks provide them with food. Rent riots erupted when authorities attempted to evict tenants who were not able to pay their rent. In Philadelphia about two-thirds of white and black tenants could not make rent payments in 1933. According to Frances Piven and Richard Cloward:

> Men and women [in the United States] haunted the employment offices, walked the streets, lined up for every job opening, and doubted themselves for not finding work. Families exhausted their savings, borrowed from relatives, sold their belongings, blamed themselves and each other for losing the struggle to remain self-reliant.[50]

Other people became so desperate that they had no alternative but to accept government assistance. Still others became so angry at the system for failing to provide a livelihood for all that they demanded aid.[51] Impoverished households often came to the realization that if they could not rely on wage income, they had to obtain state-distributed survival income.[52] Demanding that the state assume more responsibility for the welfare of working people marked the beginning of a new political period. But labor's two main strata articulated this demand in divergent ways, reflecting the substantive divisions that had formed within the working class.

## State Regulation and Labor's Informal Markets

Along with parastatal organizations, state agencies regulated certain kinds of subsistence work and marketing work. The state tried to change the ways that housework and consumption took place. Petty producing work, small-scale marketing ventures, and raising "farm" animals provided alternative sources of income to urban households until the state, business and market-oriented households began to eliminate these.[53] In Philadelphia, the state diverted households from some subsistence and marketing work to wage labor. Philadelphia's Bureau of Health intervened into home and street work by imposing restrictions on petty producing and marketing, and on certain subsistence activities. By enforcing new public health standards and by regulating the ways that businesses operated, the cost of starting-up and maintaining petty producing and marketing operations increased. This forced many labor-run, micro-enterprises to close, leaving a void that larger businesses easily filled.

In the name of good health, the state intervened extensively in food preparation and distribution. By enforcing new regulations, the state nudged petty producing operators out of business and allowed commercial food producers to move into vacated market niches. By 1912, Philadelphia's municipal government began to seek greater control over food processing and marketing. Although state intervention ultimately led to better sanitary conditions for the preparing, storing, shipping and selling of food, it greatly reduced labor's informal work options.

By improving sanitary conditions, which led to the need for larger initial investments for micro-business start-ups, the state brought about a decline in household-organized food preparation and marketing efforts in various neighborhoods. The use of tags and inspection stamps, the raising of sanitary standards in slaughter houses, market places and poultry houses, and restrictions on the way meat could be distributed were all things that affected labor's market ventures. Poultry raising geared to market sales was restricted from residential areas, but subsistence-oriented poultry raising was still permitted in these areas.[54] By 1913, only 18 places in the City were licensed to raise, slaughter and prepare poultry for the market.

Increased state control meant that the City government granted fewer licenses for vending fish and poultry. Between 1912 and 1920, the number of licenses granted for vending fish decreased from 835 to 591, while poultry vending licenses dropped from 203 to 22.[55]

New packing material regulations increased the level of investment that distributors and sellers needed to make. A Council Ordinance in 1916 mandated that all foodstuffs must be covered. And Bureau of Health officials worked to ensure that "clean" paper was used at market places. Administrators ordered their inspectors to make sure that meat vendors did not use "waste news" and other "unclean" paper. Agency workers went to markets and seized wrapping paper that did not meet the Bureau's new standards. According to the agency, offenders tended to run small stores and curb market operations in immigrant neighborhoods. Small sellers complained that they could not switch to commercially produced wrapping because it was too expensive.[56]

The municipal government tried to affect the way that small marketing ventures and shops operated because they required "more social control," made police enforcement difficult, were unsightly, unsanitary, and "bred disease." Inspectors often raided direct producers' curb markets during holidays, when there were larger quantities of game and poultry that might prove "undesirable." Besides trying to control small vendors and petty marketing entrepreneurs at curb markets, the Bureau of Health decided to intervene in the operation of rag shops, junk shops and second-hand clothing shops.[57] These micro-businesses, which often were run by families, catered to improvising labor. These sales and distribution centers were vital to low-income families because they could buy and sell goods to each other, enabling households to avoid purchasing capitalist commodities with cash, which they often lacked. Many transactions within labor's informal markets probably occurred through bartering arrangements and credit extensions, as well as through cash payments.

When public health officials received complaints about meat from small grocery stores and markets, city workers investigated. The agency was particularly concerned about poultry because shop keepers and sellers handled live fowl. Neighbors complained about squawking chickens that wandered freely around cellars, back rooms, stores, butcher shops and back yards.[58]

Although only 10 percent of the City's milk was produced locally, some of this milk was processed and distributed by petty entrepreneurs in the early twentieth century. Local producers and distributors increasingly relied upon trolleys and trucks to transport their milk to buyers, decreasing their use of horse-drawn carts. Because milk was made in and shipped from so many different locations, it was difficult for the health agency to regulate its processing and distribution.[59]

Just as households could garden without owning large plots of land, households did not need farmland to raise non-domesticated animals. In improvising labor's neighborhoods, households kept "farm" animals in family dwellings, rooming houses and commercial dwellings.[60] The Bureau of Health fought vigorously to prevent households from raising pigs in the city limits and brought many to court. By 1920, Philadelphia's public health agency could claim that pig-raising had been greatly reduced.[61]

After the municipal government issued a warning, some owners removed the pigs themselves. In 1921 owners dismantled 53 piggeries and removed 1,040 pigs from the city. If they did not comply with the law, municipal workers were sent to homes to demolish pig pens. After seizures of pigs were made, the animals were taken to the stock yards and sold, with the proceeds going to the city treasury. In 1921, officials made raids on four piggeries and carted off 55 pigs to the stock yards. The next year, 952 pigs were confiscated by municipal authorities.[62]

Although health officials reduced the pig population through neighborhood raids, an employee of the Works Progress Administration counted 93 non-domesticated animals within a South Philadelphia neighborhood as late as 1937.[63]

Gardening became more restricted as cultivation in front lawns was discouraged, setting the tone for defining front yards as ornamental and not functional spaces.[64]

All these means of state intervention reduced improvising labor's options and consolidated the grip of industry and market forces over household-organized work. Surely the vigorous campaign by governmental agencies and state-like organizations to undermine labor's micro-businesses suggests that capitalist development in localities was not characterized by open and free competition, but by state support for and intervention on behalf of medium-sized and large businesses.

## State Intervention in Biological Reproduction and Health Conditions

Following the path of its parastatal predecessors, local government and it entourage of "charities" began intervening in child-rearing to help shape the working class. Intervening in parenting, biological reproduction, and the socialization of children was seen by state officials as essential because they viewed women and mothers as the key to building a healthy, long-living contingent of workers for industry.

Anna Davin argues that a similar process took place in Britain around the same time;

> To be good mothers they now needed instruction, organized through various agencies of voluntary societies and local government, in the skills of what came to be known as mothercraft, as they were defined by the medical profession. Doctors, district nurses, health visitors, all were asserting their superior knowledge and authority, establishing moral sanctions on grounds of health and national interest, and denigrating traditional methods of child care— in particular care by anyone except the mother: neighbors, grandmothers, and older children looking after babies were automatically assumed to be dirty, incompetent, and irresponsible. The authority of the state over the individual, of professional over amateur, of science over tradition, of male over female, of ruling class over working class, were all involved in the redefining of motherhood in this period.[65]

Cooperating informally with settlement houses, Philadelphia's Bureau of Health officials sought to promote population growth within the "proper" context of small families, improve the health of lower-income people, ensure control over child development, and place women under medical establishment guidance.[66]

"Better health for all" often meant gaining greater control over women's bodies and biological reproduction. Public health officials discouraged women from having abortions, which women accomplished by administering soap solutions, and sought to replace midwives with doctors. Although they had worked with midwives until midwifery declined in the 1930s, social reformers and physicians within the commercialized medical establishment attacked midwives by making ethnic slurs about them and their clients.[67] Pregnant women in low-income communities relied on local midwives. Midwifery was one of the many diverse, income-yielding skills that household and community members could claim as their own.[68]

About one-quarter of the 32,744 births in Philadelphia still were attended by midwives in 1915, with the remainder attended by doctors, either in homes or in the hospital. Midwifery was a vital service for low-income people living in downtown neighborhoods and for households living on the fringes of the city. By 1923, the number of births attended by midwives dropped to one-half of the 1915 level, physicians attending 35,379 births in 1923 and midwives attending 5,467 births.[69]

Increasingly, physicians encouraged women to give birth at hospitals rather than at home. Physicians attending home births encouraged women to go to a hospital, where they would give birth under a physician's supervision. In 1923, 27,526 babies were born at home and 13,347 were born in institutions.[70]

This medical model for social intervention played itself out in settlement houses and social reform projects, including in the House of Industry. Reformers dealt with women and girls in a very intrusive way. New female relief applicants had to have "the routine examination before admission and [were] required also to show negative vaginal smears."[71] Welfare organizations and social agencies believed they had jurisdiction over home work, social behavior, morals and values, home life, personal life and even females' bodies.

As a monitor of children's socialization, Bureau of Health officials matched mothers from monied labor (who did not want to nurse) with wet nurses seeking additional income. They also set up segregated foster care institutions for white and black children, institutionalizing racism along color lines even for homeless children.[72]

As public health campaigns undermined labor-controlled, non-waged work, they also generally brought improved health care to working people. But health care inequities continued to develop and low-income ethnic groups suffered. As laboring people became integrated into wage work and market consumption differentially and unequally, they were assigned unequal chances for leading long, healthy lives. Although mortality rates decreased in all districts of Philadelphia from 1911 to 1915—perhaps partly as a result of state intervention in housing arrangements, street life, and working-class reproduction—mortality rates varied sharply in different districts. Overall, death from disease declined, reflecting changing standards of living in the first part of the twentieth century. Because class stratification was expressed through urban geography, urban districts were characterized by different rates of deaths from disease. When tuberculosis deaths per 100,000 people in 1915 are examined, South Philadelphia had a mortality rate of 181.5, West Philadelphia had a rate of 184.8, and North Philadelphia had a rate of 159.3. These areas all had significantly higher rates than the more suburban areas of Germantown, which had a rate of 113.8, and Frankford, which had a rate of 116.8.[73]

As health conditions in the Philadelphia area improved, which reflected a countrywide trend, the infant mortality rate also dropped significantly, partly due to child hygiene projects. In 1915, the infant mortality rate in the city declined to 103.5 per 1,000 births from 121.3 the previous year. But infant mortality rates varied tremendously for different wards in the city, with high rates in some wards and low rates in others. From 1900 to 1948, the death of infants under one year declined sharply, from 170 deaths per 1,000 live births to 30 deaths. During this time, the rate of maternal deaths, the deaths of infants under one month, and stillbirths also declined.[74]

The creation of unequal health conditions meant that white ethnic groups, in general, could look forward to longer lives than African Americans. Whites had a lower death rate than blacks, and the white death rate dropped from 18.81 per 1,000 in the population in 1903 to 15.06 in 1915. By contrast, the black death rate actually rose from 20.32 in 1903 to 25.09 in 1915. The tuberculosis rate per 100,000 of the population was also significantly lower for whites than blacks. The white rate declined from 211.87 in 1903 to 145.29 in 1915, while the black rate for tuberculosis increased from 414.29 in 1903 to 468.41 in 1915, (with a high in 1910 of 534.12).[75]

An examination of tuberculosis statistics from 1915 to 1950 shows that more black women died from the disease in 1915 (many of them being housewives, housekeepers and domestic workers), while more black men died from the disease ten and 20 years later. These statistics on tuberculosis deaths simply reflect two points on the same curve. During an epidemic, many young women died first, leaving surviving women (who had been exposed to the germ) immune. Men succumbed to tuberculosis in the later part of their lives, producing high male tuberculosis rates within low-income, black neighborhoods in the 1920s, 1930s, and 1940s.[76] Tuberculosis declined and was considered to be almost eradicated in the United States in the 1970s. But during the early 1990s, "overcrowding" in homes and apartments, close contact between people in homeless shelters and jails, drug use, and Acquired Immune Deficiency Syndrome (AIDS) became associated with the rise of drug-resistant strains of the disease. Tuberculosis once again had become designated as a major public health problem.

## State Intervention into Housing and Living Conditions

State officials in localities actively worked to increase social and health-related requirements associated with housing between 1913 and 1945. During the depression, unemployed and underemployed families from both improvising and monied labor were greatly affected by the commodification of housing. The growth in middle-class housing and high housing prices, coupled with growing state intervention in housing arrangements, made stable housing arrangements more difficult to find. Many laboring people in urban and rural communities became homeless or near homeless. In addition to their own enterprising efforts, homeless and near homeless residents in Philadelphia relied on income support and services that were provided by store and restaurant owners, landlords, the state and charities.

Transient household members who wandered in search of work or who were forced into the streets by the lack of rent money, had the option of staying at three kinds of business-run or charity-run homeless shelters, which provided sleeping space that could be purchased on a nightly basis. Licensed lodging houses, run as a business, charged 25 cents or less for a night's stay. They were inspected by municipal officials, who gave the "health" stamp of approval.[77]

Two kinds of unlicensed lodging houses also provided shelter to homeless men. City officials viewed the "Flop" as the "lowest form" of lodging for transient men. Enterprising people who ran flops provided no amenities. Shelters or rescue missions collected no fee for lodging, but did charge 5 cents for coffee, bread and a wooden bunk on the floor. Men slept with all their clothes on and covered themselves with newspapers.[78]

Social reformers looked down on members of the floating population who could not "cover the cost of their banner," or the price of housing. Unemployed or underemployed homeless men found temporary work doing odd jobs, carrying signs and washing dishes. Government officials, who regulated shelters, claimed that many homeless men were "professional beggars and criminals."[79]

In order to regulate the flow of transient people, who allegedly "provided a bad example to working people," the Bureau of Health worked in concert with other social reform organizations. The agency conducted a study of numerous bands of "gypsies" that migrated into the city for the three or four coldest months of the year. As far as the Bureau of Health officials were concerned, "gypsies" were considered to be "undesirable citizens, from the hygienic as well as moral standpoint."[80] After studying "their habits of living in order to form some policy in regard to them," municipal workers discovered that they lived in empty stores that were on the first floor of buildings.[81] Archival records do not discuss the circumstances surrounding the municipal government's campaign to evict migrants from these empty stores.

Of course, health officials continued their campaign against "overcrowded" tenements. Police helped by arresting tenement residents for various kinds of "illegal" home work, for begging in the tenement houses, breaking and entering, robbery, highway robbery, larceny, and "street walking." Those who did not work and who did not have money in their pockets were often arrested for vagrancy.[82]

Housing costs increased faster than other commodities. Housing, like other commodities, was differentially accessible to working people. How and where household members purchased the roof over their heads depended on residential and employment patterns. Suburbanization contributed to increasing residential segregation.

People who relied on temporary housing space found that "low-rent" housing began to change in this period. By 1920, fewer households from improvising labor shared small apartments with other families. In low-income residential areas, there was a decline in oil lamps, water hydrants in yards and water closets. Standard housing for labor, designed for nuclear, two-generation families in mind, was slowly becoming a one-family dwelling with its own back yard, a "well-equipped" bathroom, and separate bedrooms for the parents, girls and boys.[83]

As households allocated a larger share of their income for housing, it became difficult to make large, monthly rental payments during the bitter years of the depression. The debts accumulated by working-class tenants grew. Some relief money, to cover the cost of food, clothing and coal, was provided to destitute people by the Committee for Unemployment Relief. But, transferred income from the state did not cover the cost of rent.[84]

If workers found casual and temporary employment, they could pay the rent. But if no work could be found and if landlords insisted on full payment, tenants had to move out of their apartments. The increase in unlets, or situations where people moved out of their apartments, indicated that many did not have sufficient income to cover necessary expenses. Some tenants moved into housing with lower rents. Other tenants decided to share their homes with kinsfolk or with members of other families. One social reform agency, the Octavia Hill Association, noted that many tenants were in dire straits "because individual accumulations, and accumulations of relatives have been exhausted by the long continued industrial depression."[85] Almost twice as many Octavia Hill tenants left in 1931 as compared to 1930, even after rent reductions were made.[86]

The high number of Octavia Hill unlets, or situations where tenants lacked rent money and were forced to leave, shows how difficult it was for families to rely on their meager resources during the depths of the depression. Tenants got rent reductions from landlords, and one-half of them also received relief income from other sources. When relief programs changed from giving food tickets to making cash payments, tenants had an easier time paying the rent.[87] But this was only because they cut back on food consumption and allocated money that had been spent buying food. According to social workers' observations, about every three years during the depression cycle, low-income households faced major economic crises when work and home life became uprooted.[88]

## Work, the State and African-American Communities

The commodification of work led to the polarization of ethnic, gender, and age groups. Ethnic stratification of shop work and racism in neighborhoods limited employment and informal work options for African Americans. African-American laborers could only find low-paying, menial jobs. After World War I, for the first time in the city's history, more black males held manufacturing jobs than domestic and personal service jobs.[89] According to the 1930 U.S. census, 42 percent of the 31,721 black men in Philadelphia were industrial laborers. The largest group was made up of common laborers in the building trades. Between 1920 and 1930, the number of males increased in unskilled work for railways, road and street maintenance crews, and the chemical industry. As white males moved out of these occupations, employers hired more African Americans.[90]

African-American women in the labor force before World War II often were domestic workers. The number of women increased in tobacco processing and in the production of shirts, collars, cuffs, suits, coats and overalls from 1920 to 1930.[91]

Both men and women working for large industries found employers replacing them with white workers during the depression. Employers' racist hiring and firing practices contributed to the 30 percent official unemployment rate for African Americans in 1935, which compared to the 15 to 20 percent official rate for whites. Many black women lost industrial employment during this period, forcing them to rely on wages from personal service and domestic work.[92] African Americans faced an oppressive climate of racism and white backlash, which rapidly intensified after 40,000 African Americans moved to Philadelphia during World War I. Some whites treated black people in public places in a cruel, harsh, demeaning way, sometimes even attacking them. In response to racism, recent migrants from the South and their supporters withdrew from culturally mixed churches and sometimes formed their own.[93]

An analysis by Sadie Tanner Mossell of household budgets of African-American migrants, who came from southern agricultural areas to Philadelphia in 1917 and 1918, reveals that these households generated both wage and non-waged income. Seventy-five percent of the households annually earned between $766.50 and $1,970 in wages. Of the 161 wage laborers in unskilled or domestic work that were covered in the study, 96 were fathers, 52 were mothers and 13 were children. The father's wage provided the primary income for 33 families, while the remaining 67 families depended on sizable contributions from mothers, children and/or lodgers.[94]

Non-monetized subsistence income, which was generated by transforming goods at home for direct use, was an essential component of the total household income package. Children assumed responsibility for home work when adult women worked. Children's contributions included taking care of younger children, buying food such as corn meal, potatoes and smoked meats, and preparing meals.[95]

Household members shared belongings and passed articles down from older to younger members, recycling household goods. When working children saved enough money to buy new clothes, children who did not bring in income often inherited cast-off clothes. When clothes could not be simply handed down, deft sewers remade used clothes so they would fit younger children.[96]

Households transferred income to geographically distant household members and to other households in the South that lacked resources. Families also gave gifts of money to friends and relatives who lived nearby. Thirty-eight households had relatives in the South who were somewhat dependent on them. Many relatives lived in agricultural areas in Mississippi, Alabama, Florida, Georgia, and South Carolina.[97] Community ties remained strong across great distances and were not just based on geographical proximity.

Since housing represented the largest consumer expenditure, households shared living spaces, rented rooms and conserved on home-related expenditures. In one case, two households moved from the South to Philadelphia together, rented a common house and sublet rooms. Because of unsteady incomes and the refusal of many landlords to rent to African Americans, many households could not rent houses and could only rent rooms. Houses that were rented on a monthly basis required a larger initial investment, but did not actually cost more than rooms. Many households avoided high gas bills and relied on coal for fuel and kerosene for light.[98]

Landlords, owners and managers of firms, the municipal government and white households drove many African Americans into a near homeless condition and sometimes into homelessness. During World War I, the city provided new migrants from the South with housing in "hastily repaired [long abandoned houses], stables converted into camps, shacks built of flimsy construction, and churches and other buildings."[99]

A 1921 study by the Philadelphia Housing Associates found that houses occupied by low-income whites were better equipped than those occupied by low-income blacks.[100] Researchers conducting the 1934 survey of African-American housing reached the same conclusion. Compared to whites, twice as many homes occupied by blacks needed minor repair. Four times as many homes occupied by blacks needed major, structural repair. And four times as many black homes were considered "unfit for occupancy."[101]

After two homes collapsed and killed seven black people and injured 12, neighborhood and civic groups organized to protest landlord neglect and poor housing conditions. When injuries from another neglected home sent a woman to the hospital, 36 families in the surrounding two-block area went on a rent strike and expressed their outrage to landlords. In 1937 there were eight rent strikes in the city, five in black neighborhoods.[102]

Household members found themselves working long hours at home and in the shop to pay high rents for "substandard" housing. The growing commodification of land meant inflation of both rent and the price of houses and land, which affected black consumers more than whites. Black families spent a larger proportion of their income for rent and also faced more frequent and higher rent increases. The Western Soup Society's archival records show that rents increased more for black tenants than they did for white tenants between 1923 and 1926.[103] Some non-relief, African-American households allocated 75 percent of their money income for rent. Households with money incomes less than $1,300 usually paid more than 25 percent of their income for rent.[104]

According to the Real Property and Low-Income Housing Survey, the median income for non-relief black families was $952 in 1934, while it was $1,293 for non-relief white families.[105] Given that African Americans received the lowest-paying jobs and received little income from small marketing enterprises, inequities in the housing market created a major burden.[106]

During the 1930s, "high rents and low wages meant working mothers and the necessity of taking on roomers and lodgers."[107] Households utilized the strategy of sharing living space with others in order to reduce expenses. Philadelphia's Real Property Survey and Low Income Housing Survey shows that "families of the poor were forced more and more to share homes with relatives and friends."[108] Researchers found that, compared to whites, black homes were twice as likely to be crowded or overcrowded.[109] Most "extra" black families, those that doubled up in others' homes, lived with households that received relief and at least eight percent of homes had two whole families living together. The Real Property Survey of 1939 shows that 56 percent of black households received relief as compared with 36 percent of white households.[110]

Gardening provided a source of subsistence income for less than one percent of all black households in Philadelphia. Of the 60,000 black households surveyed in 1934 (about one-fourth of the African-American population), 420 households gardened on or off their premises. Gardeners usually lived in single-family, row houses. Most vegetable gardening took place on the fringes of the urban development and not in the central, downtown area.[111]

In Southwest Philadelphia, however, more than 10 percent of African-American households gardened, providing an opportunity to grow vegetables and bring food to the table. In this neighborhood, gardeners were largely tenants who lived in row houses or in semi-detached dwellings located on major urban streets. Cultivation took place in the front, side, or back yards, as well as in court yards.[112] Octavia Hill social workers observed that, although more poor people once relied upon food gardens, fewer low-income people grew vegetables by 1940.[113]

Some black families did not use new utility services, even when they were available. In Southwest Philadelphia, 25 percent of households decided not to buy gas for cooking, even though gas lines may have been installed. Some households relied on electric lights but did not own a "mechanical" refrigerator. Many African Americans heated their homes with wood or kerosene and some did not heat their homes at all. Home work was carried out within residential settings that sometimes used kerosene, coal or wood for a cooking fuel.[114]

Compared to European-American homes, homes occupied by African Americans in Philadelphia had fewer utility hook-ups and household appliances—refrigerators, washing machines—powered by gas or electricity. Less reliance on centralized utilities and market conveniences meant that families spent longer hours doing home work and that they faced greater health and safety risks. But families also reduced consumer expenditures by not using gas and electrical power. Only 60 percent of households had hot and cold water inside the house in 1934. A small proportion of houses had no water at all or only water in the backyard, which may have been shared between households. One-quarter of homes did not have bathrooms.[115] These new basic conveniences simultaneously enabled some subsistence work to be carried out more efficiently and, at the same time, created a greater dependence of households on utility systems, consumer goods, and often wage labor itself. Access to centralized utilities meant more income needed to be coming into the household in order to cover the high cost of utility services and gas- and electric-powered consumer durables.

## The Reconstruction of Gender and Age Divisions

Because household members often returned to a pattern of sharing more wage and non-waged work, economic necessity led to the reduction in work-related, gender and age stratification in some households. Even though economic deprivation could bring a sharing of diverse work roles and greater equity to gender and age groups at the household level, it did not always do so. As the social influence of employers' stratification system temporarily faded into the background, the cultural influence of ethnic communities and informal work systems may have increased, invigorating more family-centered assumptions about gender and age. Sometimes family and ethnic traditions were more equitable, but in other instances they were not. When hard times led family members to share diverse work roles, they probably did so in a more limited way than they might have 50 years before.

Household work histories show that during the 1930s, women assumed "male" responsibilities by bringing home wages and men assumed some "female" tasks in the home. Because families lacked income security from employment and needed to be flexible about income-generating strategies, work activities of gender and age groups were less "sex- and age-typed" than they were 25 years later, when income security for monied labor was based on the adult male's paycheck. Cyclical economic considerations propelled household members to make relatively short-term decisions about sharing more work responsibilities. Economic adversity nudged impoverished households to relax distinctions about work relations, minimizing the impact of the division of labor between gender and age groups. After World War II, stratification's secular trend brought the creation of highly segregated wage labor and informal work roles for females and males, for young people, adults, and elders.

Interviews conducted with more than 2,000 working women in Philadelphia and in the Lehigh Valley north of the city provide evidence that economic needs led to the reorganization of gender relations in the late 1920s. The women interviewed came from white households that had immigrated to the United States from Europe. These households had been in the United States for 15 to 25 years. In this study, Caroline Manning interviewed women who came from households that had to contend with the economic consequences of male underemployment and unemployment.[116]

Wage income, usually earned by at least two wage laborers, provided the basic source of income for these households, which formed part of monied labor. The median wage for female laborers in Philadelphia, the area with more unemployment, was only $15 per week, while for Philadelphia's men the median wage was $23 per week. Laborers received higher wages and worked longer hours in the Lehigh Valley. Women received a median wage of $18 per week and men received $26 per week. Female laborers in Philadelphia produced woolen and worsted goods, as well as clothing. Their female counterparts in the Lehigh Valley worked in cigar and silk factories. Men from Philadelphia worked in textiles, the metal trades and in unskilled labor, while men from Lehigh Valley households produced steel and cement.[117] Wage levels and occupational patterns, therefore, clearly reflected unequal gender relations in the labor force.

Both Delaware Valley sites had households with income-pooling patterns that indicated wage income alone was insufficient for sustaining families. Unemployment created economic insecurity in Philadelphia and the unsteadiness of work unnerved laborers in Bethlehem. Philadelphia's Bureau of Municipal Research determined in 1923 that laboring households needed $1,854.28 for annual monetary income. The Bethlehem Family Welfare Association calculated that households needed $1,109.60 each year for food, clothing, rent and fuel.[118]

When examined in relation to wages and the uncertainty of wage income, these standard budgets show that household members had little choice but to work together as a unit. When adult male laborers became unemployed, women frequently entered the labor force.[119] These women worked a "double day" in the labor force and at home.

> The day of these housekeeping wage earners began long before the hour of the arrival in the factory or in the shop. Breakfast had to be prepared and lunches put up before leaving home in the morning, and one worker said she formed the habit of doing her buying at 6 o'clock, before her day at the factory began. After 9 or 10 hours in the factory these women returned home to prepare the family meals, and spent the evening washing, ironing, cleaning or baking.[120]

Although work relations at home also were shaped by gender- and age-related expectations, there was considerable flexibility about work assignments at home.

Adult women, who usually organized home work, understood the economic relationship between subsistence work, wage work, and market consumption. Long hours in the labor force, which meant larger paychecks, reduced the number of hours women spent preparing food from scratch. Women earned higher wage incomes by extending the hours spent doing wage labor. A lengthening of the wage-earning part of the day meant devoting less time to food preparation. According to Manning, women "bought canned vegetables rather than lose the time from the shop to prepare them."[121] The multi-dimensional, overlapping character of female shop and home work enabled women to juggle household tasks and wage labor in ways that demonstrated that they still recognized the economic value of both types of work. Manning writes, "Married women referred to in a casual way to the time when they had kept boarders or had done cleaning by the day or had taken in washings."[122] Before the depression, these women contributed to household income primarily through doing informal work at home.[123]

Although work was defined along gender and age lines, boundaries between adult male and adult female home work remained fluid at home. Men were concerned about the physical demands placed on women by their longer hours in wage labor. One husband, who worked shorter hours in the steel mill than his wife did at her job, commented, "[S]he has two jobs. Begin half past 5 every morning, 10 o'clock, 11 o'clock at night she finish."[124] Since female cigar workers had longer factory hours than men, frequently men from these households started the dinner when they returned home from work in the afternoon. According to Manning, "In many families the sharing of household tasks was accepted as a matter of course."[125] During one of her interviewing sessions, "the woman interviewed was washing clothes, while her husband was wringing them and her brother-in-law was washing dishes."[126] Long working hours in the labor force and at home, where income-generating subsistence work took place, made household members share a common set of tasks, reducing the internal and external pressures promoting the polarization of household members along the lines of gender.

Job insecurity and the high cost of housing led to cooperative housing arrangements, where households shared a living space, but maintained separate access to their own private belongings. Almost one-third of Lehigh Valley homes contained more than one economic unit. Households cooked and stored their food separately, washed their own dishes and clothes, and had private belongings and bedrooms. Women cleaned common areas of the house together, but this cooperative effort was limited to the kitchen, stairs and doorsteps.[127] Although households reduced housing costs by sharing living spaces, the way home work was carried out indicated that these families valued private property and private space.

In the early 1920s, adult female wage laborers in industrial neighborhoods in Philadelphia contributed vital income to their households. According to Gwendolyn Salisbury Hughes' study of mothers working for industrial enterprises, women and their families generated income primarily through wage labor, but also through non-waged work and income transfers. The 728 women who were interviewed came from households where the adult male had either low wages or no wages. In almost half the cases, the husband was sick, had died, or had deserted the family. These women were single female heads of households. "[A]lmost one-third of the women with husbands earned half or more of the family income," Hughes writes.[128]

Wages were so low that additional income was needed, so these women worked in unskilled, low-paid manufacturing jobs, domestic and personal service, and trade and clerical work. Income for these units was below the minimal level of $1,633.79 a year or $31.42 a week, as it was defined by the Bureau of Municipal Research of Philadelphia in 1918. Home work and income transfers yielded crucial non-waged support. These households took in lodgers or boarders, did petty producing work, moved in with relatives or shared a living space with others, received transfer payments in kind or in money from the state, social agencies and fraternal organizations, received free child care from relatives or from an organization, and obtained free institutional care for husbands, a transfer payment.[129] As in the case of the immigrant households in Philadelphia and in the Lehigh Valley, the concept of the one-male-wage-earning family had little meaning.

## Economic Development and Italian-American Communities

As the commodification of work proceeded, Italian-American households restructured home and shop work activities. Italian-American households often relied on wage income from farm and industrial work. As they had before, low-income families helped support themselves by doing agricultural labor in New Jersey's and Delaware's berry fields during the summer months and by doing industrial labor for clothing and other firms in Philadelphia during the winter.[130]

After a summer of agricultural work, vegetable and fruit pickers returned to Philadelphia and carried out home and shop work. Labor contractors returned to shop work or worked in pool rooms, at fruit stands, or as janitors. According to the Ethnic Survey conducted by the Works Progress Administration:

> A host of rag pickers were represented [within the summer migrant labor pool], many street sweepers, pick-and-shovel men, on streets, in construction work; a fair percentage of the younger men and some women worked in glass and cigar factories, some in machine shops or iron foundries: for the most part, however, they were the typical pick-and-shovel workers. Some of the young women were from candy shops, artificial flower-making, manufactories making shirts, overalls, or women's garments, or even sweat-shops. Some seemed to work in Italian stores, baker's and the like. Many girls worked in box factories and many women worked in "tailoring sweat shops."[131]

Although income from farm work helped support these workers during the winter, they also relied on "borrowing money and living on credit," indicators that some community ties remained.[132]

By the 1930s, Italian-American families relied more on wage income, which was brought into the household by adult males, adult females and children. While men worked in factories, women and children worked as wage laborers on home orders for clothing firms and their middlemen. The Works Progress Administration's Ethnic Survey describes this wage labor, which took place at home:

> Italian women, with their younger children at their sides helping, spent a large part of their day and evening at this occupation. Starting shortly after sunrise after preparing lunches for working members of the family, except for interludes taken up for housework and marketing, the whole day until midnight

> was spent sewing and cutting bundles of garments. Frugal housewives worked under the light of street lamps to save on their gas bills. At the end of the week the work netted them an average wage of two to three dollars.[133]

The working day at home was spent doing "putting-out" work from the shop, though time was taken out from piece-rate work to do housework and marketing. This garment work increased income and reflected an unspecialized division of labor and work. Even within factories, the limited development of the technical division of labor still permitted families to work together at the same bench.[134]

The technical division of labor within clothing factories and workshops divided family members along gender and age lines. Hand sewers were most often women, though particular hand sewing operations were divided between women and men. Women basted armholes, canvas and sleeves, while men basted linings, which was considered more skilled.[135]

When sewing in the home, children threaded needles, sewed buttons, and pulled basting threads. As younger females hemmed pants and sewed buttonholes, older females sewed coat hems. Adult women, who supervised manufacturing work in their own homes, relied on established understandings of gender and age to set up "assembly line" production. This happened even though they could have created other ways to work and different kinds of work relationships.[136] As home operations were moved into factories, and as factory owners began relocating their operations overseas (to Cuba, for example) and to areas in the United States with lower-paid labor during the 1930s, working women in urban areas lost this source of wage income.[137]

Italian-American households tried to reduce the level of economic hardship by engaging in wage work in the home and in the shop, doing informal work, and by transferring income across household lines, either as gifts or as loans. The practice of bringing in lodgers created additional home work for women, who assumed responsibility for related cleaning, laundry and cooking work. In Germantown, lodgers added an amount that was at least one-quarter of the adult male's wages. When boarders shared a bed with someone who worked on another shift, they were able to reduce housing expenses even more. Many Italian-American households cultivated vegetables as a basic subsistence strategy. They also relied on loans with a ten percent interest rate. Wealthier households in Italy gave these loans to families that migrated to the United States.[138] Although there were many exceptions for particular households and in particular U.S. regions, Italian Americans and other "recent" white immigrant groups from Europe generally became part of monied labor by 1945.

## The Redefinition of Self-Sufficiency, 1913 to 1945

In the United States, the depression between 1913 and 1945 eliminated many smaller producers and non-waged operations. It led to the consolidation of large enterprises and the growth of transnational corporations. The transformation from non-industrial production processes to industrial production continued during this period, but the depression interrupted production and brought unsteady wages to even industrial laborers.

The history of community life before 1945 became more intimately linked to the consumer market through money and credit, the circulation and reinvestment of profits, and world finances. These relationships gradually brought improvising labor more into the fold of wage employment and market consumption, even though many families still needed to keep one foot planted firmly in the sphere of informal work.

What was significantly new during the pre-World War II period was the tremendous decline of non-waged options. Informal work, with the exception of domestic work, began to erode because of state-engineered interventions, economic expansion, and the transformation of laboring households from multi-dimensional "producing" units to more one-dimensional, wage-reliant units. As a result of economic imperatives and choices made by families, non-waged activities continued in spite of the decline of urban poultry and pig raising, begging, stealing, prostitution, and alternative housing arrangements.

Even by 1930 it had became more difficult for labor to secure food, clothing, and shelter on its own terms. Informal curbside markets had largely been dismantled before the depths of the depression, resulting in the decline of non-waged producers directly selling goods to each other. The growth of intermediary producers and merchants increased the overall costs of production, raising the price of market goods for consumers and petty producers. As laboring households relied less on securing goods from each other, they relied more on parastatal assistance and on state transfer payments.

The growing dependence on state transfer payments ultimately intensified the division between improvising and monied labor, strata which were composed of clusters of hierarchically layered ethnic groups, as well as gender and age groups. By 1945 the proportion of improvising labor in the United States probably fell to about 20 percent of the population. The decline of household-organized work and improvising labor's growing dependency on the state had a contradictory impact. Household income became somewhat more secure, but because improvising labor sometimes could rely on the state, household members relied less on their own diverse work skills. Thus state dependency allowed working families to withdraw more from informal work, to stop practicing and developing skills associated with remaining informal work options, and to lose control over what once was a large segment of household members' working day.

The state gained tremendous strength during this period and began managing the money wage. The new emphasis on money wages alone mystified the constitution of various elements in households' income and demeaned the continuing importance of non-waged activities. After 1945 the economic importance of housework and other subsistence work, which was associated with adult females, was devalued even more than it had been. By focusing attention on the adult male's money wage and by undervaluing women's work, firms were able to launch a devastating assault on home-based housework and commodify other kinds of informal work, including street vending and "taxi cab" driving typically done by men. In this way, businesses were able to deskill not just shop work, but to provide the impetus for deskilling home work as well.

One characteristic of improvising labor in the United States after 1935 was that it occasionally and sporadically became dependent on the state for income transfers that supplemented low wages. At the same time, monied labor became dependent on wages from employers and secondarily dependent on state income transfers, which were related to workers' wage earning histories. To be sure, households from both strata continued to have mixed dependencies on various income sources. To make ends meet, improvising labor relied on doing non-waged work and received income transfers from kin or other households, while monied labor counted on non-market income from housework and intergenerational income transfers from relatives. For both improvising and monied labor between 1920 and 1970, women from these strata found themselves sharing similar structural positions primarily because they did "female" housework, but also because they did "female" low-paid wage work. These two types of income dependencies led to the entrenchment of different levels of economic well-being for improvising and monied labor, and the development of different cultural and political orientations.

The following chapter traces the development of non-waged and wage work and the stratification system from 1945 to the present. Although non-waged work declined during the period of U.S. global dominance between 1945 and 1970, economic forces and social movements eventually led to the growth of self-employment and its reappearance as a contemporary public policy issue.

## Notes

1. Alexander Keyssar, *The First Century of Unemployment in Massachusetts* (Cambridge: Cambridge University Press, 1986), 274–280.

2. Records of the Kensington Lighthouse, Pennsylvania Historical Society, Philadelphia, 21st Annual Report, December 1915, 7, 32; August 1917 *Lighthouse Lantern*; July 1917 *Lighthouse Lantern*; September 10, 1917, *Lighthouse Lantern.*

3. Gabriel Kolko, *Main Currents in Modern American History* (New York: Harper and Row, 1976), 71, 74.

4. See Harry Braverman, *Labor and Monopoly Capital: The Degradation of Work in the Twentieth Century* (New York: Monthly Review Press, 1974).

5. Gladys Louise Palmer, *Philadelphia Workers in a Changing Economy* (Philadelphia: University of Pennsylvania Press, 1956), 10.

6. Ibid. 14, 22.

7. Kolko, *Main Currents,* 73, 84, 92.

8. Ibid.

9. Suzanne de Brunhoff, *The State, Capital and Economic Policy* (London: Pluto Press, 1978), 26.

10. Kolko, *Main Currents,* 88, 168.

11. David Brody, *Workers in Industrial America: Essays on the 20th Century Struggle* (New York: Oxford University Press, 1980), 14–15.

12. Ibid.

13. Kolko, *Main Currents,* 69–71, 80, 146, 149.

14. de Brunhoff, *The State,* 19.

15. Mimi Abramowitz, *Regulating the Lives of Women: Social Welfare Policy from Colonial Times to the Present* (Boston: South End Press, 1988), 254.

16. Michael B. Katz, *In the Shadow of the Poorhouse: A History of Social Welfare in America* (New York: Basic Books, 1986), 237.

17. Ibid. 237, 247.

18. Frances Fox Piven and Richard Cloward, *Regulating the Poor: The Function of Public Welfare* (New York: Vintage Books, Random House, 1972), 72, 74, 92, 96.

19. In the following paragraphs, the ideas expressed largely are a summary of those developed in: 1) Suzanne de Brunhoff, *The State, Capital and Economic Policy* and 2) Ernest Mandel, *Late Capitalism* (London: New Left Books; Atlantic Highlands, New Jersey: Humanities Press, 1975).

20. Mandel, *Late Capitalism,* 415–416.

21. de Brunhoff, *The State,* 48.

22. Ibid. 47.

23. Mandel, *Late Capitalism,* 416.

24. de Brunhoff, *The State,* 26, 31, 33, 35, 63–64, 68.

25. Stuart Ewen, *Captains of Consciousness: Advertising and the Roots of Consumer Culture* (New York: McGraw-Hill, 1977), 54.

26. Robert S. Lynd and Helen Merrill Lynd, *Middletown: A Study in Modern American Culture* (New York: Harcourt, Brace and World, 1956), 21.

27. Ibid. 49.

28. Heidi Irmgard Hartmann, "Capitalism and Women's Work in the Home,

1900–1930," Ph.D. Dissertation, Yale University, 1974 (Ann Arbor: University Microfilms, 1975), 87, 147, 167.

29. Mandel, *Late Capitalism,* 194, 319–320, 346–347, 230–231, 246.

30. Sam Bass Warner, *The Private City: Philadelphia in Three Periods of Its Growth* (Philadelphia: University of Pennsylvania Press, 1968), 162–181.

31. Caroline Golab, *Immigrant Destinations* (Philadelphia: Temple University Press, 1977), 140, 193.

32. Palmer, *Philadelphia Workers,* 92, 78. Also see J.H. Viscount Nelson, "Race and Class Consciousness of Philadelphia's Negroes with Special Emphasis on the Years between 1927 and 1940." Ph.D. Dissertation, University of Pennsylvania (Ann Arbor: University Microfilms, 1969).

33. Palmer, *Philadelphia Workers,* 25.

34. Photography Archives, Hagley Museum and Library, Greenville, Wilmington, Delaware. Works Engineering Department, W.E. EM. Co., South Philadelphia Works, Negative Numbers 24878, 23663, 23665, 23664, 23578, 23577. Information was drawn from these photos, which depicted different stages of production.

35. John Bodnar, "Immigration and Modernization: The Case of Slavic Peasants in Industrial America." In ed. Milton Cantor, *American Working Class Culture: Explorations in American Labor and Social History* (Westport, Conn.: Greenwood Press, 1979), 347–348.

36. Golab, *Immigrant Destinations,* 134. Data gathered from "Report of Division of Immigration and Unemployment," *First Annual Report of the Commissioner of Labor and Industry,* 1914, 277–278.

37. Claudia Goldin, *Understanding the Gender Gap: The Economic History of Women* (New York: Oxford Univ. Press, 1990). Goldin writes, "the Depression reinforced and extended already existing bans against the employment of married women," which reflected "various prejudices" of firm managers.(164)

38. Golab, *Immigrant Destinations,* 135–138.

39. Ibid. 139.

40. Frances Fox Piven and Richard Cloward, *Poor People's Movements: Why They Succeed, How They Fail* (New York: Vintage Books, 1979), 46.

41. Frances Fox Piven and Richard Cloward, *Regulating the Poor: The Functions of Public Welfare* (New York: Vintage Books, 1972), 50.

42. Irving Bernstein, *The Lean Years: The History of the American Worker, 1920-1933* (Boston: Houghton Mifflin Co., 1960), p. 320.

43. Piven and Cloward, *Poor People's Movements,* 48.

44. Bernstein, *The Lean Years: The History of the American Worker, 1920–1933,* 321–322, 507.

45. Ibid. 325.

46. Ibid.

47. Piven and Cloward, *Poor People's Movements,* 47, 49–50, 53, 56.

48. Records of the Western Soup Society, Urban Archives, Paley Library, Tem-

ple University, Philadelphia. Annual Report, 29 November, 1921, 173; June 21, 1920, 149.

49. Records of Lorena Hickok, in eds. Richard Lowett and Maurice Beasley, *One-Third of a Nation: Reports on the Great Depression* (Urbana: University of Illinois Press, 1981), 51, 4–5, 361.

50. Piven and Cloward, *Poor People's Movements*, 48–49, 47.

51. Ibid. 49, 53, 56.

52. Piven and Cloward, *Poor People's Movements,* 47, 49–50, 53, 56.

53. Alan Dawley, *Class and Community: The Industrial Revolution in Lynn* (Cambridge, MA.: Harvard University Press, 1976), 52–53, 57. Unlike Dawley's argument, the case is made here that land ownership and accessibility to large plots of land was not a prerequisite for gardening or raising non-domesticated animals.

54. Bureau of Public Health, City Archives, Philadelphia, PA. 1912 Annual Report, 470–471; 1920 Annual Report, 231.

55. Ibid.

56. Ibid. 1920 Annual Report, 212–213.

57. Ibid. 1916 Annual Report, 481, 504; 1920 Annual Report, 210.

58. Ibid. 1922 Annual Report, 149.

59. Ibid. 1916 Annual Report, 511.

60. House of Industry, Urban Archives, Paley Library, Temple University, Philadelphia. "History of the South-East Area," Works Progress Administration, Report, 1937, 12.

61. Bureau of Public Health, 1914 Annual Report, 312; 1920 Annual Report, 218; 1921 Annual Report, 242; 1922 Annual Report, 111.

62. Ibid.

63. House of Industry, "History of the South-East Area," 1937, 12.

64. Bureau of Public Health, 1914 Annual Report, 315; 1916 Annual Report, 481, 504; 1920 Annual Report, 210.

65. Anna Davin, "Imperialism and Motherhood," *History Workshop Journal,* 5 (Spring, 1978) 9–65, 13.

66. See Lynn Y. Weiner, *From Working Girl to Working Mother: The Female Labor Force in the United States, 1820–1980* (Chapel Hill: University of North Carolina, 1985). Social reformers were no doubt concerned because in 1918 in Philadelphia, "more than a third of the children aged from five to sixteen in the families of working mothers had no formal supervision after school. Infants and children were for the most part tended by relatives in their own homes, or watched over by neighbors."(121) Parents often organized child care on this kind of informal basis.

67. Bureau of Public Health, 1916 Annual Report, 470; 1917 Annual Report, 226, 228; 1920 Annual Report, 195–196. See Richard Wertz and Dorothy C. Wertz, *Lying In: A History of Childbirth in America* (New York: Schocken Books, 1979), "Government Involvement," 201-233.

68. For an outstanding resource on women's bodies and on childbirth, which

turns the medical establishment's view of women's bodies on its head, see Emily Martin, *The Woman in the Body: A Cultural Analysis of Reproduction* (Boston: Beacon Press, 1987).

69. Bureau of Public Health, 1915 Annual Report, 25; 1923 Annual Report, 13.

70. Ibid.

71. House of Industry, Annual Reports, 1929, 9.

72. Bureau of Public Health, 1916 Annual Report, 470; 1917 Annual Report, 226, 228; 1920 Annual Report, 195–196.

73. Ibid. 1915 Annual Report, 14–15, 54–55; 1912 Annual Report, 102.

74. "Public Health Survey," 1949, City Archives, Bureau of Public Health, Figure 31, 47. Mortality Rates for Infants and Mothers, and Stillbirths, Philadelphia Residents, 1900 to 1948.

75. Bureau of Public Health, 1915 Annual Report, 76–80.

76. Ibid. 1915 Annual Report, 76–80. Interview with W.S.R. Dickinson, Public Health director, 1983.

77. Bureau of Public Health, 1914 Annual Report, 354.

78. Ibid. 354.

79. Ibid. 358.

80. Ibid. 1916 Annual Report, 492.

81. Ibid. 492.

82. Ibid. 1915 Annual Report, 358–361.

83. Octavia Hill Association, Annual Reports, Pennsylvania Historical Society, Philadelphia. 1906 Annual Report, 7–9.

84. Ibid. 1906 Annual Report, 1–2; 1914 Annual Report, 5; 30th Annual Report, 1927, 1.

85. Ibid. 35th Annual Report, 1931, 9; From "Notes to the Supplement to the 7th Annual Report for 1971."

86. Ibid.

87. See the records of Lorena Hickok, in eds. Lowett and Beasley, *One-Third of a Nation,* 4–5, 361. Hickok writes that "the protest groups in Philadelphia asked for cash instead of food orders, clothing, medical care, more consideration at the hands of interviewers and caseworkers, and, above all, something nearly approaching adequacy."(51)

88. Octavia Hill Association, 40th Annual Report, 1936, 9, from "Notes"; 41st Annual Report, 1937, 9, from "Notes"; 45th Annual Report, 1941, 9; 58th Annual Report, 1954, 10, from "Notes."

89. Golab, *Immigrant Destinations,* 23.

90. Ethnic Survey, Works Progress Administration, Balch Institute for Ethnic Studies, Philadelphia. Job 53, "Economic and Industrial Handicaps: Blacks in Philadelphia," 8–9.

91. Ibid. 10–11.

92. Ibid.

93. Sadie Tanner Mossell, "The Standard of Living Among One Hundred Negro Migrant Families in Philadelphia," Ph.D. Thesis, University of Pennsylvania. Reprinted from the *Annals of the American Academy of Social and Political Science*, 97, November 1921, 6–9.

94. Ibid. 12–13.

95. Ibid. 16, 18, 25, 35.

96. Ibid.

97. Ibid.

98. Ibid. 27–29.

99. Records of the Western Soup Society, Urban Archives, Paley Library, Temple University, Philadelphia. "Social Development: Housing," March 13, 1939, 5–7.

100. Ibid. 3–4.

101. "Report of the Philadelphia Real Property Survey," City Archives, Philadelphia. 1934, Vol. IV, Family Accommodations by Number of Rooms, Federal Works Progress Administration for Pennsylvania, Project 4744, Roll #2, Colored Housing 1932 as Related to Census Districts, "Introduction to Colored Housing," no page number.

102. Western Soup Society, "Social Development: Housing," 11, 13–14.

103. Western Soup Society, "Social Development: Housing," March 13, 1939, 5–7.

104. Western Soup Society, Findings from "The Real Property Survey and Low Income Housing Survey of 1939," conducted by the Philadelphia Housing Authority and the Works Progress Administration, 52–56.

105. Western Soup Society, Findings from the Real Property Survey and Low Income Housing Survey of 1934, conducted by the Philadelphia Housing Authority and the Works Progress Administration, 52–56 in original source; 12 in Ethnic Survey.

106. Thomas Lee Philpott, *The Slum and the Ghetto: Immigrants, Blacks, and Reformers in Chicago, 1880–1930* (Belmont, CA.: Wadsworth, 1991). Philpott describes similar living conditions in Chicago at the time.

107. Western Soup Society, Findings from the Real Property Survey and Low-Income Housing Survey of 1939, "Social Development: Housing," 9–11.

108. Ibid. 9–11.

109. "Report of the Real Property Survey," 1934, City Archives of Philadelphia. Project 4744, Roll #2, "Introduction to Colored Housing," no page number.

110. Western Soup Society, Findings from the Real Property Survey and Low Income Housing Survey of 1939, 52–56 in original; 12 in Ethnic Survey.

111. "Report of the Real Property Survey," City Archives, 4, 8.

112. "Real Property Survey," Colored Housing, see 8, 17–20.

113. Octavia Hill Association, 40th Annual Report, 1936, 9, from "Notes"; 41st Annual Report, 1937, 9, from "Notes"; 45th Annual Report, 1941, 9, from "Notes"; 58th Annual Report, 1954, 10, from "Notes."

114. Ibid. Section on Southwest Philadelphia.

115. "Philadelphia Real Property Survey," City Archives, Colored Housing, Summary Section and Section on Southwest Philadelphia.

116. Caroline Manning, *The Immigrant Woman and Her Job,* U.S. Department of Labor, Bulletin of the Women's Bureau, No. 74. Washington: U.S. Government Printing Office, 1930; Reprint Edition, Arno Press, Inc., 1970, 20.

117. Ibid. 45–47, 135.

118. Ibid. 48–49.

119. Ibid. 75.

120. Ibid. 97–98, quote on 97.

121. Ibid. 61–62.

122. Ibid.

123. Ibid.

124. Ibid.

125. Ibid.

126. Ibid.

127. Ibid. 64–65.

128. Gwendolyn Salisbury Hughes, *Mothers in Industry: Wage-Earning Mothers in Philadelphia* (New York: New Republic, 1925); Reprint Edition, Arno Press, 1977, 13–14, 22, 31, 96, 152.

129. Ibid. 33, 98, 102, 107, 111, 105, 119, 123, 127.

130. Richard Nicholas Juliani, "The Social Organization of Immigration: The Italians in Philadelphia," Ph.D. Dissertation, Temple University, (Ann Arbor: University Microfilms, 1972), 197.

131. Ethnic Survey, Balch Institute for Ethnic Studies, Philadelphia. Conducted by the Works Progress Administration, 1940–1941, Job #66, "Italians in Philadelphia," written by Bonze, 2 April 1940, 6. From "Immigrants in Industry," Part 24, Recent Immigrants in Agriculture, Vol. 2, Hammonton (New Jersey) and Vicinity, Microfilm. Also see Shradeley, 13; Interview with Philip De Luca, organizer, 14.

132. Ibid. Bonze, 6; Shradley, 12.

133. Ibid. Shradley, 13; Interview with Philip De Luca, organizer, 14.

134. Ibid. See Judith E. Smith, "The Transformation of Family and Community Culture in Immigrant Neighborhoods, 1900–1940," in eds. Herbert G. Gutman and Donald H. Bell, *The New England Working Class and the New Labor History* (Urbana: University of Illinois Press, 1987). According to Smith, in Providence more than 50 percent of Italian-American adult men had brothers in the same occupation in the first decades of the century. She analyzed the following occupational categories (which show the percent of adult males in each category): laborer (19 percent); craft artisan, self-employed (19 percent); factory operator (17 percent); craft artisan, employee (14 percent); retail, self-employed (11.5 percent); retail, employee (11.5 percent); skilled (6 percent); and professional (2 percent). (159–183)

135. Rosara Lucy Passero, "Ethnicity in the Men's Ready-Made Clothing

Industry, 1880–1980: The Italian Experience in Philadelphia." Ph.D. Dissertation, University of Pennsylvania. (Ann Arbor: University Microfilms, 1978), 291, 315, 155, 317–318.

136. Ibid.

137. Ethnic Survey, interview with De Luca, 14; "Industrial Life," 8.

138. Ibid. Fanelli, interviews, 1.

*German-American farm women sewing a quilt, southeastern Pennsylvania, ca. 1930. Courtesy of the National Archives, Washington, D.C.*

# Seven

# Class Formation and the Emergence of New Social Identity Movements, 1945 to 1993

## Corporate Power and the Rise of Monied Labor

The lost history of tightly knit communities and cooperative work arrangements can be reconstructed by studying non-waged work relations before World War II. Although improvising labor—or "Third World" America—formed a larger part of U.S. labor before 1945, "Third World" America continued to develop throughout the United States between 1945 and the present, especially in southern rural areas, the Appalachian mountains, the border areas between Mexico and the United States, de-industrialized areas in the West and Northeast, depressed Midwestern agricultural areas, highly urbanized centers, and other locations. After 1945 most working-class neighborhoods had lost their own informal work and marketing networks, which enabled families to support each other within a communal context. Today vestiges of communal work and inter-household survival networks still can be found, even in North America's largest cities. Whether it is possible to apply knowledge about labor's support networks, both past and current, to today's regional economic development efforts remains to be seen. This seem like a logical area for social change agents to explore.

After 1945, monied labor in the United States rose and improvising labor only made up about 20 percent of the working class. Looking back a bit, both monied and improvising labor became restructured during the New Deal. Both strata's dependence on the state grew after this point, even though many people today just focus on benefits the poor received. After World War II, monied and improvising strata received higher wages than they had before, though the wage gap between the poor and the middle class persisted. In addition to the divergence in wage levels, they now received different types of state transfer payments, with members of improvising labor still having to prove that they needed help and the middle class automatically being entitled to state support.

As the economy expanded, U.S.-based businesses paid high wages to so-called skilled laborers, which served to further widen the domestic market. Between 1945 and 1970, development created images of a wage-labor monoculture, monolithic state and corporate power, insatiable consumerism, growing unions and secure wage pacts for men, with middle-class housewives confined to private life. This was the era of "one-dimensional man."[1] But these powerful media images over-simplified the relations that simultaneously pulled families and communities apart and bound social groups together in new ways.

After World War II, the United States used its new economic, political and military might to direct global development. Wage stability ensued, particularly for monied labor. Between 1945 and 1970, the United States filled the position that Britain did one century earlier and acted as the industrial, commercial, and financial center of the world.[2]

During the period of economic growth between 1945 and 1970, multinational corporate activity promoted the further, but still incomplete, commodification of household work. Monied labor's nominal wages and benefit packages developed in conjunction with changes in industrial organization. Managers of large-scale industries in the United States became less interested in coercing discontented laborers and more concerned with securing labor's general consent. By permitting grievance procedures and collective bargaining, the state gave unionized laborers, who worked for large corporations, new rights and obligations. New control based on consent was accompanied by increasing state and business intervention in market relations. In return for monied labor's new contractual rights, such as seniority and unemployment benefits, firm owners and managers benefited from a more stable labor force.[3]

Industrial managers applied time measurement to work, further reducing laborers' skill and control over shop work. Marketplace competition forced firms to offset the rapid increase in the overhead costs associated with Taylorist time management by increasing productivity. Under this regime, laborers were allowed little time for unscientific movements based on human need or innovation. According to Alfred Sohn-Rethel, "The cumulative pressures of the monopolistic economy of time devolved upon the work force by an ever-increasing speed of operations."[4] As work became more specialized and labor became more deskilled in the shop, labor was further deskilled at home in traditional subsistence activities. Still, adult family members who now bought "means-of-production" consumer goods maintained some informal work skills associated with home construction and cabinet-making, house painting, car maintenance, and the sewing of clothes. The loss of some previous non-waged sources of income and rising market consumption, which replaced less commodified home work, meant that the labor's diverse work relations at home and in its communities continued to crumble.

Labor's monied and improvising strata in the mid-Atlantic region were shaped by particular regional developments, which centered around Philadelphia's large manufacturing sector. Firms engaged in the production and transport of consumer and producer goods, such as petroleum products, coal and agricultural goods.[5] Industries produced textiles, clothing, processed food, chemicals, refined oil, paper goods, leather goods, electrical equipment, transportation equipment and metal products. The big growth industries after 1945 included food processing, paper box production, the production of televisions and electronic equipment, and oil refining (which increased as car and truck transportation became more important). Oil tankers dominated Philadelphia's port as the Delaware Basin became the largest refining area on the Atlantic coast.[6] As monied and improvising laborers worked more for companies in these industries, the development of the "automobile suburb" and the "decentralization of business" brought a dramatic increase in racial and ethnic segregation.[7]

In the United States, developments in industrial organization continued to alter home and shop work after 1945. As large-scale production grew, traditional means of subsistence declined, particularly in urban areas. The cultivation of large vegetable gardens, raising chickens and goats, canning, and bread making occurred less frequently. Households purchased more food and non-food items and engaged less in "producing" and transforming food for direct household consumption.[8]

Working-class households from both improvising and monied labor acquired a higher standard of living and purchased more consumer goods from grocery stores, department stores, appliance shops, and car lots. As firm's wages and state-based support for laboring households increased, there was a corresponding decrease in household-organized, income-yielding work. The growing indebtedness of the working-class enabled companies to sell more real estate and homes, as well as consumer durables to fill these privatized dwellings. Households bought more goods through the market and helped to foster the growth of the service sector and fast-food restaurants.[9]

But while unbridled commodification was on the agenda for especially monied labor until the 1970s, the further integration of stratified ethnic groups and their households into the capitalist orbit was uneven and unequal. Low-income ethnic groups and labor in impoverished areas of the country had little economic security, even though most U.S. labor received indirect benefits from U.S. hegemony. The divisions between monied and improvising labor became expressed through access to different and unequal state transfer payments, occupational stratification, stratified consumption patterns, and unequal access to quality education, governmental services and health care. In part, improvising labor's continuing reliance on some income from informal work distinguished it from monied labor.

Household-organized work changed in profound ways, especially for monied labor. Expenditures on market commodities replaced the need to do certain types of home work, particularly domestic work. The substitution of consumption for some informal work occurred at the same time that more women worked for wages and young people stayed in school longer. Monied labor and, to a lesser extent, improvising labor purchased more services related to child care, elder care, house cleaning, fast food and restaurant food, house and yard maintenance, car repair, personal care (such as hair cutting), psychological health, and overnight travel accommodations. In fact, the expansion of the services sector provided for many new, low-paid jobs, which were filled by less educated workers. As full- and part-time employees, improvising and less-educated segments of monied labor provided these services, which were paid for by higher-income households.

Many of these "service" tasks once had been done by low- to moderate-income families themselves, and many had also been done by families in monied labor. Even when informal work at home continued to be carried out by monied and improvising labor, most "means of production" were purchased on the market. Household members no longer made their own tools, grew all their vegetables, or raised animals for food. As families needed more consumer goods and relied more on the market to sustain themselves, women's wages provided often necessary income, even when high-paid, adult males contributed to the household income pool.

More women became employed on a part- or full-time basis by the private sector, state agencies, and government-supported social service organizations. Women's subordination at home and within the labor force became exemplified by the growth in female part-time employment. Although only 18 percent of women were part-time wage laborers in 1940, 31 percent of women were part-time wage earners by 1970.[10] Women's subordination also became exemplified by the double day of home and shop work; male wage earners did not carry an equal share of home work.[11] As households become more dependent on the market, women's wage labor increased and sexism became more institutionalized within firms and households. Growing market dependence actually ensured employers that there would be a growing supply of lower-paid, adult female laborers.[12]

Industry benefited from consumerism, which was an outgrowth of the distribution of higher wages. Wage income formed a growing proportion of especially monied labor's total income packet. The creation of new culturally defined needs led workers to purchase leisure commodities, recently advertised goods, consumer durables, education cars, and homes. Many commodities required families to go into debt, tightening the economic connection between working and buying. The creation of new consumer needs and buying patterns, in turn, stimulated a general increase in wages.[13]

During the period that the United States dominated the center of the world's economic stage, monied labor became more reliant on the market to fulfill almost all its consumption needs.[14] Families became more isolated from other families and became more mobile. Social life itself revolved more around market transactions. Monied labor helped companies realize profits every time purchases were made and wages earned. Low-income households, which also were becoming more money-oriented, remained somewhat removed from endless consumerism, partly because community ties had not completely dissolved. But for the vast majority of working-class families, the meaning of community bonds—which had once been based on mutual connections to informal work, inter-household exchanges and sales, mutual assistance, local organization of work relations, and redistributive and low-cost informal markets in neighborhoods—had been largely erased.

The decline of farming households and of land for subsistence cultivation occurred as more land was used by large producers. By 1970 open space in the countryside almost disappeared, reducing households' access to hunting and cultivation land. The heavy reliance of land as a commodity for capitalist production resulted from growing crop specialization, the consolidation of corporate control over agriculture, and mechanization. In general, available land became a capital resource that allowed production for the market. It became used less for growing subsistence food and serving as a resource for families engaging in informal work. When unemployment ravaged urban areas, however, some former farming households returned to rural areas, where they often discovered that even these areas been largely commodified.[15] But even with all these changes, commodification still was not complete, nor will it probably ever be.

After World War II, members of low-income households lost many non-waged work skills and, due to educational inequities and lost opportunities, failed to acquire new skills for shop work, which yielded high pay, adequate benefits, and promotional opportunities. The women and men—who still carried out housework, inter-household swapping, and some subsistence activities (such as child and elder care)—typically retained some informal work skills, which were somewhat transferable to wage employment. For example, people who cooked for large groups could become short-order and institutional cooks. As a result of painstaking work in fields, subsistence farmers may have acquired patience and gained mechanical skills, which helped them find troubleshooting work on assembly lines. Rural and urban women who coordinated church volunteer events may have found that they had organizational skills that applied to office work. Some non-wage earning women from monied labor carried out individualized housework, minimizing their control over the total work process and reducing their ability to acquire work skills that applied to other types of home work and shop work. Adult males from monied labor acquired new skills through shop work, which sometimes were transferable to self-employment efforts during hard times.[16]

In summary, when improvising and monied labor depended on either the state or employers for income, these economic ties affected future income-generating possibilities. Relying on the state meant reduced opportunities for acquiring and upgrading skills for shop work. In a context in which non-waged activities were declining, many families lost a chance to develop and apply skills from non-waged work. Relying on employers meant a chance to acquire and upgrade skills in shop work and to benefit economically from state transfer payments related to labor force participation. Ironically, women's housework, petty producing and marketing work, and community "volunteer" work provided women with their most consistent opportunities for developing non-waged work skills. The skills they acquired from remaining types of informal work sometimes helped give women organizational and other work skills that were transferable to wage employment.

Just as informal work served as a training ground for wage employment, wage employment may become recognized as a training ground for informal work. And surviving traditions of informal work and informal community organizations in the United States may be recognized as a training ground for economic and community development efforts that center around self-employment. New approaches to utilizing the common skills from wage and non-waged work may emerge as community developers study the relationship between wage labor and the history of informal work, communal work activities, and self-sufficiency patterns in different American and overseas communities.

## Fractured American Communities and Movements of New Social Identity Groups, 1945 to 1993

As the reorganization of work took place in the mid-twentieth century, communities splintered even more than they had in previous decades. The new social identity groups defined by gender and age continued to emerge from this structural, long-term change. When communities and families, which once were bound together through informal work and family labor, proceeded to splinter, social identity groups strengthened. This process further separated household members along gender and age lines. As a result of the structural reorganization of work, groups made up of individuals from different households (such as women from different households) began to form "abstract communities" defined by the social division of labor.

New abstract communities developed from the social identity groups of females, males, young people, adults, and elders. Unlike the personal, face-to-face quality of ties between family and community members, new social bonds became established because the social division of labor was changing. Although this has largely been a process hidden from the public eye, some group members recognized that social inequality had created similar social circumstances, power relationships, and work identities for them. The young assumed a similar identity related to school and young people's low economic status, and elders shared an identity based on retirement and Social Security. When females, youth, and elders identified with members of their culturally subordinate groups, they did so because of largely impersonal connections that became established through working patterns, state policies, and consumption patterns, as well as through literature, newspapers and magazines, television and radio, movies, and corporate advertisements. And just as culturally subordinate social identities emerged, so did the social identities of males and adults, which comprised labor's culturally dominant gender and age groups.

In this way, the widespread and long-term disruption of community-oriented informal work actually helped produce the new social movements for equality, which took off in the 1950s and 1960s. Social struggles began pulling "internally marginalized" strangers together with common political platforms and common social identity banners. Separate social movements, with some overlapping connections, developed for women, youth, elders, men, gays, and the physically challenged. Both social movement and social policy issues began to be more defined on national and global levels, leaving behind the nineteenth century pattern of social issues primarily reflecting local and regional concerns. The transformation of community life in the United States thus shaped the contemporary parameters of political, social, and economic world.

The creation of new ethnic identities was similar to the creation of new, more polarized, gender and age identities. But gender and age identities took shape within the broader context of ethnic identity, which was shaped by class considerations. By the 1950s and 1960s, even ethnic identities were newer and more abstract than they once were. After World War II, ethnic identities became more based on impersonal, long-distance relationships that stressed general ties of similarity derived from the stratification system. But there was a greater continuity in community ties for subordinate ethnic groups—especially for African Americans in improvising labor—than for the mass of culturally dominant ethnic groups (many which experienced upward mobility and moved from improvising to monied labor by 1945 or 1950.) Although early twentieth-century communities largely were defined along ethnic lines, as were post-World War II ethnic communities, new ethnic identities partly emerged through impersonal connections created by work, the state, the market, and the media. In general, labor's ethnic groups congealed into "black" labor (or "labor of color") and "white" labor. Although membership in these strata became readjusted cyclically, African Americans were disproportionately represented in improvising or "black" labor, while European Americans were disproportionately represented in monied labor, or "white" labor. Labor's strata became defined by households' differing degrees of reliance on wage labor, not by "color" per se.

It is probably too soon to tell whether contemporary gender, age and ethnic social identity groups will remain as polarized as they became by 1970. In five to ten years, people living in industrial countries may discover that the social division of labor has taken a different direction. In the period between 1970 and 1993 in the United States, it is unclear how economic recession and work force reorganization altered the way gender, age and other social identities were socially created by capitalist institutions. The structural intersections between ethnicity and labor's improvising and monied strata also remain unclear. Is the creation of these social identities essentially a secular trend, one that took off after World War II? This would suggest that social polarization and social movements based on gender, age and ethnic identities will endure for some time. Or are these social identities being fundamentally reshaped by the secular impact of the decline of U.S. power and the simultaneous impact of the economic recession? This would suggest that a regrouping of intra-class forces may occur, bringing different culturally subordinate and sympathetic dominant group members together. Until the U.S. economy begins to thrive once again, it will not be known how the contemporary aspects of cyclical and secular change have been affecting the long-term development of social identity groups and their social movements.

When this research process began, it seemed that social identities were derived from on-going secular forces, which remain undiluted and ever-present today. It was prematurely assumed that social identity groups would occupy their own, separate places on the world stage well into the twenty-first century. As the research was conducted, more complex patterns appeared. At this point, the fundamental shifts in work and the state suggest that social change may be taking place faster than ever, possibly erasing some dividing lines and bringing socially subordinate groups closer together.

In today's world, regional development (as exemplified by the creation of separate, ethnically defined countries) is initiated by ethnic nationalities with medium levels of power in response to uneven development perpetuated by very powerful corporate and inter-state global networks.[17] It can be anticipated that this trend toward regionalized responses to uneven development and social inequality will become more pronounced in the United States in the near future. If U.S. ethnic groups seize control over their own economic destinies, this most likely will take place within the established political system, which, on paper, has strong guarantees of individual rights and civil liberties. Because of this new trend toward regionalization and local control, "unexpected" political and economic patterns may emerge for different social identity groups.[18] Gender and age identity groups may function in different ways than do culturally subordinate, ethnic identity groups. Or they might do so in some circumstances, but not others. When social change agents do make future interventions to improve economic security and to increase democratic deliberations, they will need to have a clear sense of how the social division of labor is creating social identity groups and how these groups have responded to the hierarchical system.

One historical theme stands out for those people who read history in order to see how intentional change can be promoted. Rather than working against secular trends and cyclical rhythms, it is easier to develop egalitarian and democratic social change strategies and programs that are partly fueled by the energy of actual social forces. These social forces derive their momentum from long-term secular trends and the cyclical rhythms of economic expansion and contraction. Social movements, in particular, derive part of their momentum from the social processes that created them.

Social movements also derive their momentum from a shared criticism of hierarchy, monopolies, state policy, and/or environmental destruction, for example. The critique of the system by social movements has led to new social patterns (such as more involvement by fathers in child rearing, the growth of gay and lesbian communities, back-to-the-land movements, and grassroots community revitalization efforts), which have been some of labor's responses to the social division of labor. These movements may show that people try to use family and community bases to fight systemic pressures, but they do not necessarily mean that the capitalist social division of labor is taking a new direction, a less polarizing direction that serves to reduce inequities. Although certain dimensions of social life may be improving, the source of these improvements might come from without the system or from people's collective influence on the state.

Although it is important for social change agents to recognize the structural source of social identities and related social movements, it also is important to be able to begin visualizing how to reorganize the connection between the economy and social movements. The critique of society fostered by social movements questions, but also reflects, work inequities and the stratification system. Because social identity movements were born from social inequality, they reject specific inequities; but they may not go beyond trying to redress one inequity. Even though the economy has fragmented working people and their social movements, this does not mean that these dividing lines need to be accepted as eternal and irreconcilable. These dividing lines only roughly reveal where social identity groups are lined up now; they provide a starting point, not an ending point. Social change agents need not have their vision limited by the specific critiques and alternatives that emerge from fragmented and often polarized social movements. If new social relations are to be developed, social change agents need to be able to chart the common vision of different social movements and to draw pathways that weave their way through the material world of work, leading to a more egalitarian, democratic society. Greater equity and democracy will only be able to flourish if labor learns how to heal its divisions by building on the strengths of social identity movements.

## The Transformation of Wage and Non-Waged Work and Social Hierarchy, 1970 to 1993

The way that home and shop work were organized and, consequently, the way that ethnic, gender and age divisions were expressed, began to change when the United States lost its hegemonic control around 1970. The period of long-term structural change, which brought the period of U.S. hegemony from 1945 to 1970, came to an end. A new period of long-term structural change began to unfold. The structural features of this period are only now beginning to be formed. The period of contraction from 1970 to the early 1990s, therefore, brought the demise of U.S. power and the rise of a new global structure. Just as the features of social life in the 1870s became more pronounced by 1910, the features of social life in the 1970s will become more pronounced in the next 20 years of economic expansion.

There are several essential changes in wage work and production that affect the lives of working people in the United States. Robert Reich in *The Work of Nations* stresses the importance of the transformation from high volume production, which characterized production in the previous structural period, to high value production, which increasingly characterizes the most profitable production today. He also usefully identifies the three main groups of workers—the symbolic analyst, the routine production service worker, and the in-person service worker—who will carry out most of the work for firms.[19]

In order to become more globally competitive, firms carrying out some of their operations in the United States are undergoing major restructurings, including the shifting of production overseas and the shifting of production to areas in the United States that offer higher profits through lower wages, cheaper land and resources, and lower transportation costs. One major component of this business reorganization has been laying off permanent employees and using more temporary and self-employed or contract workers for professional, factory and office tasks. Firms created a large mass of self-employed workers, many who have lower wages, no benefits, and inadequate skills for remaining self-employed. When it suited firms' interests to down-size, business forced self-employment on large numbers of unprepared, unwilling workers, who may have no opportunities to become high-paid wage laborers again.[20]

Some of this organizational restructuring has taken place under the ideological banner of Total Quality Management and related business approaches. Total Quality Management (TQM) attempts to increase the productivity of each worker by creating a high performance work organization. This new way of organizing production gives front-line workers more responsibility for making decisions and reduces the number of managers.[21] Overall, labor costs are reduced by eliminating many middle-level managers and by transferring managerial functions to front-line workers, who begin to carry out increasingly automated production tasks, along with new managerial tasks. As primary sector firms now operate with down-sizing in mind as a basic premise, secondary sector firms just now are beginning to feel the initial ripple effects of this industrial reorganization. This reorganization of work in the private and public sectors indicates that, unless major governmental and community-based interventions are made, there will be fewer wage labor positions for American workers. Furthermore, there will be more workers who, without new education and well-funded, community development programs, will be unprepared to successfully run their own businesses.[22]

What will lower employment levels mean for the unequal division of the working class? Since 1970, when the United States declined as the hegemonic power, there has been a widening of the gap between rich and poor in this country. According to Robert Reich, between 1977 and 1990, "the average income of the poorest fifth of Americans declined by about 5 percent, while the richest fifth became about 9 percent wealthier."[23] By 1990, the poorest fifth of Americans had only 3.7 percent of the country's total income and the richest fifth had over half of the income.[24] According to the National Center on Education and the Economy, not only have "real average weekly earnings in the United States fallen by more than 12 percent," but incomes of the "top 30 percent increased while those of the other 70 percent spiraled downward."[25]

During the 1980s, Reich notes that the gap between male and female wages "closed by about a third," bringing the convergence of wages and benefits between "even relatively uneducated men and women."[26] The closing of the wage gap between women and men occurred between 1980 and 1990, Reich indicates, because male and female wages converged. Male wages fell and female wages increased to some extent; female wages did not rise to the very high level where male wages once were.[27] It is not clear if these changes express secular changes or cyclical variations. The wage gap between women and men has remained between 1990 to 1993, indicating that perhaps a wide gender gap will continue to be a structural feature in the future.[28] Just as wage work relations between women and men are unclear, it also is unknown how evolving social structures will influence how women and men relate to each other through the sphere of non-waged work.

Although divisions between groups continue to reflect the long-term structures that emerged from 1870 to 1970, it is possible, among the increasingly larger "bottom" tier of working people, that both adult females and males will receive relatively low wages and become excluded from the material benefits that accrue to households located in the top tier. If substantial unemployment and underemployment continues during the next cycle of expansion, the cultural polarization between women and men in labor's growing "bottom" tier (which includes improvising labor and portions of monied labor) may begin to lessen, even if a wide wage gap continues to divide men and women in the work force. The lessening of cultural polarization may occur as family members are forced to turn to other ways of generating income.

Within the laboring population, labor-based polarization between age groups has shifted somewhat, as employed elders find that they may be forced to work a longer portion of their lives and assume a larger share of the burden of covering the cost of their reproduction. This includes covering more of the costs associated with retirement and health care. For low-income groups that are increasingly shunted from wage labor's sphere, the phases of the life cycle—youth, adulthood, and "old age"—may be melding together, as members of culturally subordinate ethnic groups find that they do not have the possibility of becoming "socially productive" adults who receive wages and support dependent household members. Adulthood, as we have known it, is now being denied to large sectors of the working population. Rather than being overworked, many laboring people are excluded from the wage work force, at least for long portions of their lives.[29] And many young people are growing up knowing that they probably will not be able to support themselves and their families by defining their work within the context of wage-reliant and state-dependent self-sufficiency. By contrast, within the secure tiers of monied labor, gender and age divisions may continue to emerge in much the same way that they have, as this stratum becomes more wage- and market-dependent. More in-depth, historical research is needed before comparisons can be made between the types of stratification that are now developing within monied and improvising labor.

Women's work has been intimately connected to changes in the definition of self-sufficiency. Like informal work, the history of women's work in the United States has involved parastatal and state policy, changes in the definition and organization of self-sufficient behaviors, and the transformation of work activities in neighborhoods, regions, and the larger world. Non-waged work and unpaid work gradually emerged as a truly undervalued category of work in the United States. Home-based work became undervalued as working people relied more on higher-paid wage labor and less on their own income-yielding activities, which were undermined, but not completely destroyed. The historical examination of home work shows that the history of women's work forms a part of the history of all non-waged or informal work, which was organized by laboring households in the streets and in their homes. Seen as a whole, labor history includes the history of shop work and the history of home-based work.

Today women's work in industrialized countries serves as the primary, but not exclusive, reminder of a once vibrant world of work that laboring people organized in their homes and in their neighborhoods. Other reminders include contemporary non-waged work performed by recent low-income immigrants, street vending done by micro-business owners and by homeless or near homeless people, and "traditional" subsistence activities conducted in rural areas. As non-waged activities were discouraged by the state and business firms over the last 150 years, there was a transformation of non-waged work as a whole and of women's work in particular. The transformation of women's work, or the gradual distilling of what came to be known as female housework from other variations of non-waged work, essentially took place by 1945 or 1950. Readings on industrialized areas suggest that a similar structural transformation occurred in other highly industrialized countries at this time, including in England and the Netherlands, but before common patterns can be noted in a definitive way, further research needs to be conducted on the similarities and dissimilarities between the transformation of home-based work in industrialized countries.

Women's non-waged work in First World countries appeared to emerge as a distinct, "female" activity when other types of non-waged work, or "Third World-like" work, declined during the nineteenth and twentieth centuries. Women's work was born from the ashes of the gradual demise of household-organized work, which once was carried out by all members of the basic economic unit in society: the household. First World laborers have begun to come full circle because, now that employers and the state are not providing a basic income for growing numbers of working people, unemployed and underpaid working people have begun to rekindle families' informal work activities. In order to contend with today's pressures of cyclical contraction and the longer-term restructuring of the world-economy, households are supplementing "women's domestic work" with additional types of non-waged work.

For lower-income households in the United States, this process of supplementation has been taking place all along. Low-paid and underemployed people have been generating some non-waged income and maintaining weak neighborhood-based relations of reciprocity and "equal exchange." These income-supporting efforts, often carried out by Americans whose ancestors have been in the country for generations, have been largely unrecognized by middle-class and upper-class Americans. This group of well-rooted Americans, who were systematically disengaged from home and street work, did not benefit the way they could have from the continual, intergenerational transfer of diverse home work skills, had the state and business not discouraged informal work in the past. But many of the skills were reinvented on a generational basis, evolving from specific configurations of neighborhood and urban life.

Although low-income people in the United States historically had their informal work and its work ethic taken away from them, there is a popular conception today (partly fostered among U.S. companies with overseas interests) that the work ethic of Third World workers and some recent immigrants is virtuous, hardworking, and untarnished by the soft, easy, cushioned life that abounds in North America. Although the media now expresses many reservations about the presence of immigrants in the United States, those who advocate using Third World labor mention the character of immigrants' informal work, noting that immigrants supposedly have a strong "work ethic" and supposedly work long hours for low wages. Little reference is made of the fact that new immigrants often come from environments where informal work is economically necessary and where there have been uninterrupted intergenerational transfers of home work skills. This glowing portrayal of Third World and U.S. immigrant workers' behavior is often contrasted with the behavior of low-income U.S. workers, who, interestingly enough, are seen as having no work ethic. Because low-income U.S. workers have been relabeled as lazy and lacking initiative once again (as rural people were during the early days of factory production and as descendants of Africans were during the days of enslavement on Southern plantations), another excuse has been created for bypassing some low-income people and for hiring workers who help create the largest profits. This artificial, ahistorical contrast between low-income Americans and low-income Third World people (many who have become Americans by residency and by citizenship) is more than just another instance of pitting groups of workers against each other. It is another case of blaming the victims of a stratified system.

The history of the period from 1970 to the present includes much more than the history of workplace reorganization and growing underemployment for large numbers of U.S. workers from improvising and monied labor. As work has changed, so did the state and its relationships with laboring families. Changes in state transfer payments have accompanied the restructuring of the work force. Although there have been some attempts to strengthen welfare benefits by providing comprehensive health care and day care services (benefits lobbied for, in part, by feminist organizations and gradually adopted by state and federal governments for diverse programs), new social policies of federal, state and local governments often have reduced subsidies to low-income people and restricted their access to state transfer payments.[30] Therefore, the welfare reform process in the late 1980s rationalized the system by providing for more flexible ways for states to distribute benefits and, simultaneously, to restrict access to benefits or to penalize other welfare recipients. Low-income families with two parents and children, for example, are still not entitled to benefits in most states. When "working poor" parents qualify for benefits, which are lower than the benefits for single-parent families with children, one parent may have to "pay" for these benefits by doing menial "community service" work for 16 hours a week. This menial work, which may involve picking up roadside trash or wiping cafeteria tables in public buildings, does not provide job skills or additional income.

Currently both federal and state governments are experimenting with adjusting benefits and tightening up on eligibility requirements. The Clinton administration would like to expand social services, such as job training and child care, but simultaneously limit most welfare support to two years. Some members of Congress want to reduce food stamps and prevent most immigrants from enrolling in welfare programs. Congress will consider whether welfare recipients, who have been dependent on welfare for over two years, should engage in full-time, public service "workfare" and work off their benefits.[31] And as part of a proposal to allow welfare recipients to save income for family improvement activities (such as education or small business start-ups), the Clinton administration may decide to give $5,000 subsidies to corporations that hire welfare recipients.[32] In 1994, federal policy makers even introduced the possibility of completely eliminating the existing welfare system.

While Congress is considering changes in welfare policy, states are carrying on their own welfare experiments, many which have a punitive character. Some states have adopted or are considering measures that reduce welfare payments for incoming residents, forbid welfare payments to new immigrants, limit payments for welfare families that have additional children, and pay a premium to single welfare recipients who get married. As federal and state allocations to municipalities are reduced, and as local revenues from business taxes have decreased, General Assistance programs for women and men without children and for homeless people simultaneously have contracted or sometimes even vanished. Because the well-being of low-income Americans is more threatened now than it has been for decades, social reformers in federal, state and local governments have begun looking at innovative approaches to reducing poverty, including the encouragement of self-employment.

## Organizational Efforts to Create Greater Self-Sufficiency and to Strengthen Family and Community Relationships

This historical study, which examines how informal work was discouraged, suggests that community-based organizations and public policy advocates would be remiss not to pursue self-employment as one economic development option. In the last five to ten years, governmental officials and community organizations actually have started to experiment with developing self-employment model programs. But funding for these pilot and experimental projects has been limited and unstable. This move toward considering the benefits of self-employment has happened for a number of reasons. First, the encouragement of home-based work and community-defined self-sufficiency represents one way to add new income-yielding positions and to create greater economic stability for families. Furthermore, there is recognition that more "worker control" is needed at work, as Total Quality Management advocates argue. In addition, the dissolution of community life and the growing lack of community control has impacted schools, neighborhoods, and family life. By preparing working people to assume more responsibility for generating their own income, for controlling more of their work, and for shaping community life, some community developers from private non-profit organizations and governmental officials believe that the overall quality of life would be improved for growing portions of labor.

In short, there is a growing recognition by some grassroots community developers and state officials that, because the state and business cannot guarantee working class security to even the limited extent it did, labor needs to assume more responsibility for organizing its means of sustenance and for shaping community life. There is debate about how the state should be involved in this process and if it should be involved at all. As this new orientation grows, which sometimes emphasizes the importance of placing the working class at the center of economic and workplace decisions, business is trying to get the state to assume more responsibility for cultivating a good business climate and for assuming more of its on-the-job training costs (including through contract education programs at community colleges.)[33] So, while the state assumes less costs for labor's reproduction, it also seems to be assuming more of the operational costs for business.

Since the Progressive era, it has taken 60 to 70 years for a small number of community developers and social reformers to develop a new orientation about labor's social role in initiating and controlling work. Interestingly enough, the general work skills and leadership qualities that contemporary public officials, business owners, educators, job trainers, and social service personnel are trying to inculcate in working people once were produced "naturally" when working people had greater control over how they earned income and how the working day was structured.[34] The informal work context automatically produced skills and attitudes that led to greater self-reliance from employers and the state, greater neighborhood-centered networks of mutual support, and greater leadership development and community-organizing skills. Some of today's social reformers—who have only garnered weak state support so far—are trying to teach laboring people the same skills that their grandparents and great grandparents once possessed. These new social reformers also are trying to get working people to build new community relations and community structures that encourage mutual support and community decision-making, just as yesterday's community networks once did.

Currently many social policy and program options are being explored at the grassroots, regional and national levels, with the hope of alleviating poverty, providing quality job retraining that will command high wages, strengthening work-related education, and meeting community needs. As a result, a diverse constellation of social change agents—state agency officials, state legislators and governors, members of the U.S. Congress, leaders of community-based organizations, and directors of many national non-profit and educational institutions—are trying to identify ways to develop and support micro-businesses, small businesses and worker-run cooperatives, and to strengthen family and community relationships.

Today there are more than 200, often poorly funded self-employment programs in the United States, many which are run with government support. A pilot self-employment program run by Washington State, for example, has allowed workers receiving unemployment benefits to use subsidies to become self-employed. Similar efforts have been initiated in Canada, which seems to have expressed a greater commitment to increasing self-employment. In several states (including Iowa and Minnesota), a similar pilot project provides an opportunity for welfare recipients to use their subsidies as start-up funds for micro-enterprises. Although it focuses on training elders for job placements, the Department of Labor's Title V Program for older workers (who are often skilled informal workers) has enabled low-income elders to become trained and educated for self-employment for more than two decades.[35]

Community-based organizations, national private non-profits, and some state officials have pushed self-employment issues into the public policy realm, where issues are debated and considered by the general public. The emergence of democratic and participatory social movement organizations has provided a major impetus for placing self-employment, cooperatives and alternative trade on political agendas in localities and in state and federal governments. This new participatory social movement—which is built on the energy of everyday people, who practice democratic decision-making at the neighborhood level—has gathered its momentum as similar movements developed in other countries, especially in the Third World. Controlling and benefiting from one's own work has been a part of this effort to strengthen democratic traditions in everyday life. Expanding income-generating options, redirecting the economy so it benefits all, and controlling and benefiting from work have become components of what might be called a global movement. To function in effective ways, economic reorganization programs need to draw on local traditions and customs. For the most part, this aspect of economic reorganization has been lacking in the United States because the history and traditions of past and contemporary informal work, which often have formed an integral part of ethnic and multi-ethnic community life, have been lost, forgotten, or overlooked.

As a result of their commitment to changing the context in which work is carried out, some community-based organizations in neighborhoods, often with the help of federal and state funds, help working people become self-employed or become connected to worker cooperatives.[36] If carried out effectively, these programs might begin to revitalize urban and rural areas alike and recultivate income-yielding activities that are similar to those that were displaced at the turn-of-the century by the actions of parastatal organizations, state agencies and medium-sized and corporate enterprises.

Along with self-employment programs, many organizations have tried to meet the needs of economically disadvantaged groups (women, youth, elders and cultural minorities) without becoming narrow interest groups. These organizations try to bring different social identity groups together in order to solve social problems. They may work within ethnic or multi-ethnic contexts. Bringing together females and males, youth, adults and elders within an ethnic community is an enormous task alone, without attempting to build organizational connections with other ethnic groups.

Religious organizations and community churches sometimes try to pull together various segments of a community, while others (such as San Francisco's Glide Memorial Church) try to pull together different ethnic groups and simultaneously heal their internal divisions.[37]

Organizational leaders sometimes design their programs so that they connect directly with other groups, too. The National Association for the Advancement of Colored People (NAACP) recently suggested that the needs of African Americans can be more effectively met by working with other people of color. As a result of its new orientation, the NAACP sponsored a conference in Kansas City and brought together young men from different ethnic groups. The conference provided an opportunity for young men to talk to each other about their common needs and to do group problem solving on how to create peace between different gangs. In fact, grassroots and national efforts to bring peace between gangs and to end urban violence has been called the civil rights struggle of the 1990s.[38]

Substance abuse problems are beginning to be addressed within a comprehensive framework by former substance abusers themselves. "Circle of Recovery" groups have been established all over the United States, many through non-profit organizations. These "offshoots" of large 12-Step groups (which discourage "cross-talk" during meetings) enable smaller groups, made up of socially similar members, to explore many areas related to recovery, including romantic relationships, relationships with spouses and children, parental issues, family violence, self-identity and self-esteem issues, and school and job reentry. Although some have both men and women, these recovery groups are typically composed of individuals from similar class backgrounds and with common ethnic, gender and age identities. Some groups are largely composed of HIV positive members or members who have been in prison.

These "Circle of Recovery" groups have organized regional and national conferences and provided leadership development and training to members in other groups. Members of one California group initiated a "Midnight Basketball" program, which provides job assistance in a comfortable, fun place and at a convenient time for young men.[39] Rather than setting up standard social service offices, which are open during business hours from 9 to 5, social change agents from this partly volunteer-run, recovery program have gone into communities to work with local people in their own environments and during the hours when they are on the streets.

In order to build community relationships, the Family Resource Coalition in Chicago addresses a variety of related issues, including family support and case management, schooling, community development, and public policy. The work of this Chicago coalition, along with work done by similar local advisory councils and non-profit planning committees, follows in the footsteps of early feminist job training and counseling programs, which stressed that reentry students and workers required comprehensive supportive services. A comprehensive approach to family and community life builds on the recognition that women's needs can only be met if whole families have their needs met. This means, for example, a reentry middle-years woman will not be able to keep her new job unless all her needs and responsibilities are addressed. This may require social service providers to help women make provisions for adequate child care or elder care, health care, dental and eye care, transportation, personal or substance abuse counseling, additional education and training, finding new or cheaper housing, obtaining new work clothes, and identifying a support group. Fortunately, governmental bodies have begun to recognize the importance of providing some of these services for low-income people, though funding for these supportive social services is grossly inadequate.

In addition to organizations that encourage self-employment and that focus on particular social identity groups, educators and community developers have been working on the general project of preparing community people to become leaders. This includes teaching community volunteers how to identify and assess needs, design programs to address these needs, implement these programs, and conduct on-going evaluations. This educational process, known as community development education, is carried out by various organizations in the United States, including the Western Institute for Social Research, a school in Berkeley, California and the U.S. Cooperative Extension Service at land-grant universities.[40]

For the last century, the U.S. Department of Agriculture's Cooperative Extension Service (CES) has carried out community development education through its statewide and county-based offices. Not only is the Cooperative Extension Service the largest educational organization in the United States, but it is also the country's largest volunteer organization. The Cooperative Extension Service acts as the outreach arm of land-grant universities in all 50 states. The democratic mission of the Cooperative Extension Service is to help community people help themselves by working together to solve their common problems. It is no coincidence that this educational movement arose in rural areas, where strong community ties lasted well into the twentieth century. When community groups or individuals request information, Extension educators are supposed to present university-based knowledge in a way that is learner-centered and that encourages everyday people to make informed decisions. So long as its educational efforts continue to move more toward interdisciplinary programs (leaving specialized programs behind, which artificially separate problems and groups affected by them), the Cooperative Extension Service may serve as an important, already institutionalized network for promoting community development education.

Many grassroots organizations work to help local people become community leaders by encouraging them to address their common problems. Some well-known examples include: the Highlander Research and Education Center in New Market, Tennessee (which once trained civil rights leaders and now prepares local people to fight environmental problems); Communities Organized for Public Service (COPS) in San Antonio, Texas (which meets social needs by empowering community members to bring about change); and Congress for a Working America (CFWA) in Milwaukee, Wisconsin (which helps welfare recipients and other poor people find work, raise their income levels, and become policy advocates).[41] Small organizations like these, especially if they have a global framework for understanding common problems faced by economically deprived groups in the United States and abroad, may provide the greatest opportunities for communities that want to define what self-sufficiency will mean to them.

The last chapter reconsiders classical social scientists' conclusions about urban industrial society and examines contemporary social and public policy issues that relate to underemployment, welfare, job creation, self-employment and community development.

## Notes

1. See Herbert Marcuse, *One-Dimensional Man* (Boston: Beacon Press, 1964).

2. Doug Dowd, *The Twisted Dream: Capitalist Development in the U.S. Since 1776* (Cambridge, MA: Winthrop, 1974), 208.

3. Michael Buroway, *Manufacturing Consent: Changes in the Labor Process under Monopoly Capitalism* (Chicago: University of Chicago Press, 1979), 193, 110, 113. Also see David Brody, *Workers in Industrial America: Essays on the 20th Century Struggle* (New York: Oxford University Press, 1980), 9.

4. Alfred Sohn-Rethel, *Intellectual and Manual Labour: A Critique of Epistemology* (London: Macmillan, 1978), 161, 173. Refer to Karl Marx, *Capital: Volume I,* (New York: International Publishers, 1974), Chapter XV, "Machinery and Modern Industry."

5. Gladys Louis Palmer, *Philadelphia Workers in a Changing Economy* (Philadelphia: University of Pennsylvania Press, 1956), 20, 23, 30, 32, 41.

6. Ibid.

7. Sam Bass Warner, Jr., *The Private City: Philadelphia in Three Periods of its Growth* (Philadelphia: University of Pennsylvania Press, 1968), 169–172.

8. Ernest Mandel, *Late Capitalism* (London: New Left Books, 1975), 390–391, 400–401.

9. Ibid.

10. Claudia Goldin, *Understanding the Gender Gap: An Economic History of Women* (New York: Oxford University Press, 1990), 173.

11. See Arlie Hochschild, *The Second Shift: Working Parents and the Revolution at Home* (New York: Viking, 1989).

12. Mandel, *Late Capitalism,* 390–1, 400–1.

13. Ibid. 390.

14. See Giovanni Arrighi, Terence K. Hopkins and Immanuel Wallerstein, eds. "1886–1986: Beyond Haymarket?," *Antisystemic Movements* (London: Verso, 1989), 77–95. In most of Europe in the late 1960s, there had been a significant reduction in the number of peasants, shopkeepers, small traders, and artisans. "The overall picture was now that between 60 and 90 per cent (depending on the country) of the European labor force had come to depend on wages or salaries for its subsistence. On the basis of this purely formal criterion, the European labor force had become as fully "proletarianized" as it possibly could.(82–83)

15. Mandel, *Late Capitalism,* 378, 381–383, 387.

16. This examination of the ability of men and women to transfer informal work skills to wage employment is based on the author's research and experience working with older adults and women in various statewide, regional, and national employment, training, and educational programs.

17. See Robert K. Schaeffer, *Warpaths: The Politics of Partition* (New York: Hill and Wang, 1990).

18. Some environmentalists argue that development should be organized within bio-regions, or areas that share similar geographical and ecological characteristics. Activists often have embraced non-waged work and self-sufficient behaviors as ways to create a sustainable global environment.

19. Robert B. Reich, *The Work of Nations: Preparing Ourselves for 21st Century Capitalism* (New York: Vintage Books 1992), 81–86; 171–184.

20. Norton Grubb, Torry Dickinson, Gail Kaplan, and Lorraine Giordano, "Betwixt and Between: Education, Skills and Employment in Sub-Baccalaureate Labor Markets," National Center for Research on Vocational Education, University of California (Berkeley, School of Education, 1992). For example, one-third of the electronic industry's employees now are temporary workers. Because production lines change so rapidly in high-tech industry and efforts are made to reduce labor costs (expenditures on capital-intensive equipment are considered mandatory), there is little likelihood that this industry will offer more stable employment in the future, or that it will go back to the old pattern of keeping employees from the time of their college graduation until their retirement. This information was gathered during interviews with over 50 supervisors and personnel managers in high-tech industries.

21. Refer to W. Norton Grubb, Torry Dickinson, Lorraine Giordano, and Gail Kaplan, "Betwixt and Between: Education, Skills and Employment in Sub-Baccalaureate Labor Markets." This paper also explores the skills students are taught in vocational programs and how these skills relate to the primary sector's efforts to increase productivity through Total Quality Management and the secondary sector's efforts to utilize diverse production technologies. Also see National Cen-

ter on Education and the Economy's Commission on the Skills of the American Workforce, *America's Choice: High Skills or Low Wages!*, (Rochester, New York: 1990), 1–3. For a discussion of educational changes that are needed in order to increase productivity, refer to The Secretary's Commission on Achieving Necessary Skills, U.S. Department of Labor, *Living a Learning: A Blueprint for High Performance*, April 1992.

22. See John Judis, "The Jobless Recovery," *The New Republic*, March 15, 1993, 20–23.

23. Robert Reich, *The Work of Nations* (New York: First Vintage Books, 1992), 197.

24. Ibid.

25. National Center on the Education and the Economy, *America's Choice*, 1, 19–22.

26. Reich, *The Work of Nations*, p. 207.

27. Reich, *The Work of Nations*, 207.

28. *New York Times*, 18 October, 1993. This study, carried out by Claudia Goldin et al. is based on median, full-time yearly wages. This article speculates that the dip in women's wages in the last three years has to do with the recession and that women will do better as time goes on. Further information on the wage gap question is provided in the *New York Times*, 5 September, 1994. According to a 1994 study by the Economic Policy Institute, wages paid to men with bachelor degrees have continued to deteriorate. Men with college degrees watched their median hourly wages slip to $17.62 in 1993 (from $18.16 in 1987), while college-educated women saw their wages increase only slightly, making their hourly earnings about $4.00 less per hour than their male counterparts.

29. See Juliet B. Schor, *The Overworked American: The Unexpected Decline of Leisure* (New York: Basic Books, 1991.) Schor argues that wage workers or labor force participants (not the entire body of working people) are overworked, compared to earlier times. I argue that many groups of working Americans were excluded from wage work, once non-waged work declined and white adult males became the primary wage earners. It is unclear what work trends may develop as the economy expands and new global structures emerge.

30. The process of cutting back on welfare support began in the 1970s. See Frances Fox Piven and Richard A. Cloward, *The New Class War: Reagan's Attack on the Welfare State and Its Consequences* (New York: Pantheon, 1982); Michael B. Katz, *The Undeserving Poor: From the War on Poverty ot the War on Welfare* (New York: Pantheon Books, 1989).

31. *New York Times*, 11 November, 1993.

32. *New York Times*, 28 November, 1993. Needless to say, this plan would not increase the number of jobs and would fund corporations to conduct business as usual.

33. Grubb, Dickinson, Kaplan, and Giordano, "Betwixt and Between: Education, Skills and Employment in Sub-Baccalaureate Labor Markets."

34. Grubb, Dickinson, Giordano, and Kaplan, "Betwixt and Between." It is ironic to note that businesses have started to recruit workers who have multi-dimensional skills that are reminiscent of improvising labor's skills. Based on my interviews with high-tech employers, I discovered that employers sometimes seek workers who have "fix-it" farm skills, mechanical skills, and electronic skills. Some employers even specify that they really like recruits who have worked in production processes characteristic of different times periods: farming or ranching, high-volume mass production (from which they might have been laid off), and electronic production (which they studied in college). In other words, the ideal entry-level recruit has had two "careers" in the past and has been trained for a third. Employers now appreciate the multi-dimensional worker, who thinks about the whole production process and does not let departmental divisions fragment his/her thinking. Employers mention the importance of the "old independent work ethic," which is still assumed to flourish in farming and ranching areas, including in rural Arizona and Montana. Employers seek flexible, hardworking entry-level workers with team spirit, diverse technical skills, strong troubleshooting abilities, and strong written and verbal communication skills (the latter which seems to exclude many applicants who do not have English as their first language.)

35. The author conducted an extensive review of self-employment programs in the United States and Canada, which indicated that government, foundation and private financial support was weak. Some of these programs have strengthened since then [such as San Francisco's Women's Initiative for Self-Employment (WISE)], but insufficient funding continues to remain an obstacle. WISE now is implementing a project in Oakland, which will experiment with the use of a peer-lending model (a model used successfully in Bangladesh).

36. Through its newsletter and pilot research project (which applies Bangladesh's Grameen Bank peer-lending process to a micro-enterprise project in rural Pennsylvania), the Grassroots Economic Organizing Project at Bloomsburg University in Bloomsburg, Pennsylvania works to promote micro-enterprise development. This includes sharing information on the development of cooperatives in southeastern Ohio, which have utilized the production approach developed by the Mondragon cooperatives in Spain. The Spanish business cooperatives are based on flexible, temporary production networks. See *GEO: Grassroots Economic Organizing Newsletter,* Issue 4 (May/June 1992) and Issue 7 (January/February 1993).

37. See Cecil Williams, *No Hiding Place: Empowerment and Recovery for Our Troubled Communities* (San Francisco: Harper, 1993).

38. Reverend Benjamin Chavis' separation from NAACP occurred in part because of the gender and age divide, which has fragmented disenfranchised ethnic groups.

39. Midnight Basketball, which started in Maryland, has become a program that is run by diverse organizations around the country. The national crime law of 1994 recognizes the impact that Midnight Basketball could make, if it is implemented all over the country. Whether it continues to appeal to young men depends

on how this program is developed and implemented at the local level.

40. Paulo Freire, *The Politics of Education: Culture, Power and Liberation* (New York: Bergin and Garvey, 1985). The process of community development education is outlined in Freire's book.

41. Eliot Wigginton, *Refuse to Stand Silently By,* (New York: Anchor Books, Doubleday, 1992).

*Buying and selling livestock and household goods at a corner curb market in Philadelphia, 1915. Courtesy of the City Archives, Philadelphia.*

# Eight

# The Reorganization of Work and Social Hierarchy

## Social Change and the Transformation of Self-Sufficient Work Behaviors, 1830 to 1993

The study of changes in informal or non-waged work leads to a new understanding of how the contemporary working class was formed. The study of work relations from a non-waged perspective provides a way to integrate fully lower-income people and culturally subordinate groups within the analysis of the historical transformation of working class people in the United States. By viewing changes in the underside of economic development—informal work—it is possible to see how changes in self-sufficiency transformed the meaning of community itself. The history of informal work provides insights into what structural changes in the last century may mean for community development efforts today.

Rather than starting with historical assumptions based on the relatively short-lived phase of prosperity between 1945 to 1970, this research began by going back in time and discovering how household members actually made ends meet.[1] Just as simplified notions of completely wage-dependent families need to be abandoned, one-dimensional conceptions of the adult male wage laborer and the adult female housewife cannot be transposed back in time and assumed to be the starting point for understanding how work and community life changed.

The formation of the working class in the mid-Atlantic region, and most likely in the United States as a whole, was a complex, multi-faceted process that involved the reorganization of both non-waged and wage work. This study opens in 1830, when steam-powered industrial development was just getting underway in the United States. At this time, the laboring class was not at the initial stage of capitalist development, as some have assumed. Many laboring households had already become somewhat dependent on wage labor in various production contexts, perhaps relying on 50 percent of their income from wages. But it was not yet largely (let alone completely) dependent on wage labor and market consumption. Rather, labor became more dependent on wages and market consumption in a very gradual way. It was not until 80 to 90 years after steam-powered factories appeared that two-thirds of the laboring class could be considered to depend on wage labor for at least 65 to 70 percent of its income in the Delaware Valley. By 1920, improvising labor had become the clear minority stratum and monied labor emerged as the culturally dominant stratum, a reversal that shaped the face of twentieth-century working class politics and culture.

In the nineteenth and early twentieth centuries, working-class families used to engage in many types of informal work. Before 1850, at least one-half of the laboring families used to generate a substantial portion of their own income. In much the same way that Third World families do today, these families organized and carried out subsistence, petty producing, marketing and rental activities. Sometimes this informal work required borrowing, renting, or buying "means of production," such as a horse, cart, or tools. This pattern continued for almost one-third of labor until the New Deal took place, when limited state transfer payments enabled some families to supplement low wages with state benefits. The decline in these informal activities meant that laboring families lost the skills required to carry out many self-supporting types of work. The loss of labor's informal work skills accompanied the deskilling of labor on the factory floor. As labor lost many of its informal skills and spent more time doing wage labor, families bought more goods from the capitalist market.

Along with the decline in non-waged work came the decline of improvising labor's non-capitalist, marketing sphere. Families in improvising labor once "produced" goods for their own household-based consumption. They also made goods to sell, barter, and exchange with other families. A thriving informal work sphere meant that families organized and controlled part of their work. In addition, informal work meant that an informal market sphere prevailed, which enabled low-income families to buy and sell from each other. Although monied labor's consumer taste buds were whetted long before the turn of the century, improvising labor purchased fewer market goods, had developed fewer consumer needs, and often depended on cheap or secondhand goods that were acquired through informal markets. During the period that non-waged work flourished, working class people organized local informal markets and displayed strong organizational skills. The decline of informal work probably also brought the decline of labor's community organization skills, which had been used to set up informal markets.

The organization of work here refers to both the organization of non-waged and wage work, the opposite faces of work that developed in tandem. The complex of non-waged and wage work became reorganized between the nineteenth and mid-twentieth century. Although most low-paid families once relied heavily on work they organized themselves, approximately two-thirds of U.S. laboring families relied heavily on wage labor by the second decade of the twentieth century. The majority of laboring families used to be located at the mid-point on the wage dependency continuum. That is, they used to rely on non-waged income to supplement low wages and displayed household work patterns that resembled Third World work patterns. By 1950, almost 80 percent of U.S. labor was located at the "wage dependent" end of the historical continuum. Even though the vast majority of laboring households have high wages and acquire most of the goods they consume through the market, "Third World" America—or improvising labor—still continues to form a relatively small, but growing, portion of U.S. labor.

The social division of labor resulted, not only in the reorganization of non-waged and wage work, but in the attendant reorganization of gender, age and ethnic stratification. When low- to moderate-income laboring households relied on diverse sources of non-waged income, all members of the household (over the age of 4 or 5) engaged in some non-waged work. At the same time, most members of the household at least sporadically engaged in some wage work. Although gender and age demarcations appeared in both non-waged and wage work, households responded in a flexible way to informal work opportunities and to changing market conditions. Diverse work responsibilities tended to be shared by family members. Gender and age distinctions within families and communities tended to be more blurred than they were in the work force, where profit-makers organized the labor process and decided how to utilize groups of laborers.

Modern conceptions of gender, age and even ethnicity evolved as families began to earn at least two-thirds of their income from wage labor. At this "two-thirds" wage-earning turning point, families sent their children to school, instead of having them sell food or newspapers on the street. Girls began being preparing for their future (and culturally primary) occupation as housewife. Boys began being cultivated for their future role as the primary adult wage earner. Adult women, while they may have earned low wages or generated non-waged income, began listening to social reformers, who told women that they were responsible for creating a healthy, consumer-oriented, domestic environment. Men brought home larger, but still sporadic, paychecks and began expecting that they would not work until the end of their lives. Elders found that employers no longer considered them to be productive members of society and began to find themselves living in ethnically segregated "old age" homes.

The Civil War marked the end of legal enslavement for many U.S. workers, but highly segregated wage labor relations, educational patterns, and residential separations followed. American working families found themselves being divided into "black" labor and "white" labor, which roughly corresponded to the division between improvising and monied labor. The color line became etched into the changing social landscape. The state and business helped bring about the change from partly household-defined gender and age relations to the definition of gender, and age relations primarily through the capitalist, social division of labor. Early state policy and business directives dissolved informal work options and "assigned" household members to gender- and age-segregated occupations. Gender- and age-based occupational divisions solidified. Adult white men secured higher paying industrial jobs and women started to become relegated to lower paying jobs and to housework. By the 1950s and 1960s, social identity groups and identity group politics emerged as a result of and in response to the incorporation of family members into the orbit of capitalist institutions, the hallmark of this stage of long-term social change.

Charity organizations, workhouses, settlement houses, and municipal agencies became intimately involved in shaping how the working class evolved in the city. The evaporation of informal work would not have taken place to the extent it did without the intervention of parastatal organizations and municipal agencies. Through the implementation of "progressive" reforms, federal and state governments also shaped working class formation. By implementing their policies, state agencies and state-like organizations pushed working class families, especially low-income ones, to work more for others and to buy more consumer goods from the capitalist market.

Without the discouragement of informal work by state officials and early social workers, non-waged work would not have declined as much as it did. These social change agents squelched non-waged work and either coerced or urged families in improvising labor to drop "distracting" informal activities and emphasize wage labor, the standard way of organizing work in the industrial production process. "Self-sufficiency" was redefined by state functionaries, neighborhood organizations and middle-class volunteers to mean a more complete reliance on wages from capitalist firms, and not reliance on a shifting complex of wage and non-waged work. And when families were eventually forced to rely on welfare for part of their income, agencies stigmatized families applying for benefits. It was only in more recent times, after U.S. power declined and the economy contracted, that state agencies and local organizations began to experiment with promoting self-employment, cultivating labor's community development skills, and encouraging labor to volunteer to revitalize communities (as workers had once done automatically, when they controlled more local market activities).

The rise of big business and the consolidation of manufacturing and retail industries also reduced the number of labor's micro-businesses. Through its involvement with charity and workhouse boards, businesses encouraged people in low-income neighborhoods to become "more industrious" by working more for employers. Not only did the state establish an unfettered business climate for large companies, but the state's new health regulations forced many of labor's small operations to go out of business. The growing real estate industry benefited from state intervention into shared housing arrangements, as some low-income families began to pay for more expensive individual units. As more laboring households depended primarily on wages, advertisers promoted corporate goods and retailing establishments offered a growing variety of consumer goods. When labor did not become fully proletarianized because employers did not cover the full cost of reproducing families, state agencies then stepped in and provided limited transfer payments to supplement wages. Today elderly sons and daughters of yesterday's businessmen and state officials, who put a damper on informal work, are calling on low-income people to "pull themselves up by their own bootstraps," bootstraps long tied in knots by state officials themselves.

The efforts of state officials to more fully integrate families into an expanding market economy began to turn against the interests of middle-class and poor people by 1970, when U.S. fortunes began to unravel. As a result of its activities in the late nineteenth century and first half of the twentieth, the evolving state was unwittingly creating the social problems of the late twentieth century: a deskilled, underemployed work force and, what many critics of governmental subsidies have called "welfare dependency." The so-called lack of self-sufficient behaviors and attitudes, which accompanied the destruction of communities' informal work, eventually came to haunt state officials, employers and working people alike by the end of the twentieth century. Interestingly enough, the innovative, informal market skills of recent immigrants and Third World people are now admired by many employers and laborers. There is no recognition that North Americans, too, once had these same skills and a similar work ethic, or that they were destroyed and replaced by limited, wage labor skills and a narrower work ethic.

Just as wages alone did not support yesterday's working-class households, wages during the period of U.S. hegemony rarely provided complete support for even professional families. Likewise, during the last decade of the twentieth century, non-waged income continues to help sustain families today, even if it forms a much smaller proportion of total household income than it did during the first decades of the century. Today culturally subordinate groups rely more heavily on informal work than do white ethnic groups and many adult men.

A history of informal work in different communities suggests that U.S. labor may be coming "full circle" and is once again depending on more non-waged income, including from street vending, fixing cars, providing personal services, and selling homemade products. The lack of sufficient high-paying jobs and the high cost of living has led to growing numbers of homeless individuals and families. As the restructuring of industry continues and trade barriers between North American countries are lifted, laboring people may be forced to increase substantially their non-waged work. Because of their knowledge of informal work and building local networks that help sustain families, representatives of lower-income ethnic groups and lower-status gender and age segments of monied labor may be able to provide leadership as the United States and other countries address underemployment and unemployment.

Inserted in the history of the transformation of non-waged work, one finds an important kernel, which, when burst open, contains the quietly kept secret of how the working class and its hierarchy became formed. The historical analysis here leads to the development of a comprehensive framework for understanding how the formation of the U.S. working class took place. Unknown to many scholars, the formation of the working class and its hierarchical structure was related to changes in the full range of non-waged work and of wage labor. With the exception of some analyses, which often focus only on women's domestic work, this aspect of U.S. working class life is still largely unwritten.

When one-half to one-third of working class families organized their own work to generate at least one-third of their total family income, family members had complex and overlapping work identities. It might be said that they had several occupations at one time, and many occupations over the course of the household's life cycle. This early period, which covered the time from 1830 (in addition to the colonial and early post-colonial period) to almost 1920, was characterized by work diversity for households and by greater flexibility in gender and age relations.

By 1910 or 1920, when almost two-thirds of American labor depended heavily on wage income and left behind diverse work patterns that were characteristic of improvising labor, family members began to have more fragmented, specialized work histories. These work histories developed in relation to the new gender, age and ethnic hierarchy, which defined groups of workers as "productive" or "less productive" groups in relation to wage labor. In this way, household members became separated into the productive grouping of males and adults and the less productive grouping of children, elders and females. Economically subordinate ethnic groups, females, youth, and elders now shared a similar structural position, a position that had become defined in opposition to the adult male.

Of course, household members had overlapping social identities. Women were both unproductive (relative to men) and powerful (relative to children). When they were children, boys were subordinate to adults, but as males, they were dominant (relative to females). Although both children and elders were culturally subordinate to adults, the gender identity of family members shaped intergenerational relationships. All household members went through the process of being considered less productive at the beginning and at the end of their lives. The new wage labor-based stratification of gender and age groups ultimately led to increased divisions between household members and to increased divisions within the working class.

As family members became polarized along gender and age lines, families became internally wounded by these divisions and community life became more polarized and fragmented than ever. Within the general context of the polarization of ethnic groups, the age identity of engendered family members became reconstructed as they moved through their individual life cycles. Changing age identities were overlaid on more fixed gender identities. By the 1950s, family members had changing and oppositional identities that reflected society's hierarchy, its conflicts, and its specialized organization of work. In general, even though age relations provided variability in power relations as individuals moved through their life cycles, household members from the same gender group in the 1950s and 1960s had more specialized, less diverse work than did low-income women and men at the turn of the century.

Although household members' work become more specialized, the working class as a whole became more fragmented and splintered. Labor continued to be divided into two main strata: improvising and monied labor. These strata were divided along ethnic, gender and age lines. Rather than assuming a homogeneous character, the formation of the working class led to greater heterogeneity. Although it sub-groups shared the common fate of becoming more wage dependent, labor became more divided and more heterogeneous.

Both improvising and monied labor shared the common position of working for wages, but differences in wage levels, consumer patterns, and types of linkages between households and the state separated these strata. Segments of labor shared the common position of being culturally subordinate, but there were major differences between the specific social relations that created particular ethnic, gender and age identities. Contrary to the expectation that large-scale production created a laboring class with a great deal in common, it appears that the reverse has taken place. Industrialization and urbanization has led to a highly divided laboring class, whose segments share little in common at the family, neighborhood, regional, and countrywide levels.

Capitalist development in the United States seems to have led to the construction of small, sometimes overlapping communities defined by class, ethnicity, gender and age, which themselves are further divided along lines drawn between social identity groups. Community life has changed from a constellation of fairly personal, social relations where members participated in diverse and shared work experiences to a set of abstract, social relations that reflect work-based inequality and produce social identity groups. Over the course of the last century, the meaning of community has changed from referring to tight, local, informal networks that helped sustain families to fragmentary groupings that reflected ethnic, gender and age divisions and resulting bonds of solidarity.

When women and men today confront their contemporary situation, they face an historical irony. Although labor's ancestors worked to get out of economic deprivation and poverty (and left community life behind in the process), today many Americans want to live within a social context that has tightly-knit communities, strong families and close inter-personal relations. In the process of becoming economically stable, Americans became so divided along gender, age and ethnic lines that they can now hardly talk to one another. If community in a collective sense is possible, it will have a new meaning, partly because civil society's boundaries contracted.

As some Americans work to create a new commonwealth, they face the following challenges: sustaining a level of economic well-being; redistributing wealth within the population; creating more income-earning opportunities that support all families; creating more democratic traditions of direct participation in politics and economics; developing equitable and accessible education, health care and social services; and building community life so that it sustains everyone economically, culturally and emotionally. These goals, which relate to becoming more self-sufficient in a holistic way, might be reached more easily if Americans recognized that the activities and human creations that the capitalist market has not yet placed a value on might offer the most hope for people seeking a new commonwealth.

## The Loss of Work Diversity and Its Social Impact

The way that economic and state development took place in urban-industrial society resulted in the loss of work diversity and the sharpening of divisions within laboring households. Classical economists and sociologists began to see related social and economic patterns by the early twentieth century. It is useful to review the literature after the research process reveals unexpected patterns of development. To benefit from the perspectives of classical social scientists, who studied long-term trends in work and stratification, a review of selected social scientific writings will now be made.

In *Industrial Evolution,* Carl Buecher speculates about what the decline of the household-centered sphere and the rise of the market economy has meant for households and household members. He argues, on the one hand, that the "primitive union of labor at home. . .and in the earlier division of labor" was characterized by "a warm breadth of social fellowship," economic independence, and direct producers using the goods they had made.[2] But he also argues that the modern division of labor is characterized by "the cold, cutting winds of calculation, contract, and greed of gain."[3] And the modern division of labor "forc[es] large masses into a condition of dependence" where consumption goods are produced by unknown workers.[4] As consumers, people become more alike each other, but as workers they become more dissimilar, according to Buecher. An occupation becomes more like a life-vocation and the mind becomes narrowed. "In our sphere of activity," Buecher writes, "we have lost in fullness of life, and the worker has not the old joy in his work. . . . [H]as the division of labour merely made life richer in pleasures, but poorer in real joy?"[5]

Looking at the consequences of development in industrialized societies from a psychological viewpoint, and not from the perspective of changes in workers' activities, Sigmund Freud saw a similar lack of satisfaction and joy in life in the twentieth century. In *Civilization and Its Discontents,* Freud argues that the individual and society became more opposed to each other. By 1900 in the United States, he writes, individual development (in the middle class) became very restricted. Freud asks, "What good to us is a long life if it is difficult and barren of joys, and if it is so full of misery that we can only welcome death as a deliverer?"[6]

In *The Protestant Ethic,* Max Weber argues that capitalist development paralyzes the human spirit. "Specialists without spirit," he writes, "sensualists without heart; this nullity imagines that it has obtained a level of civilization never before achieved."[7]

In a similar vein, Emile Durkheim concludes that most people have continued to find that even steady work is an insupportable servitude. In *The Division of Labor in Society,* he writes, "Is it true that the happiness of the individual increases as man advances? Nothing is more doubtful."[8]

The arguments and conclusions advanced by these social scientists still have relevance, if one identifies and considers the consequences of the decline of informal work, the intervention by the state into non-waged work, and the rise of industrial production. These processes reshaped family and community life, contributing to the dissatisfaction with work that classical social scientists noted.

In *The Division of Labor in Society,* Emile Durkheim provides important insights into social change in the capitalist world. He emphasizes the importance of changing forms of conscience and the centrality of conscience (or consciousness) as "a source of life" and "vitality."[9] As industrialization proceeded, he argues, the forms of group solidarity and conscience changed in fundamental ways.[10] Durkheim's understanding of social change can be applied to the reorganization of urban-industrial life in U.S. communities between 1830 and the contemporary period.

According to Durkheim, mechanical solidarity emerged when all members of a group tended to be formed within the full range of social relations, a process that produced bonds of social likeness. He argues that the "general and indeterminate attachment to the group" resulted from common "harmonious" and "collective movements."[11]

> The greater the diversity of relations wherein the individual makes his actions felt, the more it creates links which attach the individual to the group; the more, consequently, social cohesion derives completely from this source and bears its mark.[12]

In terms of work relations, bonds of social likeness emerged when group members shared "qualitatively similar but mutually indispensable tasks."[13]

Although Durkheim saw non-capitalist societies as exhibiting mechanical solidarity in its most ideal-typic form, it can be argued that early U.S. communities also exhibited characteristics that resembled mechanical solidarity. When examining income-generating patterns in yesterday's low- to moderate-income communities, it can be argued that similar tasks held members of nineteenth-century households together. As non-waged work declined and as market imperatives directed more work and buying activities, household members became less bonded together by relations that created social likeness.

As the social division of labor unfolded, Durkheim argues, society became organized as a "system of different special functions which definite relations unite."[14] Mechanical solidarity declined, he posits, as special tasks escaped the action of collective conscience.

> The more specialized they [special tasks] are, the more circumscribed the number of those cognizant of each of them. Consequently, the more marginal they are to the common conscience.[15]

Old bonds of social likeness were broken by the division of labor. Conscience became more differentiated, Durkheim writes, typically along occupational lines. New bonds of social likeness developed, which attached individuals to the operating mechanisms of modern industrial society as whole. Modern industrial society was characterized by a new type of solidarity: organic solidarity.[16]

The division of labor within the market economy created more specialized tasks for the labor force. The reciprocal and redistributive aspects of community life, which evolved because the market economy only partially supported labor, were largely undermined as the market economy grew. As household-organized work became more commodified, household members carried out relatively more specialized tasks at home. Household solidarity, which once had emerged because households members had been shaped in similar ways through home and street work, began breaking up. Strong family bonds gradually eroded as new forms of status group solidarity developed from gender, age and ethnic divisions.

In *The Division of Labor in Society,* Durkheim presents an oversimplified picture of how new types of solidarity emerge. He assumes that organic solidarity is based on occupational association.[17] According to him, people who have the same occupation will be bonded together socially. Durkheim suggests that people had just have one occupational affiliation in industrial society. However, it has been shown that family members often had multiple occupations in early industrial society, a pattern that still occurs today for women and members of low-income families. The ethnic, gender and age hierarchy is expressed partly through occupational differentiation, which includes occupational differentiation in informal work. Occupational differentiation meant that gender-, sex-, and ethnic-typed occupational groupings developed, not that individuals just had one occupation. Durkheim also fails to stress that occupational differentiation reflected and perpetuated social inequality.[18]

This study shows that social differentiation created by the division of labor disrupted household integrity and created new social bonds, which were based on unequal work relationships in the labor force, inequities in state support, inequities in working class-based organizations, and the gender and age hierarchy at home.[19] Bonds of social likeness created on the basis of gender and age, as well as through the redefinition of ethnicity, led to the growth of new, enduring types of solidarity that had never really been seen before. New gender, age and ethnic solidarities stepped out on the stage of economic and social life, where they remain to this day.

Strangely enough, the new social identity solidarities of the second half of the twentieth century resemble the type of mechanical solidarity that developed over a century ago in some urban neighborhoods and rural regions. Like yesterday's social inequities, the contemporary stratification of gender, age and ethnic groups occurs because each group is created generally in a similar set of work relations. Social solidarities became differentiated as sets of gender, age and ethnic workers carried out qualitatively similar tasks in a divided work force and within socially defined gender and age tasks at home.[20] Unlike the old mechanical solidarity, the new mechanical solidarities of gender, ethnicity and age were not cultivated through shared and overlapping relations of all family members and neighborhood residents. And while more personal connections once thrived, impersonal and contractual work predominates today. Overall, because sufficient similarities remain between mid-nineteenth century mechanical solidarity and the new social identity solidarities, it is possible to argue that modern society produces new mechanical solidarities, which reflect labor's internal divisions.

Economic and social inequities, and the resulting social polarization, meant that labor was redivided into new strata of the "haves" and "have nots." In monied labor, household members found that extensive commodification established the basis for particularly strong age and gender solidarities. For low-income ethnic groups, the strengthening of ethnic solidarities partially offset the divisive and questioning characteristics of gender and age solidarities. Typically, strong gender and age identities decreased the extent to which whole households found themselves held together by bonds of social likeness. However, because these divided groups told the story of how society was not egalitarian, they carried the potential to transform social relations in a more equitable direction. For this reason, gender, age and ethnic social identity groups can provide a starting point for defining alternative visions and for building new social relations.

The ways that work activities are organized can help promote economic sustainability, greater control over work, and a more equitable social world. Ethnic-, gender-, and age-integrated organizations, along with community and state-directed efforts, may be able to respond to contemporary economic and social challenges by developing more inclusive, equitable mechanisms that direct market developments, state activities, and community- and household-based work activities.[21] Through their connections with families, social identity groups, employers, and the state, laboring people today may be able to help establish more equitable work relations in the home and the shop, build democratic organizations at the grassroots level, and connect different social identity groups, both here in the United States and across national boundaries.

## Conclusion: Social Policy, Self-Sufficiency, and Community Development

This historical overview of the transformation of work and self-sufficient behaviors contributes to an understanding of how social change can be brought about more effectively today. Based on an analysis of cyclical and secular trends, a suggested summary will be made of the interventions that might be carried out in order to improve the quality of work, home, and community life. Suggestions will focus on interventions that will expand labor's options for becoming more self-sufficient in a holistic way and create stronger democratic traditions at neighborhood, city, regional, state and national levels.

Even the best-intentioned reform movements in U.S. history helped create future social problems. As this social history demonstrates, the officials and reformers who discouraged informal work and cultivated wage relations in the name of capitalism, whether they behaved intentionally or unconsciously, set in motion long-term, processes of social change that partly worked against the interests of working people. Although parastatal managers, settlement workers, Progressive reformers, state agency directors, and business leaders may have thought they were helping the economically disadvantaged, in the long run they removed a critical source of economic and cultural stability. Although households that were highly dependent on non-waged work generally went along with the reorientation toward consumerism and wage labor, local state agents and social reformers actively promoted the demise of subsistence, petty-producing and marketing work. State officials and social reformers, who themselves earned relatively high wages and bought market goods, squelched non-waged work and helped carry out the wholesale destruction of many informal, neighborhood organizations. These officials did not understand that non-waged work in low- to moderate-income neighborhoods provided options for generating critical income, being trained in non-waged work, securing exchanged or low-cost goods, and supporting family-centered and community networks.

Because municipal officials and social reformers often caused irreversible damage to local networks and informal work relations, it is vitally important today that working class people begin to have a voice in economic and social decisions that directly impact them. This means that residents from low-income neighborhoods and impoverished rural areas, as well as members of culturally subordinate social groups, should provide leadership in and direct the development of programs involved in starting micro-enterprises and community revitalization. Local people who have experienced economic deprivation and "internal marginalization" understand the inherent strengths, work skills, and reciprocal behaviors of people.

Contemporary efforts to promote local economic democracy need to be initiated from the grassroots level. The new economic democracy movement represents an effort to rebuild society from the ground up. But it is unrealistic to assume that grassroots organizing and the creation of alternative institutions, without widespread and sustained support of the state, will have the economic power to transform regional economic patterns or the society as a whole. Once neighborhoods and localities begin organizing themselves, they should consider seeking support for their work from governmental bodies and even businesses. After all, making democracy work and creating economic opportunities for all is a countrywide issue. This is a movement that can help America reach its true potential. It is also a social movement that relates to people in other countries, who are trying to achieve political and economic democracy.

As grassroots efforts build a more democratic, sustainable economic system for all, participants in this movement can benefit from the knowledge of others, who have started similar and related projects. They also can learn from those who have an informed, practical understanding of how cyclical and long-term trends now affect, and may eventually affect, neighborhoods, cities, regions, the country, and perhaps even the world.

Along with having the right to vote (which women and African Americans acquired at a time when low-income communities were being stripped of non-waged work options), democracy means making decisions about the economy and becoming involved in economic developments that affect everyday life. Because the economy is anarchic and the course of future historical events is not known, the best-placed grassroots efforts may not always work. But economic planning can be based on a considered analysis of what direction(s) social change may take. Rather than responding primarily to institutions that are already in place, labor should try to shape the overall contours of economic history and build egalitarian social networks in which people can lead economically secure and fulfilling lives.

Social change agents, including social workers and program developers, must make dedicated efforts to learn from economically disadvantaged people and improvising labor, and from women, youth, elders and members of culturally subordinate ethnic groups. Today social reformers should start supporting neighborhood people and help them lead redevelopment projects. For non-local professionals who have earned their living by working on poverty issues, this reorientation may mean that they cannot count on being high-paid directors who "serve" a class of people that they see as beneath them. If this democratic orientation starts to operate, professionals may find their salaries reduced and dead-end programs may be eliminated or revamped. Rather than finding themselves tempted to make a living from other people's impoverishment, professional social change agents should be honest about what approaches do not work and should do their best to work with poor people to make job-creating programs effective.[22] Social change agents will need to listen to, work under, and work hand-in-hand with the people who have the most intimate knowledge of social problems and social survival networks: America's improvising laborers and "internally marginalized" people.

Social reformers differ about which social unit of analysis should be the focus of social change efforts. Far too many government and private non-profit programs work only to help single individuals become more self-sufficient. For example, self-employment programs may focus on helping individual adult females start micro-enterprises. There are typically few supportive services arranged for family members, who depend on women in self-employment programs. The absence of these services minimizes the chance that female participants in these programs will be successful. More importantly, women in these programs may be encouraged to borrow start-up funds from friends and relatives, thus—at least temporarily—depleting family and community resources. If businesses fail, as many do within the first five years, not only are individuals in these programs in worse situations, but numerous, broader networks of local people may become even more impoverished.

As some family caseworkers advocate, focus needs to placed on helping entire family units become stabilized and self-sufficient. But this may not be enough. Social change agents need to question the once progressive, but now old "social-work" assumption that the family is the largest unit that should be assisted. In addition to families, the supportive networks that sustain low-income families during hard times also need to be stabilized and strengthened. Even this approach, however, limits the scope of change. In order to begin meeting the needs of individuals, families, and supportive networks, it is essential to change the way that income-generating and marketing networks operate in urban neighborhoods and rural regions. This can only be done by community development planning, which is carried out by local residents. Self-employment options and related marketing networks can only be sustained over a long period of time if program developers decide how small producers, small retailers and buyers can support each other. This includes planning how informal workers can break away from the grip that large producers and retailers now hold over production and marketing. Partly because many government programs just measure whether individual placement goals are met, many self-employment programs fail to enhance the security of families and support networks, much less include a community development component.[23]

While liberal social policy advocates correctly point out that the U.S. government should provide greater economic support for working-class families, social reform advocates should do more than lobbying the federal government for increased family and community benefits. A European-oriented movement within the liberal American academy advocates that the U.S. government develop social programs that more closely resemble social programs in Western Europe.[24] It is an admirable goal to get the U.S. state to follow the lead of more generous Western European states. But given the history of the U.S. government's rather limited support for labor, it seems unlikely that this will happen in the near future. In fact, the U.S. state resembles the old South African apartheid state much more than it does European states. Now that a democratically elected government rules in South Africa, the United States stands alone in the industrial world as a state with substantial *de facto* segregation and weak social programs. To begin meeting social needs in the United States today, social reformers need to push both for the expansion of additional, new income-earning options—for extensive support of micro-businesses and cooperatives and for job-creation programs—and for strong, social programs with universal entitlements.

When advocates ask cities, states, and the federal government to support community development programs, state officials should recognize that these local organizing efforts offer a chance for the country to meet its promise. Rather than simply providing supplemental unemployment benefits, revising job training programs (which primarily increase workers' ability to compete for a fixed number of jobs), or reforming education, the state should also expand the number of long-term, income-yielding options. State agencies and non-profit organizations can help create new fields of work on a sustained basis by supporting the development of micro-enterprises, cooperatives and small businesses and by encouraging face-to-face organizing around community development issues.[25]

For more than a century, the U.S. state has actively assisted the rise of big business and monopolies. Social change agents today need to take a long look at what monopolies have wrought, particularly as low-wage, overseas operations are growing and as U.S. poverty is increasing. Social reformers need to try to reverse the century-long trend of active U.S. support for large corporations and its neglect of small-scale, entrepreneurial efforts. Public policy and job training programs should not just focus on helping workers catch the dangling ends of corporate global webs as a means of economic survival. As corporate networks become detached from U.S. production facilities, Americans and regional groups should develop an economic plan that more closely resembles autarky than the widening, transnational market that prevails today. This would enable self-sufficiency to develop within economic units that are smaller than the world and possibly smaller than the United States. It would also discourage never-ending consumption, which has little meaning except to the companies that market new products. Encouraging the switch to a four-day work week with only a five percent loss in wages (as France and Germany are considering) would also create jobs for underemployed workers and stabilize family incomes.[26]

Social policy makers and social change agents need to involve labor directly in the identification of key problems, the development of short- and long-term solutions, the implementation of new programs, and the evaluation of these programs. It does not make sense for the state to fund the development of self-employment programs or even to increase state transfer payments without simultaneously cultivating greater grassroots control over these programs and over community development work in general. The cultivation of small-scale, producing and marketing operations and cooperatives could be facilitated through community development education, which requires local involvement in problem-solving. This democratic process places community people at the center of assessing needs, designing community development plans, implementing programs, and evaluating their progress. This clarifies what problems remain untouched and new programs need to be redesigned and strengthened. The government, which has unwittingly taken away working people's independent and self-sufficient behaviors over the last century, now needs to support working people as they define and direct more of their work, and develop community organizations that help sustain future generations along both cultural and economic dimensions.

Reuniting labor's new communities—its divided social identity groups—forms an important part of the current struggle to improve the quality of life at work, in the family, and in neighborhoods and regions. Although laboring families and working people are now divided more deeply than they have ever been, the laboring class also has the potential to create equitable social relations more than it has ever had. Now that working people have had a history that has included both closely knit families of the past and more recent social identity groups, labor can benefit from the combined knowledge of these stages of history. The knowledge gained from the historical development of work and stratification can serve as a powerful tool that can provide direction in conceiving and creating a better world.

## Notes

1. The period of U.S. hegemony typically has provided the "standard" base for historians and social scientists studying the United States. The typical method of research has been to see what characterized this period (e.g., highly automated factories, factory-based occupational patterns, consumerism, etc.) and then to go back in time to see how these recent phenomena developed. There has been little to recapture what may have once been thriving before, but has largely been submerged. The development of women's work identity usually is traced in relation to wage work and/or domestic work, but little else.

2. Carl Buecher, *Industrial Evolution* (New York: Augustus M. Kelley, 1968), 313–314.

3. Ibid.

4. Ibid.

5. Ibid.

6. Sigmund Freud, *Civilization and its Discontents* (New York: W.W. Norton and Company, 1962), 35.

7. Max Weber, *The Protestant Ethic and the Spirit of Capitalism* (New York: Charles Scribner's Sons, 1958), 181.

8. Emile Durkheim, *The Division of Labor in Society* (New York: The Free Press, 1964), 241.

9. Durkheim, *The Division of Labor,* 96.

10. Ibid. 106, 109, 124.

11. Ibid. 106.

12. Ibid. 109.

13. Ibid. 124.

14. Ibid. 129.

15. Ibid. 127.

16. Ibid. 129, 127.

17. Gender, age and ethnic cultures now shape relationships within the working class much more than specific occupational cultures do. It can be said that occupational groupings tend to be shaped by gender, age and ethnic stratification.

18. See Ruth Sidel, *Women and Children Last: The Plight of Poor Women in Affluent America* (New York: Penguin Books, 1987), 12–13, 24, xvi, 15–16. The effects of stratification may be intensifying. According to Ruth Sidel, "[a] far larger percentage of non-whites are poor than whites."(12) Households headed by women comprised almost half of all economically poor families in 1983. Many poor people in America are children.(xvi) Furthermore, over a 21-year period, from 1960 to 1981, an alarming change took place. Between the 1960s and 1981 "the number of persons in poor families headed by women increased 54 percent, in contrast with the nearly 50 percent decrease in the number of persons in poor families headed by white men."(15–16) See Barbara Ehrenreich, *The Hearts of Men: American Dreams and the Flight from Commitment* (Garden City, New York: Anchor Press, 1983). In a similar vein, Barbara Ehrenreich argues that, as male wages are shared less with women and children, women face tremendous economic insecurity.(10–12) C. Eric Lincoln, *Race, Religion, and the Continuing American Dilemma* (New York: Hill and Wang, 1984). Lincoln writes about the perpetuation of a "color-caste syndrome," where "there is nothing new for the black masses except the permanence of their exclusion and the threat of total abandonment."(224, 217) William Julius Wilson, *The Truly Disadvantaged: The Inner City, the Underclass, and Public Policy* (Chicago: University of Chicago Press, 1987). William Julius Wilson argues that "blacks have experienced a deterioration of their economic position in nearly all the major labor-market indicators." In addition, there has often been an increased isolation of economically deprived groups from groups of "different class and/or racial backgrounds," intensifying the lack of economic options.(147, 137)

19. Dietrich Rueschemeyer, *Power and the Division of Labour* (Stanford: Stanford University Press, 1986), 141.

20. Robert N. Bellah, Richard Madsen, William M. Sullivan, Ann Swidler, and Steven M. Tipton, *Habits of the Heart: Individualism and Commitment in Amer-*

*ican Life* (New York: Harper and Row, 1986). "The citizen has been swallowed up in "economic man," write the authors.(271) "[I]t is the extreme fragmentation of the modern world that really threatens our individuation; that what is best in our separation and individuation, our sense of dignity and autonomy as persons," they write, "requires a new integration if it is to be sustained."(286)

21. Maria Mies, *Patriarchy and Accumulation on a World Scale: Women in the International Division of Labor* (London: Zed Books, 1986), 211–219; 225. Mies suggests that work and the total work day need to be reconceptualized. Work needs to be reorganized more around the creation of goods and services for use, and not so much for exchange. Americans in the United States need to consume less, to make more household goods, and to recycle goods both between household members and between households. Non-hierarchical reciprocal relationships need to be strengthened so that people can become closer to each other and to nature, thus contributing to a global ecological system. Mies urges people to rediscover the work that actual people do to make commodities. This can happen, she writes, if people trace the paths commodities have taken before they buy them in a store and bring them home. Autarky needs to be promoted, which would enable self-sufficiency to develop within economic units that are smaller than the world. (211–219, 225)

22. The problem with many employment and training programs is that they do not create new jobs, but just compete with each other to place their trainees in a limited number of positions. The rate of poverty does not change, but the individuals experiencing impoverishment might change.

23. Community development of this kind requires stability from the organizations carrying out this work. It would work best in situations where residents have little geographical mobility, but this is not a prerequisite. Because Americans move on the average once every five years, community development efforts would have a better chance of succeeding if there were a reduction in this mobility. But mobility reflects economic insecurity and industrial reorganization. Informal markets in Third World countries flourish where there is tremendous geographical mobility, but the basic market structure already is established. Informal markets in the mid-Atlantic region thrived when almost half the city's residents moved at least once every ten years. Sometimes residents stayed in their neighborhoods, so informal relations were not interrupted. And, once again, these markets already had been established. Although local and regional markets would be built on top of informal organizations and local networks, they would almost have to be built from scratch.

24. See William Julius Wilson, *The Truly Disadvantaged: The Inner City, The Underclass, and Public Policy* (Chicago: University of Chicago Press, 1987), 149–163. Wilson emphasizes the need for universal entitlements and a family allowance program in the United States. Also see Barbara Ehrenreich, *The Hearts of Men,* 177–180. Ehrenreich wants a new welfare state to replace the old source of women's income: the male's family wage. Refer to Ruth Sidel, *Women and*

*Children Last,* 172–209. Sidel would like to see an array of social service programs, which resemble Sweden's. (Due to fiscal constraints, Sweden's programs weakened after Sidel wrote her book.)

25. Because the revitalization of neighborhood life is so important, social advocates recently have suggested that the settlement house and Progressive-era organizations be resuscitated. In a neighborhood center (or modern "settlement house"), neighborhood people could get a variety of services provided in one location. This study shows that the settlement house movement hurt low-income neighborhoods because middle-class social reformers had different values and worked to undermine local, informal organizations. If local people started and ran organizations that resembled former settlement houses, this might help neighborhoods. This community-run effort, however, would diverge from the settlement house concept, which was based on the notion of outsiders planting themselves in low-income neighborhoods. In "Bringing Back the Settlement House," Howard Husock argues that settlement houses are preferable to typical social service organizations because settlement workers saw poor people as citizens, not as clients. In *Public Welfare,* (Fall, 1993) 16–25. Also see Amitai Etzioni, *The Spirit of Community: Rights, Responsibilities and the Communitarian Agenda* (New York: Crown Publishers, 1993), 118, 230–233. My study shows that while settlement workers wrote about citizenship, they tried to push neighborhood people to do what they wanted, in much the same way that many social workers treat "clients" today. The old settlement house model might be transformed by developing a critique of earlier settlement house operations and by conceiving of new ways to have diverse social service and educational programs provided in one location, a mode of service delivery known as "one-stop shopping."

26. *New York Times,* 22 November 1993, A1.

*Boy walking with horse near boardinghouse, Philadelphia, 1897. Courtesy of the City Archives, Philadelphia.*

*Child standing in front of hillside shack, which was built by a migrant construction worker, ca. 1910. Crystal Water Company Collection, Courtesy of the Balch Institute Library.*

*Migrant construction workers displaying the steer they intend to cook and eat together, ca. 1910. Crystal Water Company Collection, Courtesy of the Balch Institute Library.*

*Mrs. John B. Scott standing with her three children in front of a garden, Harrisburg? 1912. Courtesy of the Balch Institute.*

*Man working in his garden. Frank Coccagna photograph, courtesy of the Balch Institute Library.*

*Grocery and fruit vendor preparing to continue his rounds. Ricci family photograph, courtesy of the Balch Institute Library.*

*Jewish elders sitting in front of their old age home. Albert Einstein Medical Center photograph, courtesy of the Balch Institute Library.*

*Canned goods stored by German-American farming family ca. 1930. Courtesy of the National Archives, Washington, D.C.*

*Boys selling produce at a curbside market, Philadelphia, 1938. Courtesy of the City Archives, Philadelphia.*

# Index